Higher Education
As a Public Good

GLOBAL STUDIES IN EDUCATION

A.C. (Tina) Besley, Michael A. Peters,
Cameron McCarthy, Fazal Rizvi
General Editors

Vol. 27

The Global Studies in Education series is part of the Peter Lang Education list.
Every volume is peer reviewed and meets
the highest quality standards for content and production.

PETER LANG
New York • Bern • Frankfurt • Berlin
Brussels • Vienna • Oxford • Warsaw

Higher Education As a Public Good

Critical Perspectives on Theory, Policy and Practice

EDITED BY
Ourania Filippakou and Gareth Williams

PETER LANG
New York • Bern • Frankfurt • Berlin
Brussels • Vienna • Oxford • Warsaw

Library of Congress Cataloging-in-Publication Data

Higher education as a public good: critical perspectives on theory,
policy and practice / edited by Ourania Filippakou, Gareth Williams.
pages cm. — (Global studies in education; Vol. 27)
Includes bibliographical references and index.
1. Education, Higher—Philosophy. 2. College teaching—Philosophy.
3. Common good—Philosophy. I. Filippakou, Ourania, editor of compilation.
II. Williams, Gareth L., editor of compilation.
LB2322.2.H51984   378.001—dc23   2014017281
ISBN 978-1-4331-2166-1 (hardcover)
ISBN 978-1-4331-2165-4 (paperback)
ISBN 978-1-4539-1269-0 (e-book)
ISSN 2153-330X

Bibliographic information published by **Die Deutsche Nationalbibliothek**.
Die Deutsche Nationalbibliothek lists this publication in the "Deutsche
Nationalbibliografie"; detailed bibliographic data are available
on the Internet at http://dnb.d-nb.de/.

The paper in this book meets the guidelines for permanence and durability
of the Committee on Production Guidelines for Book Longevity
of the Council of Library Resources.

© 2015 Peter Lang Publishing, Inc., New York
29 Broadway, 18th floor, New York, NY 10006
www.peterlang.com

All rights reserved.
Reprint or reproduction, even partially, in all forms such as microfilm,
xerography, microfiche, microcard, and offset strictly prohibited.

Printed in the United States of America

Contents

Preface	vii

Introduction

I.	Higher Education As a Public Good: Notes for a Discussion OURANIA FILIPPAKOU	3

Part One   Theoretical Approaches

II.	In Search of a Public: Higher Education in a Global Age RONALD BARNETT	15
III.	Transparency, Accountability and the Public Role of Higher Education PAUL STANDISH	29
IV.	Higher Education, the Public Good and the Public Interest PETER SCOTT	41
V.	Institutionalising the Public Good: Conceptual and Regulatory Challenges MALA SINGH	59
VI.	A Most Public Private Matter—Changing Ideas of Economists about the Public–Private Dimensions of Higher Education PEDRO TEIXEIRA	75

Part Two Models and Policies

VII. The Paradoxical University and the Public Good 97
ANGELA BREW

VIII. Is Higher Education a Public Good? An Analysis of the English Debate 113
TED TAPPER

IX. A Cultural Value in Crisis: Education As Public Good in China 127
KAI-MING CHENG AND RUI YANG

X. Assuring the Public Good in Higher Education: Essential Framework Conditions and Academic Values 141
DAVID D. DILL

XI. Inequality and the Erosion of the Public Good 163
JON NIXON

Coda

XII. Reflections on the Debate 181
GARETH WILLIAMS

Contributors 205

Index 209

Preface

Higher education serves both public and private purposes. In the public sphere at various times universities have existed primarily to provide intellectual underpinnings for religious beliefs and to provide staff for religious organisations, to provide qualified public servants for emerging nation states, to discover theoretical laws and processes that permit understanding and some control of the natural world, and to provide thoughtful and able people in a very wide range of occupations in a modern society. At the same time those who have been able to become religious leaders or senior public servants or distinguished scientists or generally successful in their occupations as a result of their higher education have invariably obtained considerable benefits as individuals. However the balance between the public and private and what constitute the public and private benefits has swung backwards and forwards over the centuries. In recent decades the main public benefit has been seen by governments at least as the promotion of economic growth while distributing the benefits to as many people as possible as equally as possible.

This book examines how different theoretical perspectives conceive of higher education as a public good. The idea of higher education as a public good is also used as a vehicle for theorizing the study of higher education. However, the following chapters are not only theoretical analyses. Drawing upon different disciplinary perspectives, they explore how theories about the purposes and functions of higher education impinge on policy and practice.

Although in the public domain the argument is mainly about how higher education is to be funded, a wide range of issues have been drawn into the debate. What is a public good? What is the public good? What is the impact of student fees have upon access to higher education and its content? Is higher education more than preparation for relatively well-paid occupations? How do the traditional academic subjects react to this process? Are higher education institutions more than training institutions and research laboratories? Is a particular university providing a unique product that justifies commercial branding? What is quality and how is it to be assured and enhanced?

Most countries have now achieved mass higher education in terms of the proportions of each generation that at least embark on a higher education programme of study. A large and increasing share of all goods and services consumed is composed of the knowledge embodied in them and higher education is perceived as one of the most important creators and disseminators of knowledge. This raises many questions that were previously taken for granted about its purposes, content and costs.

Most countries have been experiencing a shift from public to private funding of universities and colleges. This raises the question of how the purposes of higher education are perceived: as a commodity that increasingly brings only private benefits or as a set of socio-cultural experiences that attempt to achieve a wider public good. The line is being drawn differently in different countries but the direction of change is global.

This book arose out of a conference of the Society for Research into Higher Education at New College Oxford in June 2011. All the chapters have been extensively revised.

Introduction

I. Higher Education As a Public Good: Notes for a Discussion

OURANIA FILIPPAKOU

Overview

As mass higher education evolves into universal higher education, with more than half the population taking part, massive debates about its purpose and practice are taking place. One of the most important of these is a questioning of the widely held view that higher education is intrinsically a public good. The aim of this book is to examine this debate in the context of exploring the purposes of higher education in the 21st century.

Higher education as a public good can be theorised in three broad ways: ideas of higher education, models of higher education delivery and policies where ideas and models meet the world of other, often conflicting claims and ideas. This book is as an examination of these three approaches emerging out of the current ideological struggle at the core of higher education that is reshaping policy and institutional behaviour:

1. The ways in which the idea of higher education as a public good is changing—the interpretations of higher education as either a private or a public good—in response to the pressures coming from the state, especially the political control of funding.
2. How curriculum delivery and research might be effected in pursuit of (1).
3. How institutional change might be effected in order to bring about 1. and 2.

Higher education is now a key policy arena for government and the state. The political debate centres upon the perceived role of higher education in securing the smooth functioning of a modern society. To assume that higher education is basically a private good gives it different societal functions from the interpretation which sees it as a public good.

In the rest of this chapter, I summarise the contributions of the book and an analytical framework by which we might understand the changes—at curricular, institutional, national and global levels—currently underway and which will serve as a framework within which the other contributions can be placed.

Higher Education: A Public Matter

During much of the twentieth century the provision of higher education was seen, particularly in Europe, mainly as a public good as part of the welfare state, but this view is increasingly challenged. Recently, largely under the prompting of economic analysis, that proposition has changed as the idea of a welfare state has itself changed and there has been a shift in the discourse. The focus now is upon the private benefits of higher education. Perhaps the key point to be derived from this shift in the discourse, occurring in many countries and supported by governments of different political persuasion, is that the purposes of higher education are being redefined. A consensus has evolved, which embraces the state (both its bureaucratic and political branches), an increasing range of organised interests and think-tanks, and many of the more immediate stakeholders such as employers and university governing bodies and even includes many students, parents, faculty and administrative personnel.

No longer can those engaged in the academic study of higher education take it for granted that higher education is seen primarily as a public good; that is to say, this claim carries less legitimacy than it did. But such a reconceptualisation of higher education is only the start of a question raising process. For what kinds of outcomes are being promoted if higher education is more of a private than a public good? What kind of purposes are being pursued? What kinds of compromises are possible between two conflicting ideological conceptions?

An analysis of this kind alerts us to the social dynamics at work. It also suggests that evaluations of higher education as a public/private good should incorporate questions such as:

1. What interests are served by these changes?
2. Are some interests being marginalised?
3. If there is a state agenda what are its drivers and how persistent is it?
4. To what extent is the agenda global, national or merely local in character?

These are questions for all those who are attempting to form different interpretations of higher education as a public good, whether based inside or outside the academic community; those responsible for delivering higher education including institutional managers; and those—above all students—who are influenced by its practices.

Outline of the Book

Higher education ideas are discussed in Chapters II–VII. These cover various theoretical approaches including ideological struggles between the competing ideas of higher education and offer different understandings of the public role of universities. In Chapters VIII–XIII various models and policies are presented; models which will discuss how various higher education systems have been constructed to achieve a public role; policies by which different ideas and constructions are being put into practice. The focus is on the societal implications of the two perceptions of higher education and the ensuing policy struggles.

The book is based on the premise that analyses at the different levels can help in understanding the contributions that higher education makes to the public good. Individual authors treat the questions in ways that are appropriate to their own disciplinary concerns. Collectively, the chapters provide an interweaving of issues, levels and perspectives on contemporary aspects of higher education and the public good. Also, between them, the authors offer the perspectives of those engaged in research, teaching development and policy formulation. However, the central issue running through the volume remains clear: how at different levels is the relationship between higher education and the public good interpreted and how can it be made more effective? Putting the key question that way, of course, raises a further issue: what is meant by public good?

Part I: Theoretical Approaches

In Chapter II Ronald Barnett is 'In Search of a Public: Higher Education in a Global Age'. He poses questions such as: does not the juxtaposition of 'public' and 'higher education' in the twenty first century have an element of spuriousness about it? Where in a global age is the public in question? What might it look like? Isn't there something faintly mythical in calling up the trope of 'the public' in the contemporary world? Barnett explores and rebuts such pessimistic sentiments. He suggests that, at least, such melancholia should not be embraced too quickly. The internet, the fuzzy formation of a global community, the (admittedly) hazy idea of the student as 'global citizen', the idea of a 'socialist knowledge', the idea of the new formation of a 'public sphere' and the idea of a university of wisdom: these are only some of the straws in the wind that together suggest for Barnett, so far as higher education is concerned, that not only can mileage be detected in the idea of a public but that it can even be promoted to the idea of a global public.

Paul Standish examines in Chapter III the relations between transparency, accountability and the public role of higher education focusing on the pressures imposed by a certain 'democracy of accountability' on the ways of thinking about what constitutes the university. He suggests that it does so by, first, acknowledging but gaining some distance from and complaints against performativity, and second by examining in finer detail the notion of performativity, recalling Bourdieu's helpful phrase: 'the performative magic of institutions'. As Standish suggests, on the strength of this it seems to expose the nature of the responsibility that attaches to teaching and research in higher education, especially as these are brought together in the role of the professor. On the strength of this Standish identifies two 'drives' that can characterise the university as a means for providing a richer account of what the university might be about. In the course of his chapter he goes on to elaborate more specifically on the nature of the relation between the private and the public. On the strength of this he expands on the question of the public role of higher education.

The interconnectedness of higher education, the public interest and public good are neatly demonstrated by Peter Scott in Chapter IV. He suggests that from the emergence of universities in medieval times until the present, higher education has been regarded as a matter of great public significance. In the nineteenth century new universities were established as conscious instruments of State reform, beginning with the University of Berlin in 1810, and later in the twentieth century the growth of more extended higher education was closely linked to wider social and educational agendas. According to Scott, most recently theories of the 'knowledge society' have emphasised the direct role played by higher education institutions in the production of all kinds of 'goods', public and private. However, there has been some reluctance to make an explicit, and exclusive, connection between universities and the 'public good'. There appear to be two main reasons for this reluctance. Firstly, such a connection could be taken to legitimise the subordination of universities to the interests of the State, thus threatening academic freedom and institutional autonomy. Secondly (and more recently), growing enthusiasm for the application of market principles to the funding and organisation of higher education systems has tended to diminish the emphasis on the 'public good'. Scott argues that definitions of what constitutes the 'public good' have continued to evolve and he discusses this process of evolution in two perspectives — first, in the context of the most popular conceptions of the 'public good'; and secondly, against the background of the historical development of the university (and higher education systems) in relation to the evolution of the welfare and now market state.

In Chapter V Mala Singh examines 'the power and powerlessness of public good discourses in higher education'. She argues that the ostensible consensus over, and increasing visibility of, the public good at the level of an abstract policy norm in higher education has not necessarily translated into greater epistemological depth about its meanings or the scope of its applications, nor into concrete strategies for change. The role and status of the public good within a network of organising concepts currently used to frame the contextual requirements of higher education (such as knowledge society, accountability, innovation) remains unclear. It may also be a matter for consideration as to whether concretizing the public good into operational strategies could consider drawing on 'enemy tools' from new public management like performance indicators and associated measuring, evaluating and reporting instruments. What does the public good discourse mean within the different functions of higher education (teaching, research and community engagement) and by what means does it change how these functions are conceptualised and undertaken? Finally, Singh reflects on the most strategic way of taking the public good agenda forward in higher education–whether as an ideological alternative to the current economically over-determined framings of higher education or as an internal under-addressed cognitive field and strategic pathway — or some combination of the two.

In determining whether or not change prevails over continuity in higher education Pedro Teixeira (Chapter VI) draws on an economic approach and offers 'An historical digression on the changing ideas of economists about the public–private dimensions of higher education'. He suggests that in recent decades economists have become increasingly interested in applying economic analytical tools to analyse an expanding array of topics such as higher education. The development of these interests has led to the progressive consolidation of a specialised community that has aimed at establishing an economic view about higher education, with particular attention to issues such as the individual and social costs and benefits of higher education, mechanisms of funding and their effects and the transition of graduates to the labour market.

One of the central aspects in the economic debate about higher education refers to the nature and specificity of higher education as a good and the extent to which it should be provided by private and/or public sources. In his chapter, Teixeira reflects upon the way economists' views have changed about the specificity of higher education since the nineteenth century. By doing so, he analyses how their prevailing views about the potential role of government in this sector have oscillated between a straightforward application of economic theory and an assumption of higher education as a peculiar sector to which the application of economic principles and concepts posed significant problems. Texeira argues that the adoption of an historical perspective will help us to understand how this ambivalence still frames many of the contemporary economic debates about higher education and to understand better the role that issues such as marketisation, privatisation and competition have come to play in contemporary higher education policy debates.

Part II: Models and Policies

In Chapter VII, Angela Brew pursues a vision of higher education as appropriate for life in the twenty-first century. Her text exposes some of the conflicts of values and current practices that act to limit the capacity of the university to contribute to the public good in this era. It is based on the premise that universities should be exemplars of how to live and work in open democratic societies. That they are not, cannot, be wholly attributed to outside influences such as government agendas, or the demands of industry and the professions. Universities themselves must take responsibility for critical self-evaluation leading to change. Embedded in university life are some key contradictions which trap higher education in the past. These include the juxtaposition of equality and meritocracy, the pursuit of democracy in autocratic institutions, the desire for creativity trapped by positivistic thinking, the conflict between collaboration and competition and the respective positions of university members (academics, students and professional staff) within it. Using examples, especially from innovative initiatives in Australia, to break down hierarchies, develop inclusivity among staff and students, and to involve both in the academic project of the university: the chapter highlights aspects of university life that need to be strengthened and those that need to change if universities are to contribute to the public good in the future.

Ted Tapper (Chapter VIII) suggests that it is usual for economists to view higher education as contributing to both a private and a public good. Focusing on the changing English experience, Tapper suggests that this is an analytical distinction that has also served a particular political purpose in the contemporary politics of English higher education. It has been used frequently as an argument to justify a mixture of the private and public funding of English higher education, and in particular to support the case for charging tuition fees. His chapter is organised around a number of interrelated themes: What public good does English higher education supposedly enhance, and who controls that definition? What impact, if any, does the source of funding have upon the pursuit of public ends by higher education institutions? If higher education is delivered by a for-profit provider can it also be a public good? Is the university essentially but one provider of higher education that serves different purposes from other providers? Tapper addresses these questions by drawing upon evidence from the broad development of English higher education since 1945, although much of its focus is upon the more recent years that have seen the emergence of privately funded institutions, for-profit providers, and the decline in public funding to support teaching and learning in higher education.

Kai-Ming Cheng and Rui Yang focus in Chapter IX on past and present higher education in China and reflect on public good in a political discourse. They argue that universities in the modern sense of the term emerged in China only at the beginning of the twentieth century and have been very much modelled after the western version of higher education, according to the movements in the west. According to Cheng and Yang, Chinese universities were institutions of higher education in the ancient dynasties in China. However, almost all of them were set up by the imperial authority as a means to train senior scholars in order to serve the government. This very much reflects the nature of 'education' in ancient China which was understood narrowly as preparation for selection of intelligentsia to serve the state. Such institutions have vanished with the disappearance of the dynasties. However, despite the western conventions in their structure and operations, universities are still expected by society to play a political role. Such an expectation is nonetheless under increasing tension with the rise of recent market-oriented political developments.

In Chapter X David Dill contends that a critical challenge for all researchers studying the public good in higher education is to clarify 'which public' and 'for whose good?' The focus of his chapter, based upon empirical research on higher education from the UK and other countries, is how best to regulate universities to assure the provision of education, research and public service that contributes to the public good. Dill offers an essential framework of conditions and academic value. The analysis focuses on the challenge of designing and implementing effective policies to promote variable fees through tuition caps, the provision of information to guide student choice and quality assurance policy.

According to Dill, evidence suggests most universities contribute to local and regional development, not through patenting and licensing, but primarily through traditional publications, the provision of skilled science and technology graduates and technical problem solving with local business and industry. A 'one size fits all' national policy for public service may therefore diminish socially beneficial institutional diversity. He concludes that the complexity and uncertainty of academic work may distort the efficiency of higher education markets and compromise government regulatory efforts to promote a particular public good in higher education. The most effective institutional framework for assuring the public good in higher education, therefore, appears to be providing incentives to reform and strengthen the collegial mechanisms by which the members of the academic profession monitor, socialise and reinforce the values essential to effective university teaching, research and public service.

Finally Jon Nixon in Chapter XI takes as his point of departure that goods are not in themselves either public or private. Their designation as one or the other is a matter of history or more precisely how people choose to make for themselves a history. A private gain becomes a public good only through a process whereby the public gains ownership of what was previously under private ownership. Similarly, a public good becomes a private gain only through a process whereby the public loses ownership of what was previously under public ownership. In either case that process constitutes the core of democratic politics: the struggle to define who owns what. Within that process of struggle, Nixon suggests, the notion of 'the public' is itself highly contested. Within the modern post-republican state 'the public' is literate and reasonable, critical in the defence and promotion of its own vested interests, external to the direct exercise of political power and deeply committed to the ideal of individual freedom. It comprises a more or less informed electorate. This 'modern' construction of 'the public' is, as Dan Hind puts it in his The Return of the Public, a 'public of private interests'.

According to Nixon, this privatised public remains quietly but determinedly protective of the gross inequalities that support and perpetuate its own vested interests. It is a public without a polity, a polity without a citizenry: a public, the economic sustainability of which is based not only on pre-existing levels of inequality, but on escalating inequality. That same 'public of private interests' is equally protective of the increasing privatisation of higher education and the increasing disparity of institutions across the higher education sector. League tables are a self-fulfilling prophesy whereby those institutions located at the top recruit high profile academic staff, attract the bulk of available research funding and select students from a small and highly privileged pool of often privately educated applicants.

Nixon raises the question: how then might we reclaim higher education as a public good? He argues that we might start by acknowledging that higher education is not synonymous with the university. More specifically we might re-imagine the institutional connectivity between higher education, further education, secondary schooling, primary schooling and early-years provision. We might also look at ways in which higher education might help redefine new forms of civic engagement. Finally, we might acknowledge that the public good must now be defined with reference to a pluralist world society.

Gareth Williams' concluding Chapter XII reflects on the previous chapters and returns to an old conundrum—the question of the extent to which higher education as a public good is closely linked to another question that is also frequently discussed following the explosive expansion nearly everywhere in the second half of the twentieth century: what, if anything, is the essence of the modern university?

What general conclusions may be drawn from these analyses of higher education as a public good. Higher education provides much good and many services for the public. The phrase 'public good' is ambiguous, however, and carries a range of possible interpretations:

- that society values 'higher education';
- that graduates will have to acquire those skills and knowledge that society values for their own individual economic well-being;
- that people are seen to be the most important economic resource;
- that, amidst social and technological change, continuing investment in higher education has to be made for economic competitiveness;
- that personal growth and renewal is integrally bound up with higher education;
- that the state has a social and moral responsibility to support higher education; and
- that important social problems come under rational scrutiny and are, thereby, subject to what higher education can offer in order to deal with them in an informed way.

Whatever the meaning, however, there is a public interest in higher education for several reasons. First, it can be seen as both a public and private 'good' and all citizens should have access to it. Second the quality of higher education has become a matter of public interest. Partly, the interest is linked to the emergence of mass higher education systems, in which there arises a tension between the desire for expansion of the system and finding the funds to pay for it. Partly, too, issues arise as a result of the market being given more prominence in defining its aims and character. Third—following the previous point—the issue of 'impact' has begun to get a hearing in relation to the role of academics as researchers. What are the expectations to which they feel themselves to be subjected? What are they trying to do, and what considerations might they be expected to entertain in order to fulfil their roles? How do they understand their responsibilities in promoting the 'public good'? To what extent is there, or ought there be, a public responsibility ethic underpinning their transactions?

Higher education systems across the world are subject to manifold influences and pressures and many are in a state of change. The change is dynamic because the balance of pressures is itself changing, at the global, national and local levels, as pressures and policies are modified over time. But what effects on higher education are sought as a result of its public being seen as an amalgamation of individual interests? Is there such an entity as the public for it to serve? Can these changes be justified? What societal effects are anticipated through the reshaping of higher education? In higher education we have entered a conversation about its character. There are many voices in that debate and there is no necessary end-point around which a consensus can be constructed. The different voices express differing starting points and values as to the proper ends of higher education. There need to be legitimate ways of accommodating those different points of view. For the moment, we should at least be prepared to go on with our conversations, exploring the possibilities of interpretations and accommodations. That is the aim of the following chapters.

Part One
Theoretical Approaches

II. In Search of a Public: Higher Education in a Global Age

Ronald Barnett

Introduction

Does not the juxtaposition of 'public' and 'higher education' in the twenty first century have an element of spuriousness about it? For where, in a global age, is the public in question? And what might it look like? Is there not something faintly mythical in calling up the trope of 'the public' in the contemporary world? This chapter will explore and rebut such pessimistic sentiments, claiming at least that such melancholia should not be embraced too readily. The internet, the fuzzy formation of global communities, the (admittedly) hazy idea of the student as 'global citizen', the idea of a 'socialist knowledge', the idea of the new formation of a 'public sphere' (as, in effect, 'public spheres') and the idea of a university of wisdom: these are only some of the straws in the wind that together suggest, so far as higher education is concerned, that not only can mileage be detected in there being a connection between higher education and the idea of a public, but that that connection offers new possibilities that expand the horizon of higher education itself.

The Problem of the Public

In the UK, at least, a debate is struggling to get going as to whether, and in what ways, higher education might be considered to be a public good. The debate is being promoted largely by those wanting to develop a riposte to the marketisation of higher education (in which process England is an outrider, along with Chile, it seems). The marketeers rather avoid this gambit, declining to engage directly with the defenders of the public benefit of higher education. One reading of this diffidence is that, being so sure of the presence and potential of the market, its defenders believe that time is on their side. In time—and in probably a fairly short time at that—the market will simply demonstrate its effectiveness.

Empirically, they may be right: it may just be that higher education will not meet its nemesis even as it falls under the onward march of the market. Rationally, however, this leaves the defenders of the higher-education-as-a-public-good argument on the moral higher ground for their argument remains on the table, to the effect that higher education constitutes a public good. Since the marketeers do not engage with it, those advancing the higher education as a public good argument feel unassailed, at least in terms of argument.

There is, however, an argument that the marketeers could call upon that just might unsettle the defenders of the public good idea of higher education. This is the argument that the very idea of the public good no longer makes much sense. This argument could run as follows. The very idea of a public implies a unity in a realm outside of the state, either in fact or as an end to be desired. However, either as fact or as an end to be desired, that idea of a single public makes little sense in the modern world. As a fact, so the argument could run, the modern world has many publics. That is to say, it has a multitude of interest groups who are forming themselves, perhaps ephemerally over single issues. Their formation is aided by modern communications and, as a result, some of these interest groups are global in nature. They can often wield much influence—witness an international charity such as Amnesty International or anti-abortion lobbies. As matters of fact, these interest groups are proliferating and have become a significant part of civil society.

As a matter to be desired, the idea of a single public is also problematic, for it could imply the formation of a monolithic society in which a diversity of opinion, publicly expressed, was far from encouraged. The idea of a public may make some sense in the presence of a state with overwhelming power (as in a military dictatorship) or where resources and influence are concentrated in a few hands (as in the Mediaeval period or in some developing countries today). Here, the idea of a public implies the development of an educational system and the emergence of an educated class, capable of forming and articulating opinion, perhaps aided by the circulation of pamphlets, newspapers and journals (MacIntyre, 1990, chapter 10). Such a public is a reading and thinking public, and is crucial to the formation of a civil society. However, as implied, such a public could presage an unequal society, with a narrow range of opinions coalescing around some taken-for-granted assumptions as to civil rights, respect for persons, obligations of persons as citizens to the commonweal and so forth. In short, this unitary public could be a harbinger of a lack and even a loss of intellectual and social freedoms.

Both as fact and as idea to be desired, therefore, the notion of a general public—attached to some set of universal values—is suspect. In turn, therefore, the idea of a public good is problematic. Accordingly, the idea of higher education as serving the public good is far from being self-evidently an idea that deserves our approbation. Here, surely, is an argument that the marketeers could make against the higher education as a public good lobby. Such an argument might even unsettle that lobby.

The Emergence of Multiple Publics

It is at this point that the argument could take an interesting turn. The 'higher education as a public good' lobby could admit that modern society exhibits many publics but go on to offer a variant of their own argument. Instead of higher education serving 'the public good'—whether as fact or as ideal—it could now be suggested that higher education could serve the public *sphere*.

'The public sphere' is an idea that, in recent times, has been particularly associated with Jurgen Habermas, with his book *The Structural Transformation of the Public Sphere*. First published in 1962, it predates many of the most recent developments that are associated with mass communications in an internet age and it rather depicts the public sphere as a unitary phenomenon. There is an important logic at work here, for Habermas wants to set off the idea of the public sphere both against other large spheres of life, particularly the economic sphere, the social sphere and the personal sphere. For Habermas, it is a matter of concern as to whether the public sphere in this sense has been and is being further curtailed. It has, after all, been an abiding concern of Habermas as to whether instrumental reason has been colonizing communicative reason. And it was a major concern of the Frankfurt School of Critical Theory—the intellectual predecessor of Habermassian thinking—as to the extent to which public opinion in an age of mass communication actually constituted a species of informed opinion.

But if the concept of the public sphere in Habermas' hands retains something of a unitary aspect, his treatment has three elements which are helpful to us here. Firstly, Habermas traces the historical development of the public sphere and, in so doing, demonstrates its dynamic character: it continues at least to change, even if we must hesitate before suggesting that it is evolving. Secondly, Habermas notes—in looking at the 'the model case of British development' and 'the Continental variants'—that at any one time, significant variants in the shape of the public sphere can be identified. Thirdly, as stated, the identity of the public sphere is acquired precisely through it being set off against other potential large spheres of life. More positively, the idea of the public sphere is strongly associated with the formation of civil society.

This Habermassian concept of '*the* public sphere'—in the singular—is not necessarily in jeopardy but it needs updating; and attempts are currently being made to do just that. Two apparently counter moves are made. On the one hand, in a global age, the idea of the public sphere itself takes on a global dimension. No longer tied to the nation state, a sense arises of a world community evolving (Bartelson, 2009). On the other hand, in an age that too breathes differentiation, with communities emerging oriented towards particular projects (both universal projects such as feminism and ecology, but also more specific projects of a more local nature), the sense arises that publics are replacing the idea of a public (Nash, 2011). These developments have normative dimensions, attracting their adherents working actively to realise the kind of interested and engaged publics appropriate to their projects. Supporting all of these developments are modern internet-based communication technologies, permitting more or less instantaneous interaction twenty-four hours a day.

Against these considerations, the idea of the public sphere takes on new complexities. For it now embraces multiple publics (not mere interest groups) concerned variously with all manner of large projects, even pretending to have a universal character. Accordingly, those advocating a turn on the part of higher education in the direction of the public sphere can retain the idea of such a link—between higher education and 'public'—but further work lies ahead to establish this link in these new times.

Higher Education: A Public Matter

The onus, then, of establishing a link between higher education and the public sphere lies with those who are proclaiming the higher education as a public good thesis. It is becoming a far from easy matter. The key argument up the sleeves of these advocates is that knowledge is non-rivalrous (Marginson, 2012). That is, my coming to possess some knowledge that you already have does not diminish its value. On the contrary, the widest distribution of knowledge may actually increase its value. There is, therefore, so the argument runs, an argument in favour of making higher education as widely available as possible, rather than restricting its provision as might occur where it is made available through market mechanisms.

It is noticeable that these 'public good' advocates less commonly attempt to identify a non-rivalrous quality about higher education itself. This is understandable, since it has been well understood—for fifty years or more—that higher education is a major determinant of life chances all over the world.

Following Bourdieu's pioneering work in establishing the idea of 'cultural capital' (Bourdieu and Passeron, 1979), higher education has come to be understood as providing the individual with social, creative and economic capital. Higher education is multiply beneficial for the individual. However, it is also understood that each of those forms of capital take on a collective dimension: higher education bestows benefits to society, in terms of its total cultural, social, creative and economic capital. The research on 'the wider benefits of higher education' has begun to exemplify these more collective processes at work.

Those arguing the higher education as a public good thesis may glimpse a way forward here. Can these various capitals not be seen as species of public goods? There is, surely, in each case, a public benefit. But tempting as it may be, that gambit leads nowhere. The adjectives that have come to qualify 'capital'—'social', 'cultural', 'creative' and 'economic'—are not synonymous with 'public', even if put together. For the idea of a public denotes some kind of voice and some kind of purposive stake in collective affairs. Not far distant, too, is the idea of citizenship. The different capitals may be seen as resources or powers or potentials; the idea of a public works in a different sphere. It summons up a sense of active authorship, of first-handedness *and* collectiveness. Capitals may be invested; they may or may not be put to work, even if they are collective in nature. A public is inherently possessed of itself, engaged in forging its interests.

Here we may return to the possible link that we have just noticed between 'knowledge' and 'public'. In order that a public exert its active, contributing and even critical voice, it needs to be at least in possession of some knowledge. Indeed, in a knowledge society, we should rather look to a public to be generating knowledge—of some kind—on its own account. Modern society, indeed, may be seen as a competition between different groups attempting to advance their narratives about the world. Characteristically, too, these narratives are infused with ideas, theories and evidence of various kinds. These imaginaries (to draw on a term of Taylor's [2007]) constitute 'ethno-epistemic assemblages'(Irwin and Michael, 2003). In this dialogical melting pot, fuzzy sets of values, knowledges and projects contest with each other.

The door is opening here for the higher-education-as-a-public-good advocates to press their claims via a significant step forward in the argument, by forging a connection between higher education and the idea of a public. More particularly, there are three ingredients now to put together: the idea of multi-publics; the idea of a public as having a voice with influence; and the link between knowledge and the idea of a public. What kind of mix might be available?

An argument which I would want to propose could go in the following direction. In gaining knowledge, a student can 'enter the conversations of humanity' as it has been proposed (Oakeshott, 1989; Rorty (1980, esp. chapter VIII); Young (2008); Wheelahan (2010); Bernstein (1975, Chapters 3 and 4; 1996, chapter 4)). Knowledge only counts as knowledge in virtue of its having stood the test of critical scrutiny by relevant epistemic communities. Already, therefore, in gaining knowledge (accompanied by due understanding), a student is *ipso facto* entering a community. Further, such knowledge is—as intimated—a public resource. Even though it may be esoteric and even considered to be 'sacred', still it is in the public domain, available for general access and deployment. We see this these days in situations where members of 'the public' either by themselves or in groups raid the academic literature (in medicine, in planning, in law, in environmental and ecological fields) in order to become more active and 'agentic' in matters which they see as vital to their well-being. Not infrequently, such raidings on the part of members of the public put them in positions where they are able to challenge so-called expert opinion.

The next step in the argument is this. A genuine higher education not only ensures that students acquire knowledge but do so with critical understanding. They enter a space of reason (Bakhurst, 2005, chapter 5) in which they are able to interrogate claims but also to form views of their own and defend them in a rational discourse. Furthermore, students are increasingly finding themselves situated in global networks and a genuine higher education can impart the wherewithal to engage in those networks with knowledge, understanding and critical acumen. More than that, the very idea of the student as a global citizen (Stearns, 2009) requires as a minimum that the student form a sense of herself or himself in an interconnected world, with the world having claims upon one, and having the resources to discriminate between those claims and wisely to discern those that are legitimate. (The idea of the student as global citizen could also take a strong form in which the student comes spontaneously to be sensitive to and to have a concern for the other; but we do not need to pursue that avenue here.)

There are two further steps in the argument. In engaging with the world, as an informed and critical citizen, the student will be engaging, as noted, with many publics. But, and here is perhaps the crucial step in the argument, he/she will be herself/ himself helping to shape those publics in which she or he is engaged. In so doing, the student—now as graduate, we may surmise—comes to strengthen the voice of those publics and to expand the space of public reasoning.

We have, then, in this series of contentions, linked the ideas of higher education, knowledge, multi-publics and a voice (or voices) having influence. Higher education and the idea of a public can meaningfully be put together in the same phrase but it has required several additional concepts and many steps even to sketch such an argument. Further work is called for, therefore, if this argument is to be shored up.

The Making of a Public Good

It is surely emerging that higher education is *not* a public good as such. Its possible status as a public good has to be earned; has to be realised through the kind of experiences in which students engage. This may seem a bold claim, namely that higher education is not inherently a public good. This is my position, however. To be more strictly accurate, my position is that higher education is currently far from being a public good but that it makes sense still to construe it as such.

In pressing this argument there should be, to begin with, nothing too shocking in observing that higher education is falling short of its potential as a public good. As noted, the higher-education-as-a-public-good characteristically gains its force in being a rejoinder to the so-called 'neo-liberal' turn in higher education around the world, accompanied by the marketisation of universities, and the encouragement to students to understand themselves as customers in that marketplace, with commensurable purchaser claims on their university of choice. So there is already a kind of tacit insinuation in the public debate that the public potential of higher education is not being fully realised. I want, though, to press the stronger argument that the public dimension of higher education is always falling short of its potential. There is a fragmentation of the public realm that is only indirectly related to markets such that the very idea of a public is problematic. However, that realisation should not prevent us in holding onto the idea of a strong association between higher education and the public sphere.

The idea of there being an association between higher education and the public sphere is not especially new, in that it has appeared in evidence for around the past fifty years or so. It has been heard many times over this period but it has surely largely been heard in response to successive waves, in which the policy attention has turned its attention to apparent deficiencies in the effectiveness of higher education.

Perhaps its first appearance was in the 1960s (at least in the UK), when the Robbins Report drew a connection between higher education and a common culture. That reference has surely to be understood against the background of an emerging sense that higher education was an education for an elite (as indeed it then was). It emerged again in the 1970s during debates over the 'relevance' of higher education when the state (again, in the UK at least) began to take a strong interest in the shape, position and purposes of higher education. At that time, there were concerns in the public debate that higher education was insufficiently oriented towards providing the skill base needed by a growing technological economy. So there were concerns expressed about the utilitarianism of policy framing and calls to consider the wider public interest. Subsequently, in the context of a unification of the UK's higher education system, voices could be heard espousing a link between higher education and general purposes of the university. At this time, too, there developed a debate as to the 'general transferable skills' that universities should impart, in addition to any vocationally specific skills. More recently still, as concerns about the financing of higher education have come to the fore, an attempt has been made—and is being made now—to promote higher education as a public good. At the same time, higher education has come to be understood in virtue of its positioning in the global economy and calls for the student as a 'global citizen' have arisen. It can hardly be coincidental, too, that there is renewed interest in the idea of 'general education'.

If this crude sketch has any historical validity, two points may be derived from it. Firstly, that the idea of the public good has been framed in different ways over time. Accordingly, the term 'the public good' is but a holding umbrella term, under which sits a cluster of ideas and sentiments, including those of 'common culture', 'liberal education', 'public interest', 'general education' and 'global citizenship'. Not far away, too, is emerging the idea of a 'university of wisdom' (Maxwell, 2012). Secondly, the idea of the public good, taking its different forms over time, has been pressed often in response to the dominant public agenda and the wider societal and global positioning of universities and higher education. To use a term once favoured by philosophers of education, to some degree at least, it turns out that the idea of 'the public good' in this context is *parasitic* on the wider debate and contemporary shifts in higher education, especially in the wider economy. Those espousing higher education as a public good may feel that they are thinking and acting autonomously but, in fact, they are thinking and acting in large part purely in response to emerging circumstances of which they disapprove.

This set of observations may, for some, seem dispiriting. Behind all the scholarship and energy in driving forward a 'higher education as a public good' argument lies—to a significant extent—mere responsiveness and even defensiveness. But this judgment should not be drawn too hastily. A first qualification is that the higher education as a public good argument has taken on a new strength of late. It has become more sophisticated (drawing on large and wide theoretical and empirical frameworks) and it has sought to situate higher education in its new global context. It has also sought to stimulate a public debate as to the purposes of higher education and to give that debate a broad and substantial base. So the defence for higher education as a public good cannot be lightly dismissed as purely reactionary.

A second qualification lies precisely in the charge of defensiveness. Which interests are being alleged to be defended or advanced by the public good adherents? To say the interests being defended are their interests makes little sense, unless we say that the public good advocates are seeing themselves as members of a public. Which is to say, that they are voicing their arguments from a disinterested point of view. It may have taken a utilitarian turn, or an undue vocationalism, or a strident neo-liberalism to bring out the public good argumenters and their arguments, but at least they can hardly be accused of acting in their own interests. We have a right to believe that they are actually voicing their arguments—and taking their actions—in defence of a generalised set of interests.

The Possibility of the Public Student

The title of this chapter will be recalled: 'In Search of a Public: Higher Education in a Global Age'. The juxtaposition of 'public' with 'global age' and the idea of going 'in search' of a public implies—indeed, is meant to imply—that there is some difficulty in detecting a public in a global age. Our explorations in this chapter have surely shown just that. The idea and the existence of a public are elusive. After all, features of the contemporary world such as multi-culturalism and cosmopolitanism take their bearing from a sensitivity to social and cultural complexity. 'Public' turns out to stand for multiple 'publics'; concern over higher education as a public good seems only to take off in response to contrary sentiments in the policy framework; the knowledge base on which a public became an engaged public is fuzzy; and the relationship of the student to the idea of a public sphere is hazy at best. It seems that sightings of a public, still less of a tight connection between higher education and 'public', are fleeting.

But there have already been glimpses of such a connection. Can they not be brought more clearly into view? We have two challenges here: trying to say something a little more substantive about the idea of a public; and sketching out a potential link between the student and the idea of a public. Clearly, too, these two tasks need to be conducted in sight of each other.

Let us say at the outset that there is something disturbing and even shocking about this task, against the horizon of Western higher education as it has unfolded over the last two centuries. For higher education has come to be understood as, at its heart, the unfolding of a student. One might be tempted to speak of the unfolding of the mind of the student; but that might seem to betray an overly cognitive conception of a student. At any rate, crucial to this idea of higher education has been the idea of an individual student, who is stretched by being placed in challenging situations; and then is largely assessed for his or her individual accomplishments, tested by the relevant intellectual and professional criteria. To import the idea of a public sphere into such an individualist conception of higher education could be to undermine the idea of higher education itself.

This is not an avenue to be explored here, but it is worth noting the point for it emphasises the daunting nature of the challenges at hand, of bringing the idea of the public sphere into a relationship with higher education. Against this horizon, there are two gambits available: either to find the public realm within the student's immediate higher education experience, or to find it in the student's relationship with the wider society. Perhaps both gambits may be pursued together; perhaps they even support each other.

Let us look at the higher education experience pathway first. The public sphere can be glimpsed in the student's immediate experience in at least four ways; in the knowledge that the student encounters; in the curriculum; in the settings in which those epistemic encounters happen; and in the pedagogical processes. We have already encountered the idea of knowledge as public, as an entry into a public space of reason and, thereby, into the 'conversation of mankind'. The curriculum can expose the student to the public sphere by opening up the social dimension and then extending it into the public sphere (for example, by looking at potential public claims in social policy, and in the social implications of issues under discussion, whether in chemistry or philosophy). So far as the student's knowledge settings are concerned, the public sphere can come into play through the student being invited to be active in the community, even through social networking. And lastly, the pedagogical processes can enable the student to enter into a space of critical reason, understood as a space of public reasoning in society.

In exploiting these four domains in which the student experience can invoke and reach out to the public sphere, the idea of the student as a 'global citizen' could begin to take shape; for students would be being encouraged to see themselves ultimately as discussants against a global horizon within which differences of viewpoint were (and are) contending.

The student might also connect with the public sphere through his or her relationship with the wider society. Alongside the course of her studies, the student can be engaged in all manner of 'lifewide' activities (Jackson, 2011), either locally or even internationally (and perhaps her university might have established a mechanism for recognising, and even accrediting, that activity). Through the course of her higher education experience, the student can be given the wherewithal to be able to critically engage with the wider society in having her career within one of the professions. More widely, the student-as-graduate can help to widen the public space of reason by contributing to reasoned offerings in public debates (either locally, nationally or internationally). As a graduate, the student should have the capacities to draw on research to inform the development of her profession and even possibly engage in small-scale research while being a professional.

These two forms of public engagement could coincide. For example, within her studies, our student might be exposed to the wider society during her work experience, perhaps say in the clinical situation. Or, to suggest another possibility, a class (in a university department in one country) could be connected with a comparable class in another country. Making use of interactive technologies, such students might even venture into joint projects, so forming kinds of international collaboration. En route, such students might also become more understanding of another culture, another language and another set of social situations.

In a less structured way, students might well extend their often sophisticated computer skills to engage with the increasing amount of open source materials made available by universities across the world, in promulgating their research output. Such knowledge distribution, approaching what is being termed 'socialist knowledge' (Peters and Besley, 2006, chapter 3) encourages a new kind of epistemic responsibility on the part of the student, in developing appropriate epistemic demeanours in the company of a near infinity of data sources. Beyond her studies, and not untypically, a student might also be involved in, say, voluntary work in another country (and even, as I once witnessed, set up a student society so as to raise funds for students wishing to embark on such ventures). In all these ways, and others, substance might be given to the formation of students as 'global citizens'.

Of course, mere exposure to the wider society is not synonymous with an exposure, still less an engagement with the public sphere. The public sphere will only open if it enters the being of the student as having a claim on the student. To a large extent, curricula can be designed with the development of—as we might term it—knowledge citizenship in mind. But what is at stake here is also the encouragement of suitable epistemic dispositions, for students (and graduates) are increasingly going to be called upon judgmentally to sift the information sources so as to discriminate between them. They are also going to be put increasingly into situations where they are enabled to add to existing open source materials (in the sciences, universities have such enormous data sets that they are inviting the public to assist them by engaging directly with that information, so participating in the 'creative commons'). Here, the public is not beyond the student or graduate but rather the obverse: the student or graduate is herself or himself a member of the public engaging in knowledge creation.

Conclusions

The idea of the public sphere is beginning to make headway in the contemporary debate but the concept is somewhat fuzzy and ill-developed at present. Partly, this perfunctoriness in the concept can be traced to the idea being proposed rather defensively as a reaction to the onward march of the marketisation of higher education. Less noticed in this debate is that the very idea of a public—still less *the* public—is in difficulty. The world is now a repository of numerous and multiplying communities with their own positions and outlooks. It is not clear that there remains the basis for secure talk of a public realm.

Under these conditions, a trite and immediate observation beckons: in relation to higher education, the public is everywhere and nowhere. In this age, the public sphere is elusive. For all the talk of 'public universities', of universities having a public role, and of the 'public benefits of higher education', the category of the public turns out to be problematic. There is no grand public wanting or ready to receive the largesse that universities have to offer. If the term 'public' still bears weight in a differentiated, fluid and internet age, it may no longer have the substance it once enjoyed. We seem to be in an age of multiple and fragmented publics; and to say this is almost to imply that the notion of 'public' is dissolving. Its earlier connotations of a unity, of the members of a society in communication with each other and feeling bonds of community with each other, are in jeopardy.

However, a further and more optimistic interpretation has surely opened here. If we go in search of a public on behalf of higher education, perhaps—even in a global age—some sightings of a public may just be glimpsed. More than that, it may be that higher education has both new possibilities and, thereby, new responsibilities to play its part in gaining new senses of 'public' in this complex age. This venturing in search of a public might even herald a recovering of the idea of a public spirit. The connection between higher education and the public sphere can never now be sure and strong, for now the location of a public has an inevitable elusiveness about it. But it still makes sense, with some hopefulness, to continue to search for a public; even for a global public. This very search may even help to bring about the connection—between higher education and the public domain—that it seeks. It may even justify a linking of the idea of the university with the idea of universality; but that must remain another story.

References

Bakhurst, D. (2005) *The Formation of Reason*. Chichester: John Wiley.
Bartelson, J. (2009) *Visions of World Community*. Cambridge: Cambridge University Press.
Bernstein, B. (1996) *Pedagogy, Symbolic Control and Identity: Theory, Research, Critique*. London: Taylor and Francis.
Bourdieu, P., and Passeron, J. C. (1979) *The Inheritors: French Students and their Relation to Culture*. Chicago: University of Chicago.
Habermas, J. (2005/1962) *The Structural Transformation of the Public Sphere*. Cambridge: Polity.
Irwin, A., and Michael, M. (2003) *Science, Social Theory and Public Knowledge*. Maidenhead: McGraw-Hill/Open University Press.
Jackson, N. (ed). (2011) *Learning for a Complex World: A Lifewide Concept of Learning, Education and Personal Development*. Bloomington, IL: Authorhouse.
MacIntyre, A. (1990) *Three Rival Versions of Moral Inquiry*. London: Duckworth.
Marginson, S. (2012) The 'Public' Contribution of Universities in an Increasingly Global World, in B. Pusser, K. Kempner, S. Marginson and I. Ordirika (eds), *Universities and the Public Sphere: Knowledge Creation and State Building in the Era of Globalization*. New York and Abingdon, England: Routledge.
Maxwell, N. (2012) Creating a Better World: Towards the University of Wisdom, in: R. Barnett (ed), *The Future University: Ideas and Possibilities*. New York and Abingdon: Routledge.
Nash, K. (2011) *Transnationalizing the Public Sphere: Nancy Fraser et al*. Cambridge: Polity.
Oakeshott, M. (1989) *The Voice of Liberal Learning*. Timothy Fuller (ed). New Haven and London: Yale.
Peters, M. with Besley, A. C. (2006) *Building Knowledge Cultures: Education and Development in the Age of Knowledge Capitalism*. Lanham: Rowman and Littlefield.
Rorty, R. (1980) *Philosophy and the Mirror of Nature*. Princeton: Princeton University.
Stearns, P. N. (2009) *Educating Global Citizens in Colleges and Universities: Challenges and Opportunities*. New York and Abingdon: Routledge.
Taylor, C. (2007) *Modern Social Imaginaries*. Durham and London: Duke University.
Wheelahan, L. (2010) *Why Knowledge Matters in Curriculum: A Social Realist Argument*. Abingdon and New York: Routledge.
Young, M. D. F. (2008) *Bringing Knowledge Back In: From Social Constructivism to Social Realism in the Sociology of Education*. Abingdon and New York: Routledge.

III. Transparency, Accountability and the Public Role of Higher Education

Paul Standish

Regretting Performativity

In 1979, in a report to the Government of Quebec about the nature of its higher education provision, Jean-François Lyotard coined the term 'performativity' in order to capture what he diagnosed to be the character of universities, and so much else, in the postmodern condition, the phrase that famously gave his report its title. What Lyotard meant by that phrase is expressed most succinctly in the Report in the following terms: 'The true goal of the system, the reason it programs itself like a computer, is the optimization of the global relationship between input and output—in other words, performativity' (Lyotard, 1984, p. 11). Since then the term has become a handy catch-all for the many ways in which measures of efficient performance have come to dominate higher education institutions around the world, measures that play a key part in what we have come to call the culture of accountability. A quick look at the research literature on higher education will make it apparent how widespread complaints against peformativity have become, and there is nothing in what I want to say that wishes to take issue with such complaints: I am quite sure that higher education has been impoverished by performativity. But the complaints have now become tediously familiar, and somehow or other it is time to move on. To be fair to Lyotard, it is also important to recognise that 'performativity' was not the last word he had to say about education, and his position is subtle in many respects. What needs to be noted for present purposes, however, is the way that performativity puts priority, as Lyotard rightly diagnosed, on a particular kind of evidence. The question of evidence is one we shall return to.

Not long after the time when Lyotard was developing these thoughts, and in response to increasingly frequent demands that the university justify itself in public terms, Alasdair MacIntyre made the following remark:

> The beginning of any worthwhile answers to such questions, posed by some external critic, as "What are universities for?" or "What peculiar goods do universities serve?" should be, "They are, when they are true to their own vocation, institutions within which the form 'What are x's for?' and 'What peculiar goods do y's serve?' are formulated and answered in the best rationally defensible way." That is to say, when it is demanded of a university community that it justify itself by specifying what its peculiar or essential function is, that function which, were it not to exist, no other institution could discharge, the response of the community ought to be that universities are places where conceptions of and standards of rational justification are elaborated, put to work in the detailed practices of enquiry, and themselves rationally evaluated, so that only from the university can the wider society learn how to conduct its own debates, practical or theoretical, in a rationally defensible way (MacIntyre, 1990, p. 222).

I have some sympathy with the spirit of this remark but doubts about the weight that is placed on the contrast between the 'university community' and 'some external critic', and misgivings about its tone. In what follows I hope to broach questions of the public role of the university, of accountancy and transparency, in a way that both moves beyond the complaints against performativity and avoids MacIntyre's characteristic hauteur.

What exactly is the problem? If we are concerned that the university account for itself, as in some sense I am sure we should be, then why cannot it simply describe what it is about, by assembling evidence of how things are? The accounting systems that have become an increasingly familiar feature of university practice—in some countries more than others, to be sure—attempt to do precisely this. The parenthesis here is an acknowledgment of the variation that exists between countries not only in the structures of higher education but also in the role that is played by accountants, the English-speaking countries typically employing very many more. But what is it to give an account?

Verifying Accounts

The idea of giving an account harbours complexities that I can only gesture towards at this stage. (For a fuller account, see Standish, 2010.) Suffice it to say for present purposes that accounting as understood thus far is typically a matter of bookkeeping, and as such it reiterates a particular conception of meaning. Meaning is to be found in the matching of statements to what is the case, according to procedures of evidence-gathering that are clearly established. An extreme philosophical expression of this conception of meaning can be found in the doctrine of *verificationism* developed by the logical positivists in the 1920s and '30s. Verificationism states that the meaning of a statement is to be understood in terms of its method of verification. Thus, meaning in the physical sciences, which of course constitutes the paradigm case, depends upon there being agreed ways of testing the truth of statements—that is, in highly regularised and universally accepted experimental method. A notorious by-product of this claim is that where there is no clearly established method of testing for a statement, that statement is literally meaningless. Statements relating to questions of value, in ethics and aesthetics, lack such tests for truth and so in the end are nothing more than expressions of subjective preference. This conception of ethics was formulated most fully in the doctrine of emotivism associated with the work of C.L. Stevenson—a doctrine sometimes referred to as the 'boo-hurrah' theory.

In philosophy, verificationism was discredited long ago, but this has not prevented its influence from continuing to filter through the popular consciousness. For example, its hardening of the fact–value divide reverberates today through the familiar reproach: 'Aren't you bringing values into it?' And its similar hardening of the subject–object dichotomy generates crude accounts of objectivity, where objectivity is thought to be synonymous with numerical measurement. This helps to explain why the questions that MacIntyre identifies, such as 'What are universities for?', tend to be framed within assumptions of economic productivity as the ultimate, perhaps the sole means of justification. In the end this reductivism suggests a shying away from questions of value, a lack of confidence tantamount to a kind of nihilism[1]. It conditions the now familiar pedagogical belief that, if something is not tested, it cannot be learned.

These ways of thinking accentuate the importance of a kind of transparency, and certainly, other things being equal, transparency is valued for good reason. But they reinforce also a particular conception of what is real, with the accent on what can be made *present* as evidence—here, to me, now. This, it seems, is the ultimate authentication of the real, sometimes referred to as the metaphysics of presence: all else is derivative from what is present—present temporally and present spatially. This is valued both at the personal level (I should be prepared to examine openly and honestly what I am really like) and on a larger social scale (we want the institutions of our society to be transparent). This is the bedrock of personal and institutional identity: it secures what these things are; it fixes what we *mean* by identity.

In some respects all this may seem plausible enough. After all, what could be plainer, more basic, than the idea that meaning depends upon the correlation of a statement with what is the case ('The bottle is on the table')? And yet we know, do we not, that the dominant form of statements in our contemporary accounting, in our databases and spreadsheets, has a surface precision and rigour that correlates badly with the more complex, more messy reality of institutional practice that it purports to describe? Let's allow that they correlate with *something*, but this is something we manufacture by constructing practices that correlate with them! To understand this better it is worth turning back to the idea of performativity. When Lyotard adopted the term, it was in large part because he wanted to draw attention to the ways in which such postmodern bookkeeping runs away with itself. And one might add that the more we have seen it run away with itself, the more it has been complemented—in mission statements, manifestos, marketing—by that plainly emotive aspect of modern institutional life: political 'spin'. Do the databases and spreadsheets not themselves become rhetorical forms within this spin.

But these problems can be approached better if we look beyond what Lyotard intended by the term 'performativity'. What I have in mind here are the richer implications of the idea of the performative, realised in the work of a number of writers. A suggestive entrée for present purposes is provided in Pierre Bourdieu's phrase the 'performative magic of institutions' (Bourdieu, 1991). What exactly is meant by this, and how does it relate to the verificationist account of meaning that we have been considering? Where does the idea of the performative come from?

The Magic of the Performative

To speak of performative magic is to suggest, at least, that there may be something about the life of institutions that is not amenable to transparency or to a purely calculative rationality. In order to gain some sense of what is meant here, we need to turn to 1950s Oxford philosopher J.L. Austin's original introduction of the idea of the performative. Austin is struck by the way that philosophical accounts of meaning and language are dominated by a preoccupation with statements and the way they correlate descriptively with states of affairs (*constative* utterances). He contrasts these with utterances of a similar propositional form but where the statement does not so much describe an action as *perform* one. He has in mind such statements as: 'I promise to call you later this evening', 'I name this ship 'Marybel',' and 'I do' (in the marriage service). He refers to such expressions as *performative* utterances. All this then helps to show that significant parts of our language have meaning not in virtue of their correlation with a state of affairs ('the bottle is on the table'), but rather because of what they do: it shows what we *do* with words.

This is surely a telling point, and it is one that already cuts to the heart of the central doctrines of logical positivism, which remained enormously influential in Anglophone philosophy at the time when Austin was developing these ideas. But what is also very interesting is that the more Austin pursues the distinction he has drawn, the less confident he is about how clear it is—because a performative element seems to seep into the constative. A simple example of this might be the small-talk about the weather that is quite common amongst people living in changeable climates. The meaning of 'It's a lovely day' may need to be understood not only in terms of a correlation between the statement and the sun shining, etc., but also in the light of a certain, good-humoured spirit that the expression enacts. More of our language is like this than we are inclined to admit. Surprisingly perhaps, Austin expresses a certain glee at the way his distinction breaks down.

His glee at this 'failure' reflects a way that his pursuit of what might have seemed a comparatively minor linguistic point has broken through to something of more pervasive importance, which extends beyond the usual confines of epistemology or conceptual analysis. 'It's a lovely day' depends upon timing, which is to say also that it depends upon context. This may be a trivial example, but the point applies generally to what we say. The marketing people and spin doctors have understood something of this, but they have understood it cynically, as something consciously to exploit; and philosophers are typically too earnest, too bent on uncovering the truth–value of propositions, to take seriously what such people do. But Austin's discovery reveals something that is neither simply to be exploited nor complacently to be ignored, for this is a more pervasive aspect of language that conditions who and what we are.

Hence, it is not surprising that the idea of the performative has been taken up by many subsequent thinkers (in ways much richer than Lyotard's)[2]. For example, Judith Butler (1997) has effectively demonstrated the performative nature of gender, such that it is appropriate to think of gender as a matter not so much of biology but of social institution. What is true of broad social institutions (gender, the family, religion) is true also of more specific ones such as the institution of higher education, as well as of particular instances of that institution (e.g. the University of Nottingham). Thus, they are constructed most obviously through such performative acts as opening ceremonies, the awarding of degrees and inaugural lectures; and less obviously through the complex codes through which they sustain their academic work, extending through pedagogical practices and structuring the disciplines themselves. To speak of 'complex codes' is not intended in any way to imply that these are merely arbitrary or that they have a primarily exclusionary function, etc.;

these are simply the ways in which such practices must come into being and sustain themselves. This is part of their performative magic.

Now, in trying to account further for the character of the linguistic difference he has identified, Austin speaks of constative and performative *force*. To understand the significance of this, we need to look further at how the dynamism of language works.

Transparency and Transformation

Jacques Derrida, also a fascinated reader of Austin, has provided an account of language and meaning, in stark contrast to that developed by logical positivism, and consideration of this in the present context is highly edifying. This can be explained in two stages. First, and following de Saussure, Derrida draws attention to the way that words have meaning not simply through their correlation with an object ('red' with a red colour patch) but through systems of difference (red, as opposed to green, yellow, pink ...). In fact, and to press this to a stronger point, such differences emerge for us through the distinctions that language makes. Second, however, Derrida departs from Saussure's structuralism in that he draws attention to the way that such systems of difference—in other words, the words we use—are themselves in movement. In fact, with this lack of fixity, our words (and what we mean, what we think!) always operate in a way that is beyond our full control. This is so in two respects: in the first place our words come to us with histories of usage that extend beyond anything we can know; and, in the second, whatever words we use are necessarily available to interpretation and reiteration in ways that we cannot possibly foresee. This negativity, this hiddenness and openness to possibility, is at the heart of meaning and of ourselves, and it is dynamic and transformative. At the least it should modify our expectations of transparency, both at the personal level and on the larger social scale. It should modify and deepen our idea of what knowledge, learning and the pursuit of truth entail. Far from being something to lament, this is the very condition of meaning. Far from being a tool for communication, language comes to seem more like the crucial means to our coming to have thoughts at all. And far from this being a further iteration of epistemological scepticism, we find here the articulation of sense in which doubt and certainty are possible at all.

It follows from the above that the present moment—me, here, now—does not exist as what I think of as the present moment without those systems that differentiate *me* from *you/them/it/etc.*, and *here* from *there*, and *now* from *later/earlier, etc.* Rather than isolating and identifying the present as a kind of secure point, it turns out that presence depends on what is not (not here, not now). Hence, verificationism's account of meaning cannot be right.

In an essay entitled 'The Principle of Reason: The University in the Eyes of its Pupils' (2004), and borrowing from Aristotle, Derrida reveals the operation of this negativity at another more suggestive level in connection with the nature of vision (our sight being the sense that is associated most directly with understanding—'I see what you mean'—but also more surreptitiously with surveillance). He points to the contrast between animals with 'hard eyes' (sclerophthalmic), such as crocodiles, and those with 'soft eyes', such as human beings. For soft eyes vision is possible only if it is interrupted frequently, by the closing of the eyelids: without this the eyes will dry and cease to function. An unremitting transparency is not possible; without closing our eyes, we shall go blind. Derrida writes: 'Man can lower the sheath, adjust the diaphragm, narrow his sight, the better to hear, remember, and learn. What might the university's diaphragm be? The university must not be a sclerophthalmic animal' (Derrida, 2004, p. 132).

But is this, we might wonder, anything more than a fancy analogy, a rhetorical ploy to support a claim that remains still to be argued for? What needs to be said in response to this doubt is not only that Derrida elaborates on the claim and substantiates it extensively in his writings—extending the point downwards, as it were, to the fundamental account of language and meaning that he offers, with the emphasis on negativity, hiddenness and openness to possibility noted earlier, but also that the demand on the part of the positivists for *evidence* itself depended upon a certain metaphorisation of vision, reptilian as this now plainly appears.

It also follows from this account of language that what the world is, is not separable from language. Language itself is part of the world, and it is partly constitutive of the world. (Heidegger speaks of a mutual appropriation of human being and world through language.) Given that language is dynamic, always opening onto new possibility, the world itself is always becoming, in virtue of the ways we word it: in the beginning was the word. All this makes abundantly clear the fact that meaning cannot be understood simply on the model of the correlation of a statement with a state of affairs; such correlations exist only within a larger work of wording the world.

We saw earlier that our language operates in ways that are beyond our full control, and it is important, as we saw, that in Derrida's work this recognition is not an expression of regret. The dynamic unknown, the waywardness, of language (in speech, but especially in writing) has sometimes, however, been viewed as a danger—in Plato's *Phaedrus*, for example, as a drug, a *pharmakon*, something that may work for good or ill—and there have been various attempts to suppress it. Socrates suspects writing of being like an orphaned child, without the care and protection, the direct control, of its parents. A similar, modern anxious desire for control is to be found in the reduction of language—and, *a fortiori* of academic enquiry—to a technical function, subservient to what are imagined to be the needs of society. This hard-eyed expectation is tantamount to depriving the university of the capacity to think, and to the extent that this model of thought is allowed to prevail, society is deprived of its capacity to think. Its reptilian retrogression is sufficient to arrest the university's and society's evolution.

The choice is not between, on the one hand, a dynamic language and, on the other, a language that ties everything down, for in fact language is necessarily dynamic. In the end there is no language without excess. Do we not notice the way that those most committed to efficiency and performance indicators, the spreadsheet and the corporate diary have their own poetics?

In order to draw out the significance of what is at stake here, I shall shortly identify two 'drives' that operate through higher education, relating these to the guiding concerns of this paper. But first let us recapitulate and sharpen the key points that have been made so far:

- Language does not just describe the world; it is also the arena of action, of world-making.
- Language is not simply a tool of communication, fully under our control; it necessarily exceeds our full control, opening possibilities of becoming.
- The way the world is, the way it becomes, depends in part on the way we word it.
- Our institutions are performatively constructed and sustained, and they depend upon the language we use.
- To imagine that language is just a tool of communication connected transparently to ends that we can clearly specify in advance is not to stem but rather to repress its essential dynamism—hence, foreclosing the possibilities of becoming upon which the good society (as opposed to the stagnant society) depends.
- Higher education is an arena *par excellence* in which these possibilities of language must be allowed to flourish.

The Functional and the Transformative

In the light of the above, then, I want to venture a distinction between two *drives* that run through various conceptions of the nature and purposes of higher education, a distinction that will reverberate through our practices of teaching and learning. Both are necessary, and both are liable to distortion. The *functional drive* takes the university to be an institution that serves the needs of society. Hence, the university is accountable to the public, its role being to bring benefits that are transparent to the public—such as a strengthened economy, greater national competitiveness, enhanced opportunity and class mobility. It is an arena for negotiation and *cooperation* over the realisation of our shared and individual projects. The *transformative drive*, by contrast, takes the university to be one way in which new possibilities for society and for human life are pursued. It is an arena for *conversation* in which we may come to discover what our shared and individual projects may be and may become.

The force of these drives can be seen to run through practice at the most basic level—through the content of learning, teaching, assessment. Where the functional drive predominates, it is supposed that transparency and objectivity are achieved by the specification of precise learning outcomes, with clear criteria for their assessment. Teaching and the facilitation of learning are contrived in such a way as to maximise efficiency in achieving those outcomes. Content (subject-matter) is selected in the light of what is amenable to testing in this way. Where the transformational drive predominates, the focus of attention and effort may be located in partially contrasting ways: it may be student-centred, in a manner inspired by, say, Carl Rogers or Malcolm Knowles; it may be subject-centred, in a manner associated more with, say, Michael Oakeshott, Allan Bloom, Lyotard, Derrida or Readings, this being thought in the end to provide the best possibility of growth for the student. Whatever the various ideals here, they will be other than the subservience to the status quo, the replication of society that the functional drive presupposes. They will be open, somehow or other, to new possibility.

Corrupted Drives

But both these drives can become corrupt. Overemphasis on the *functional drive*, is likely to defeat its own purposes. Attempts in the UK to widen participation in higher education as a means of social inclusion, for example, have been curiously counter-productive, the increased university places available being taken up by young people from middle class backgrounds, with a consequent reduction in social mobility (see Toynbee and Walker, 2008, pp. 119–120). But at a deeper level there is the paradox that if one aims only to serve society's needs, what is likely to happen is that those needs come to be phrased in fixed terms, foreclosing the possibilities of growth upon which that society depends. This stultifies or truncates that inevitable growth and change that are written into our language, our making of the world. Or, to put this another way, if the account of language and meaning that has been offered is correct, the *transformational drive* can never be simply suppressed, for there is a libidinal energy, here within language, that will find its way out, one way or another. Here are four current manifestations of this energy in 'corrupted' form. First, it is there in performativity, as we saw, where our postmodern bookkeeping runs away with itself. Second, it is there in what we might think of as the compensatory-therapeutic—in stress-management courses, in the development of assertiveness skills, in notions of work–life balance and in be-all-you-can-be management training. Third, it is there in various values-supplements to curricula, as if any deficit could be compensated for (and nihilism held at bay) by a kind of bolt-on ethics. And finally it is there in those new enthusiasms for 'active learning'—for learning-how-to-learn, for understanding your own learning-style, for study skills, transferrable skills, enterprise skills, communication skills. (For a fuller account of some of these 'corruptions', see Smeyers, Smith, and Standish, 2006; Blake, Smith, and Standish, 1998.)

Elsewhere I have considered more fully a distinction along these lines in relation to teaching and learning in higher education (Standish, 2005). Let me conclude here, however, by considering what these ideas might imply for the role of the professor.

The Priestly Caste

What is it to be a professor? How should we account for the professor's role? My question is fundamentally about what it is to teach in higher education. Perhaps we should begin by taking serious the idea of professing. In 'The future of the profession or the unconditional university (thanks to "the humanities," what *could take place* tomorrow)', Derrida sets out what he claims is 'less a thesis, or even a hypothesis, than a declarative engagement, an appeal in the form of a profession of faith: faith in the university and, within the university, faith in the Humanities of tomorrow' (Derrida, nd, p. 1). How far does profession (as of faith) characterise the work in which the professor should rightfully be engaged? Derrida explores ways in which the idea of profession requires something tantamount to a pledge, to the freely accepted responsibility to profess the truth. The professor enacts this performative continually in her work: what she says is testimony to the truth; as *work* it is necessarily an orientation to a to-come (*avenir*, which resounds with religious connotations of advent that are hidden in the English word 'future'). The academic work of professing must then be something more than the (purely constative) statement of how things are. (For a fuller account, see Standish, 2001).

This role of the professor, in the humanities especially (but let's generalise this at least to certain aspects of social science), cannot be properly played if it is restricted to the description of what is. The emphasis on the performative entails a change of modality, in a direction that might be thought of as subjunctivity: if the description of the world relates to the way *it is*, the work of profession involves always some attempt to see it *as if*. .... Concretely, let us say, the work of a professor might then not be just to provide an accurate description of the way things are but to offer something that adds somehow to the world, an invocation of new thoughts. Are not thoughts, after all, part of the world? This extends beyond a criticism that is fully in possession of its faculties to a readiness for risk, an openness to the event.[3] Openness to the event requires something beyond the range of predetermined categories or of a purely autonomous control (effective performance), and this is essential to the exercise and growth of the imagination that this professing requires.[4]

In terms of the *functional drive*, we can imagine the successful professor to be someone who publishes in the best journals, wins the research grants, manages her commitments efficiently, sits on the appropriate committees, etc., and who is sufficiently established in these respects to be a star in any quality assurance system. In terms of the *transformative drive*, the kind of professor we might look for would be committed to profession in the ways Derrida ventures to suggest—to risking a point of view, to setting an idea spinning, to a profession of faith, to offering an account. And if anyone thinks that this might grant too much licence, that its law somehow might be lax, let her for a moment, to paraphrase Emerson, try to live up to this principle for one day. This, if we can for a moment recall Bourdieu's phrase, would be tantamount to a priestly function—a kind of wizardry, if you like—in the performative magic on which the institution depends[5]. This in the end is a public responsibility, and it cannot be undertaken in the sclerotic conditions of full transparency.

An earlier version of this paper was presented at the British Educational Studies Association Annual Conference in 2012 and published in *Educational Futures*, 5.1.

Notes

1. This would be the kind of nihilism Nietzsche associates with 'the Last Man', whose bourgeois existence, committed ultimately to no more than a life of comfort and ease, constantly keeps at bay any direct engagement with questions of value. In such an existence there may indeed be inflated talk of 'values' and 'standards', but whatever

is referred to in these terms is moribund. Our responsibility then must be to expose false values and not to indulge in complacent reliance on those that are received. For further discussion, see Blake et al. (2000), especially Chapter 4, 'The Last Man'.
2. Lyotard mentions Austin only in a footnote in *The Postmodern Condition*.
3. In much of the poststructuralist literature to which I have been alluding, the term 'event' has a particular force. The event is to be understood as something that breaks into and in some way disrupts all plans and programmes. It is then incumbent on us to live with a receptiveness to the unknown and the unpredictable aspects of this.
4. 'The populace think that your rejection of popular standards is a rejection of all standard, and mere antinomianism; and the bold sensualist will use the name of philosophy to gild his crimes. But the law of consciousness abides.... If any one imagines that this law is lax, let him keep its commandment one day' (Emerson, 'Self-Reliance').
5. Perhaps it goes without saying that this would, in the process, retrieve the sense of vocation within the idea of teaching.

References

Austin, J. (1950) *How To Do Things With Words.* Cambridge, MA: Harvard University Press.

Blake, N., Smeyers, P., Smith, R., and Standish, P. (2000) *Education in an Age of Nihilism.* London: Routledge Falmer.

Blake, N., Smith, R., and Standish, P. (1998) *The Universities We Need: Higher Education after Dearing.* London: Kogan Page.

Bourdieu, P. (1991) *Language and Symbolic Power*, trans. G. Raymond and M. Adamson. Cambridge, MA: Harvard University Press.

Butler, J. (1997) *Excitable Speech: A Politics of the Performative.* London: Routledge.

Derrida, J. (2004) The Principle of Reason: The University in the Eyes of its Pupils, in: *Eyes of the University: Right to Philosophy 2.* Stanford, CA: Stanford University Press.

Lyotard, J.-L. (1984) *The Postmodern Condition: A Report on Knowledge*, trans. G. Bennington and B. Massumi. Manchester: Manchester University Press.

MacIntyre, A. (1990) *Three Rival Versions of Moral Enquiry.* London: Duckworth.

Smeyers, P., Smith, R., and Standish, P. (2006) *The Therapy of Education.* Basingstoke: Palgrave Macmillan.

Standish, P. (2010) Calling Education to Account, in: Smeyers, P., and Depaepe, M. (eds). *Educational Research: The Ethics and Aesthetics of Statistics.* Dordrecht: Springer.

Standish, P. (2001) Disciplining the Profession: Subjects Subject to Procedure, *Educational Philosophy and Theory*, 34:1, 5–23.

Standish, P. (2005) Towards an Economy of Higher Education, *Critical Quarterly*, 47:1–2, 53–71.

Toynbee, P., and Walker, D. (2008) *Unjust Rewards.* London: Granta.

IV. Higher Education, the Public Good and the Public Interest

Peter Scott

Introduction

The 'public' is now close to being regarded as a boo-word, such has been the influence of neo-liberal ideology and 'market' policies over the past quarter of a century. This has remained true—so far—despite the global crisis triggered by the banking crisis in 2008 which, it might have been thought, would discredit this ideology and these policies (Crouch, 2011). The 'public sector' has been stigmatised as a 'cost', a burden on wealth generation, with little regard being paid to the diversity of activities covered by that crude overarching label (transfer payments, welfare insurance, capital investment, service provision and so on). Just as, according to Marx, surplus value accrued to owners of capital by denying workers the full value of their labour, it is now argued—equally crudely—that the 'public sector' is incapable of generating wealth and can only sustain itself by 'taxing' the wealth of others. In contrast during the third quarter of the twentieth century the development of the welfare state was justified largely in terms of investment, in the context both of economic development and of social improvement. Only in the final quarter of the last century, and during the first decade of the twenty-first century, has social expenditure come to be regarded as an overhead, more or less necessary depending on political viewpoints. Both the centre-right and the centre-left share this broad orientation.

Notions of 'public policy' have also been transformed by the increasing resort to quasi-market mechanisms, notably in education and health care, as substitutes for political priorities generated through democratic processes. The State's interest, once defined in terms of fiduciary principles and later of developmental dynamics, too has been redefined either as a 'trader' in its own right, providing quasi-consumer services in return for the taxes it levies (and/or, increasingly, the payments it receives from users), or as the regulator of other providers of these services, whether for-profit companies or voluntary organisations. These changes have been described in various ways—as the replacement of the welfare state by the market state, or in terms of the 'hollowing-out' of the State. But a paradoxical effect is that, while the ideological drive behind this transformation of political culture remains a crude demonisation of the 'public', its practical consequence has been to replace a relatively clear demarcation between public-sector and private-sector domains with a much more fuzzy environment within which a powerful third sector of privatised and out-sourced services, no longer State provided but not fully private either, has emerged. These changes have also encouraged a shift in the organisational culture of many public institutions, towards more explicitly managerial forms. These forms have been described as the (no longer so new) 'New Public Management', the broad intention of which has been to model the management of education, health and other public services as closely as possible on what is assumed to be good practice in the commercial sector (Ferlie, McLaughlin and Osborne, 2001).

For higher education—and, in particular, traditional universities—this transformation of political culture has posed a serious challenge. In the United Kingdom universities were firmly located within what has come to be defined as 'civil society', insulated from both political command-and-control and also from the immediate pressures of the market. Their status as 'public' but not 'State' institutions reflected this positioning. However, both the concept and territory of 'civil society' have been undermined by the neo-liberal shift. First, the ability of the State to provide financial support for civil-society institutions has been compromised as globalisation has aided the 'tax flight' of multi-national corporations and as democratically elected Governments have lost the nerve (and often the will) to maintain moderate or high-tax regimes. As a result the State has been forced to retrench, concentrating on core responsibilities such as national security and safety-net social welfare. In the case of higher education this has been manifest in the pressure on public expenditure. Secondly, the new third sector of privatised industries and out-sourced services that now occupies the space between the (hollowed-out) state and the true market has little in common with the traditional notion of 'civil society' as a protected space. As a result there has been pressure on universities to redefine themselves as state-licensed delivery organisations, a definition that is difficult to reconcile with traditional conceptions of institutional autonomy and academic freedom. Their characterisation as 'public but not State' institutions makes less sense in this new context. Some higher education institutions, particularly elite universities, now prefer to align themselves more categorically with the 'private' sector, as wealth generators in the global knowledge economy. This realignment has also been reflected in a growth of more managerial and less collegial forms of governance.

This chapter will explore some of the tensions arising from this shift—from the welfare state, within which traditional universities were comfortably nested enjoying a high degree of public financial support but an equally high degree of institutional autonomy, to the market state, in which public financial support for higher education has been reduced but new accountability regimes have also been developed. It is divided into four sections. In the first section various conceptualisations of the 'public' are explored, in continuation of the discussion already begun in this introduction. In the second section the historical evolution of university–state relations (and, more broadly, articulations between higher education and the public domain, both themselves subject to frequent and sometimes fundamental change) is considered. The third section concentrates on the 'public good', in terms both of collective goods and of wider socio-cultural considerations. In the fourth section the 'public interest' is similarly examined, again in both narrow and more open definitions. Finally, these discussions are brought together to consider how higher education is positioned with regard to both the State and wider 'civil society' and also to contrasting definitions of the 'public interest' and the 'public good', returning full circle to the preliminary discussion in this introduction.

Definitions of the 'Public'

The idea of the 'public' is the counterpoint to the idea of the 'individual'—not as opposites but as different aspects of the deconstruction of older notions of community such as corporation or affinity, family or guild. Both were (and are) liberating ideas—the former asserting a wider public interest transcending sectional interests, and the latter creating scope for individual expression less constrained by group norms. In their beginnings not only were both embodied in new political and social structures (the state or the nuclear family) but they also reflected a new sensibility. They emerged across the span of three centuries from Machiavelli's classic text on statecraft *The Prince* to Goethe's equally famous account of the fate of the individual, *Young Werther*, although both were not fully realised before the emergence of a truly modern society in the nineteenth and twentieth centuries.

Both ideas, the 'public' and the 'individual', were expressions of a re-ordering of space characteristic of modernity. The former was embodied organisationally in the bureaucratic forms of the state and ideologically in terms of universal principles—for example, of 'liberty' guaranteed by the state as opposed to the 'liberties' (or privileges) of corporations and guilds. The latter was embodied in the private space reserved for individual expression and action. A new idea—of 'civil society'—emerged to order the in-between space previously occupied (and commanded) by corporatist bodies. At times this in-between space has been celebrated—for example, as David Cameron's 'Big Society' (Cabinet Office, 2011). At other times it has come close to extinction—for example, in Margaret Thatcher's infamous assertion that 'there is no such thing as society; only individuals'. The market, in a recognisably modern form, was (and is) a hybrid space, incorporating features of bureaucracy (in the form of the modern corporation and the evolution of 'brands') but also reflecting individual choices (as expressed through consumer selection).

It is important to place more detailed consideration of the relationships between higher education (both institutions and systems) and notions of the public interest (or public good) within this wider context. The idea of the 'public' is not, as neo-liberal ideology would assert, easy to define; nor categorically distinct from, and opposed to, ideas of the 'private', the 'individual', or even the 'market'. Rather it has been contested and remains problematic, as the choice of labels to describe its political construction suggests. The most common label today, of course, is the 'State', which tends to emphasise the legal and constitutional aspects of government. However, almost as popular is another label, 'republic', which today is used to denote a particular form of state but in its original Latin formulation, *res publica*, expressed a wider idea. A third variant is the 'commonwealth', a label still preserved in the titles of states in the United States such as Massachusetts and Virginia, which in turn recognises the synergies between government and community.

The university occupies more than one of these spaces. In its medieval European origins it belonged to the corporatist world of guilds and their 'liberties'. But it flourished hugely under the rule of bureaucratic and later democratic states. It was also a key institution in the in-between world of civil society—and is presently a key enabling institution within so-called 'open societies' as opposed to authoritarian and totalitarian societies. The growth of higher education in the twentieth century was both an expression and a reflection of the expression of individual life-choices and realisation of life-chances, as less prescriptive forms of personal identity replaced older categorisations based on gender, class, ethnicity and religion. Most recently higher education institutions have become increasingly entwined with the operation of markets—in student choices, skills valued by employers and knowledge that is 'impactful' (and sometimes tradable). However, it may be misleading to regard these connections as sequential and exclusive. Rather higher education continues to occupy all these spaces, even in the twenty-first century. Also these spaces, in particular the standard distinction between 'public' and 'private' domains, have always been fluid and contingent categories—and their fluidity and contingency have tended to increase.

Higher Education, the State and the 'Public'

The earliest universities cannot be described as either 'public' or 'private' because such a distinction did not yet exist. Some universities, notably those in medieval Italy, were dominated by student interests; others, for example Paris or Oxford, by those of scholars and teachers. But all were identifiably guilds or corporations in their pre-modern form (de Ridder-Symoens and Rüegg, 1992). Although licensed by Popes or monarchs they prized the 'liberties' they had been granted. These 'liberties', or privileges, generally prescribed their organisational forms. But funding, the overwhelming preoccupation today (and typically the demarcator between 'public' and 'private' institutions), was almost never considered. It is tempting to regard these archaic forms of the university as almost entirely irrelevant to the organisation of the mass higher education systems of the present. But echoes remain; perhaps the most important is that many universities continue to be organised as 'corporations' with tightly prescribed forms of government.

When recognisably modern universities began to emerge (or be re-founded) in the nineteenth century, the connections between the development of higher education and evolving notions of the 'public' began to tighten:

- First, the new bureaucratic states became increasingly significant customers, in the sense that universities educated the new elites needed to govern these states. The establishment of the University of Berlin in 1810 was the prototype for this new relationship. Although medieval and early-modern universities had always educated clerical and courtly elites, it was during the nineteenth century that these links between universities and the civil service (and wider bureaucratic regimes, including the professional and corporate sectors) became systematically established;
- Secondly, the role played by universities (and also higher technical institutes) in producing the cadres of experts in professional society—doctors, engineers and teachers—was also enhanced. These links played an important part in the growth of 'civil society', whether in terms of the development of autonomous professional organisations or of notions

of 'civic-ness' closely linked both to the growth of urban civilisation and of democratic cultures. The establishment of so-called 'civic universities' in the United Kingdom between 1850 and 1914 is a good example of these strengthening links;
- Thirdly, the importance of higher education with regard to economic development was more widely recognised. Universities not only trained technical experts but also acquired an increasing stake in scientific research and dependent technologies. It was in this context, more specifically of agricultural development, that the 'land-grant' universities were established in the United States in the 1860s.

In the course of the twentieth century the 'public-ness' of higher education became more intense. The already established links between universities and the civil service were broadened to embrace multiple links between expanding higher education systems and the burgeoning welfare state. The identification between mass higher education and the public sector became deeply entrenched. Changes in occupational structures, and in particular the growth of new professions, stimulated—but were also stimulated by—the expansion of higher education. The success of university-based science further strengthened the assumed links between investment in higher education, technological advance and economic growth—even before the explanatory framework of the 'knowledge society' became routine. Finally, mass (and then universal) participation in secondary education, the consolidation of democratic politics and the transformation of social structures further emphasised the key role played by higher education in shaping the character of contemporary society (Scott, 1995).

However, within this historical frame of reference it is important to distinguish between different forms of public involvement in the development of higher education. The expression of its increasing 'public-ness' has been multi-dimensional. One form in which it has continued to be expressed was the licensing of universities by the State. Even under the most neo-liberal conditions, the State has generally reserved to itself the power to agree to the establishment of new higher education institutions. Another form has been the State's role as regulator, a logical extension of its long established licensing power but also an expression of more recent notions such as those of the 'regulatory state' or the 'audit society' (Power, 1999). A third form has been public funding of higher education, whether wholly or in part. Two distinct processes have been at work in this respect. First, the State has been a purchaser of specific services. Secondly, it has been a funder of last resort, making good deficits created by shortfall in other funding sources. A fourth form has been the State as provider of higher education. In many countries universities have been until recently bureaucratic emanations of the State. But even in countries where institutions have always enjoyed independent legal personalities the State has often taken the initiative in establishing new institutions. The creation of the former polytechnics in England and Wales is an example of direct State intervention (Shattock, 2012).

The multi-dimensional character of the 'public-ness' of higher education, and also of the more direct patronage or control by the State, is an important lesson that can be drawn from a historical sketch of the development of higher education systems. It is a necessary corrective to the one-dimensional characterisation of universities as either 'public' or 'private' according to a calibration of their dependence on public funding. Funding is only one indicator of 'public-ness'—and not necessarily the most important.

Public Goods

There is an extensive theoretical literature about public goods. Key characteristics are said to be that public goods can be enjoyed by everyone ('non-excludability' in the jargon), and are not diminished by the number of people who enjoy them ('non-rivalrous consumption'). Both characteristics can be contested—the first because access to nearly all goods is influenced by factors such as wealth, health, geography and appetite; the second because sensitivities about environmental limits have always suggested that almost no goods can truly be regarded as infinite or non-positional (Hirsch, 1977). As a result these definitional characteristics often do not apply to all forms of public goods. For example, scientific knowledge can be regarded as a 'public good'—provided it is freely available and has not been redefined as intellectual property (Stiglitz, 1999). But its 'free' availability is still subject to important access conditions.

In this chapter the idea of public goods is discussed in more practical terms—in three distinct modes. The first, familiar to economists, covers those goods the benefits of which cannot be allocated, wholly or in part, to individuals. The second mode denotes those goods the benefits of which can be allocated to individuals, although such an allocation produces undesirable (and even perverse) social effects that, in turn, diminish their value to individuals. So some form of collective intervention is justified. The third mode describes those goods the provision of which has been regarded historically as the core responsibility of the State. Although conceptually distinct, in practice all three overlap. The evolution of the State to become a market state and the changing dynamics between civil society and the new 'third space' occupied by privatised and out-sourced but often heavily regulated service providers, discussed earlier in this chapter, have added to this confusion.

The first mode of public goods covers a range of publicly provided (or subsidised) services. These may include health, on the grounds that improving the general health of the population and reducing the prevalence of infectious and chronic diseases produce general as well as individual benefits; social security, because reducing poverty has an impact on crime levels and respect for law and order and enhances social cohesion and solidarity; and also education, because a better educated population is likely to be more law-abiding, more likely to participate in civic and voluntary organisations as well as being more economically productive.

In these, and other, cases the definition of public goods tends to be a residual one. When all possible individual benefits have been allocated, what remain must be collective benefits (social benefits that can be interpreted in narrow or broad terms, and public benefits that are broadly equivalent with the narrow interpretation of social benefits). The difficulties produced by this narrowly economistic definition are revealed by examination of the balance of individual and collective benefits accruing from the provision of higher education (Psacharopoulos, 2009). The collective benefits described earlier—the propensity to be more law-abiding and more participative, and also the contribution to wealth generation—apply with greater force to college and university graduates than to secondary school leavers in the sense that they are more pronounced. However, it has to be recognised that disentangling private and public goods in this respect is becoming increasingly difficult. Not only does the presence of more graduates in the population increase the propensity for society at large to be more law-abiding and participative, from which all benefit; but also graduates may themselves benefit disproportionately from this propensity.

But, in any case, it is clear that the individual benefits graduates derive from higher education are also greater—in terms of starting salaries, enhanced lifetime earnings and other economic advantages (although partly because the benefits for non-graduates have been depressed by the mass production of graduates). Those who support the application of 'market' policies in higher education rely on the latter effect, and on rate-of-return calculations, to justify charging or increasing tuition fees. They tend to ignore the former, but equally significant, effect. Another significant consideration is that the spread of individual rates-of-return is greater in a mass system, with graduates of elite universities receiving substantial (and increasing?) benefits in terms of lifetime earnings while those attending less favoured institutions receive more limited rewards. This raises the interesting question of whether the latter may in fact be producing greater external benefits for society at large than they are receiving in terms of additional personal income.

This apparent paradox suggests that the balance between individual and collective benefits is not a zero-sum game. It also suggests that there is a powerful positional effect at work that also disturbs this balance (Arnett and Davies, 2002). For both reasons this first definition of public goods as a residual category once all individual benefits have been allocated has limited use in guiding policy about the extent to which universities should be regarded as public institutions funded predominantly out of general taxation, so giving priority to the collective benefits they provide, or as private institutions funded predominantly by their various 'users', so giving priority to the individual benefits they produce.

The second mode of public goods offers a wider definition—and perhaps a better justification for public provision and/or subsidy of services such as higher education. This moves beyond the narrowly zero-sum economistic calculus of individual and collective benefits, although it also tends to introduce normative considerations that are more difficult to calibrate. Such considerations might include a belief in the (moral) advantages of self-reliance or the 'right to choose' (even if the choices made are counter-productive to the individuals who make them). For example, there is evidence that more equal societies are also richer (and certainly more contented?) societies, although critics have argued about which is cause and which is effect or indeed denied any causal links (Wilkinson and Pickett, 2010). In other words all, or most, individual benefits are enhanced by wider social benefits. Not only do these public goods produce a generalised advantage, such as higher rates of economic growth or social cohesion, but they also increase individual benefits, such as lower insurance premiums or improved health. In short everyone is—potentially—a winner. Instead of regarding private and public benefits as a zero-sum game this second mode of definition emphasises their synergies.

The third mode of public goods covers those services that are regarded as the irreducible responsibility of the State, either because they appear to produce no identifiably individual benefits or because the essence of the State would be lost if it ceased to provide these services. The best example is the military apparatus of the State. It is difficult to identify the benefits that accrue to individuals from military expenditure (except those who are employed in the armed forces or defence contractors), largely because much of such expenditure is precautionary. It is also difficult to see what would be left of the State if it was unable, or unwilling, to defend its citizens. However, in the course of the past two centuries, other services have come to be defined as core responsibilities of the State—not least, education (at any rate, to the extent that the State has made it compulsory).

Also a similar argument can be applied to the State's responsibility to ensure that its citizens can compete successfully in a global knowledge economy. Under twenty-first-century conditions this competition for global economic advantage has largely substituted for armed conflict between nation states, strengthening the analogy with military expenditure. But the range of activities linked, directly or indirectly, with strengthening global competitiveness is very wide, providing—notionally, at any rate—a justification for large-scale State intervention. Just as the evolution of the welfare state in the twentieth century justified the extension of the State's assumed core responsibilities into the social arena, so the twenty-first-century shift to the market state has justified a new range of interventions to enhance competitiveness, whether through subsidy, regulation or direct provision of services (Bobbitt, 2002).

The implications of these different modes of interpreting public goods, therefore, are far from straightforward in the context of higher education policy. The narrowly economistic calculus that seeks to distinguish clearly between private benefits and public goods is of limited use, not least because it depends on the ability to make such a clear distinction. It also fails to address the positional dimension. It might have been expected that the growth of mass higher education systems would have reduced the private benefits accruing to graduates, because of the increasing supply (and proportion) of graduates in the workforce, while enhancing the public goods enjoyed by society at large. Yet there is (so far) little empirical evidence to support this conclusion—perhaps because any erosion in the graduate 'premium' has been more than compensated for by the shift towards more highly skilled jobs in postindustrial occupational structures; but also because the development of mass higher education took place, coincidentally rather than causally, at a time when the spread of incomes was becoming more unequal.

However, the wider modes of interpreting public goods are not much more satisfactory. Both to a large extent are dependent on historical circumstances and political choices. For example, there appears to be an inconsistency between increasing State investment in basic research and the growing popularity of so-called 'cost sharing' with regard to higher education, a euphemism for shifting the burden from taxpayers to students and other 'users'. The former reflects the belief that the State has irreducible responsibilities, among which now is the promotion of global economic competitiveness (because higher levels of State investment in research are generally accompanied by an increasing emphasis on 'relevance' and 'impact'). The latter, the shift towards 'cost sharing', is largely justified in terms of private rates-of-return to individual beneficiaries and appears to play down the public benefits that, arguably, have increased at a faster rate. The safest conclusion, therefore, seems to be that these various interpretations of public goods have limited value as explanatory tools for describing, let alone determining, the 'right' (or fairest) levels of private and public contributions to funding modern higher education or of justifiable levels of State intervention and regulation.

Public Interest

However, public funding of institutions is only one dimension of public involvement in higher education. Nor is it necessarily the most significant. A distinction also needs to be drawn between general public funding, in the form of block grants to institutions, and specific public grants made on a contractual basis (for example, for research). While the former may require justification in terms of the public goods produced by higher education as opposed to benefits that can be allocated to individuals, the latter is more simply justified in terms of specific deliverables. In addition when cost-sharing between students/graduates and taxpayers (in other words, higher tuition fees) has been introduced, these higher fees have generally been accompanied by the provision of loan facilities (which often include a high degree of continuing, as well as initial, public subsidy). This is the case in England where institutions are now permitted to charge fees of up to £9,000; but all students, regardless of their economic status, are eligible to receive State provided loans to pay their fees (Committee on Student Fees and Funding, 2010; Department of Business, Innovation and Skills, 2011).

Other forms of student aid, both State provided or guaranteed loans and tax exemptions on tuition fees, are also available. These financial benefits may extend to students in for-profit institutions. Finally most institutions, as charities, enjoy a wide range of other financial advantages. Taken together general public funding for institutions, specific public grants for projects and various forms of student support (including loans to pay tuition fees) represent a substantial public subsidy for higher education—a subsidy that has continued to increase despite the shift towards more explicitly 'market' systems of higher education. The complexity of these forms of public subsidy—direct and indirect, hard and soft—complicates any straightforward justification in terms of the production of public goods.

However, other modes of public involvement in higher education are as important as public funding, even in these extended forms. As has already been pointed out, state licensing and public regulation have always been significant. In fact they long predated the introduction of large-scale public funding. Arguably they are likely to become more significant again as direct public funding declines. The market state is also the audit state. Licensing and regulation will be used to express a range of public interests in higher education—from the prevention of fraud and avoidance of market manipulation, to the promotion of key social and economic agendas (for example, increased social mobility by encouraging greater participation by socially disadvantaged groups or faster economic growth through targeted investment in advanced skills and research and technology).

These wider public interests cannot be reduced to the public goods produced by investment in higher education in a narrower economic sense. They can be grouped under at least three headings—the preservation (and invention?) of cultural identity, the expression of democratic accountability and the promotion of social justice.

Cultural Identity

Universities have often played foundational roles in the construction of cultural and national identities. The foundation of the University of Berlin as a key element in the renewal of the Prussian state following the shock of defeat by Napoleon has already been mentioned. The prestige of German universities later in the nineteenth and early twentieth centuries provided an essential underpinning of the legitimacy of the newly united Germany, as Goethean Enlightenment was succeeded by 'blood and iron' (and science, technology and industry; Ash, 1997). The ancient Scottish universities were equally significant in maintaining, and enhancing, the distinctiveness of Scottish national culture after the Union with England (Davie, 1981, 1986). The establishment of the University of Wales was a decisive step in the rediscovery of national and cultural identity. In the United States the evolution of the colonial and pre-bellum college into the world-class research universities of the twenty-first century was one of the most dramatic, and well as progressive, elements in the larger narrative of American power and hegemony.

These are only a few examples of the role higher education, and especially universities, have played in shaping cultural identity. Nor is this role now of purely historical interest. It continues, often with renewed force. For example, in England the so-called 'post-1992' universities, the former polytechnics, especially those in large cities, have been key agents in shaping new multi-cultural identities by providing channels for upward social mobility to students from ethnic and religious minorities. Although social mobility has stalled, and even gone into reverse, as a result of the reforms of the 1980s, it still remains true that students from ethnic minorities are disproportionately represented in the 'post-1992' universities. More generally higher education has provided the institutional base in which new notions of culture have been nurtured, at one extreme ideas of postmodernity. In China, India and other emergent powers universities are regarded as key national institutions on which to base global ambitions. All these agendas—the 'invention' of cultural traditions, the consolidation of national identities, the shaping of grand narratives—were and are profoundly 'public'; but none had or has much to do with the public funding of higher education institutions.

Democratic Accountability

The accountability of universities to the State is also a well-established historical phenomenon. However, this accountability has taken a number of distinct (and even contradictory) forms. The clearest distinction perhaps is between fiduciary and contractual relationships. Under the former the State acts as a trustee. First, it ensures the good governance of institutions and general conformity with the principle of sound stewardship, although both of these principles have become more problematical in the age of the so-called 'New Public Management' and 'Value for Money' benchmarking exercises (and also against the background of a multiplication of missions within modern higher education system). Secondly, the State ensures that institutions remain true to their—charitable—objectives, again no longer an uncomplicated task in the age of the 'entrepreneurial university'. Finally, the State (in particular, the democratic State) ensures that universities are able to contribute to the preservation of open societies by guaranteeing their institutional autonomy and also academic freedom. There is, after all, a vital public interest in the ability of universities to provide a critical space within which knowledge can—safely—talk back to power, intellectual challenges can be mounted and scientific innovation can flourish. Admittedly there are legitimate limits to institutional autonomy. But the democratic State has a strong (self) interest in allowing the greatest possible degree of autonomy.

However, the modern State has increasingly taken on the role of a contractor. Again this is not new. Universities have always played a key role in the education of future leaders—clerics in the Middle Ages who staffed Papal or royal bureaucracies; ministers of religion in the early modern period who were the public intellectuals of their age; civil servants, (lycée. *gymnasium*, grammar and high) school teachers and members of the traditional professions such as law and medicine from the nineteenth century onwards; technical experts such as engineers in the twentieth century; later members of the new professions spawned by the welfare (and the market) state. What is new is the intensity and complexity of these contractual relationships. Now the political and academic systems interact at a level of detail and on timescales unimaginable a few decades ago. It can be argued that, as a result, the nature of these contractual relationships has been transformed. There are a number of elements in this transformation. First, since the middle of the twentieth century the State has taken a lead role in the commissioning of university research, which was initially experienced as benign largesse but more recently has come to be regarded as more intrusive and controlling. Secondly, the State has multiplied—from global governmental institutions through regional conglomerations such as the European Union, more activist and interventionist postwelfare market states to a penumbra (but plethora) of public–private organisations. Thirdly, as has already been pointed, the grand narrative of the 'knowledge society' has propelled higher education into the heart of politics—not only the UK but in Europe more broadly where the economic case for investing in higher education has been strongly entrenched since the 2005 Lisbon Declaration. Yet, as with cultural identity, only a proportion of these fiduciary and contractual relationships between the State and higher education can be explained in terms of 'public goods'—although all are 'public interests' in a wider sense.

Social Justice—and Social Identity

The development of mass systems has also propelled higher education into the heart of the social arena. As a result of the expansion of student numbers since the 1960s experience of higher education has now become commonplace, although it would be misleading to ignore the importance of workforce factors as drivers of expansion. The 50-percent participation target adopted by the (New) Labour Government in the United Kingdom in 2001 was based on projections of future demand for graduates. The debate about the importance of so-called STEM (science, technology, engineering and mathematics) subjects has been framed within the grand narrative of the 'knowledge society'. However, the main driver in most countries has been pressure 'from below', from the increasing number of 17- and 18-year-olds with the qualifications (and the motivation) to enter higher education. In other words, mass higher education has been driven by demand (rising social aspirations and increasing standards of achievement in secondary schools) not by supply (although, once again, the development of new institutional types that have appeared to be more accessible and more relevant to a mass student population has been a contributory factor).

Within the general expansion of the system there has been one especially powerful strand, a determination to make access to higher education fairer. In most countries an 18-year-old from an upper middle-class family is typically four times more likely to continue on to higher education than an 18-year-old from a working-class family. This drive for greater social justice has generally been labelled 'widening participation'. In the United Kingdom it has produced mixed results, impressive for female students and satisfactory (at least) for students from ethnic minorities but disappointing for working-class students (Reay, Crozier and Clayton, 2009). However, this is not the place to discuss the successes and shortcomings of 'widening participation'. Rather its larger significance is that it emphasises the degree to which modern societies are fast becoming 'graduate societies', in which participation in higher education is not simply necessary in the context of a high-skill labour market but also highly desirable in terms of the ability to fully function as a social and civic actor. Those denied access to higher education are, in effect, second-class citizens. Admittedly, in a society in which income generation (from paid work) and consumption patterns have become key components of social identity it is difficult to disentangle such identity from economic status. It is also true that social identity and cultural experience are melded with technical (and intellectual) innovation and wealth generation in the spatial geography of the new knowledge economy. However, experience of higher education is relevant to all these strands. In many countries, developing as well as developed, a new 'graduate culture' is emerging. Another key 'public interest' because of its multiple ramifications—but, once again, difficult to reduce to 'public goods', however liberally defined.

Conclusion

This chapter has attempted to discuss the 'public-ness' of higher education from a number of perspectives:

1. The first was the various, and multiplying, definitions of the 'public'. The conclusion was that, far from the simple-minded binary distinction between public and private assumed by neo-liberal ideology, the boundaries between the two have become increasingly fuzzy and porous. Indeed the emergence of the so-called market state has increased this complexity—and ambiguity.
2. The second perspective was the historical development of the university with regard to the State—but also 'civil society' (and the more recent 'third space' occupied by state-regulated but privately provided 'public' services). The conclusion was that, although current debates about whether universities should be regarded as public or private

institutions have been dominated by degrees of public funding, public involvement in higher education has taken many forms—of which large-scale public funding of institutions is a relatively recent form.
3. The third perspective was a discussion of how 'public goods' as opposed to individual benefits should be defined. Once again, many current quasi-market reforms of higher education depend on two assumptions—first, that it is possible to arrive at a satisfactory distinction between public goods and individual benefits; and, secondly, that current patterns of State funding do not adequately reflect the scale of individual benefits (and, therefore, amount to an unjustified subsidy of rich students by poor taxpayers). The conclusion was that the first is difficult to achieve, because the development of modern higher education systems has generated both more social benefits (or public goods) and individual benefits; that it logically follows that there is no stable basis for determining the relative contributions of taxpayers and students (and other users); and that further complexity is produced because public goods merge into wider social benefits (and also individual benefits that cannot be monetised);
4. The fourth perspective was a discussion of the wider idea of the 'public interest(s)'. Such interests create difficulties for the construction of more explicitly 'market' systems of higher education because they embrace elements that cannot readily be reduced to public goods as opposed to individual benefits. The conclusion was that, viewed through three lenses—cultural identity, political accountability and social purpose—these interests address issues that are legitimately the focus of public policy. Once again, the range, complexity and volatility of these 'public interests' in higher education offer little clue to the proper degree of public involvement in the governance, shape, direction and funding of higher education.

This analysis suggests that there may be a paradox at the heart of current reforms that seek to introduce a greater degree of cost-sharing into the funding of universities which are justified by the desire to achieve a better balance between (public and private) contributions and (social and individual) benefits. But, as has already been emphasised, the introduction of higher tuition fees has nearly always been accompanied by an elaboration of student support systems (notably the provision of State provided or State guaranteed loans to pay these higher fees). As a result high levels of public subsidy of higher education are likely to continue, certainly into the medium term and arguably for the foreseeable future. The main difference, therefore, is not a shift from public funding to payments by individuals—although often this is how it is represented because of the rules governing the construction of national accounts. Rather it is a shift from funding higher education through direct grants to institutions to indirect funding by means of student 'vouchers'.

The key difference is that direct funding of institutions offers the basis for interventions to promote the wider public interests that have just been discussed, as well as reflecting the social benefits (public goods) that accrue from this public investment. Indirect funding through students makes it more difficult to make such interventions—or, rather, such interventions must be made by indirect means through various forms of regulation. There is a risk that these wider public interests, as opposed to public goods, will become more difficult to reflect in these new funding systems. Arguably such indirect interventions will be less transparent and more difficult to manage, and so more likely to produce unintended consequences and even perverse effects.

The analysis in this chapter has been confined to a discussion of how public goods (and wider social benefits) can be defined, and how public interests, the validity of which has been endorsed by the experience of history and are only denied by a small ideologically driven minority, transcend these definitions. It—deliberately—has not addressed the wider question of whether higher education can safely be regarded as a commodity, given the essence of the transactions that are taking place between teachers and their students (or scholars and scientists and those who 'commission' their research), the necessary imbalance of authority and knowledge and the equally necessary indeterminacy of the objectives of higher education and research. However, if this wider question had been addressed, the answer almost certainly would have reinforced the sceptical tone and conclusions of this analysis.

References

Arnett N., and Davies, P. (2002) Education as a Positional Good: Implications of Market-Based Reforms of State Schooling, *British Journal of Educational Studies*, 5:2, 189–205.

Ash, M. (ed). (1997) *German Universities Past and Future: Crisis or Renewal?* Providence RI and Oxford: Berghahn Books.

Bobbitt, P. (2002) *The Shield of Achilles: War, Peace and the Course of History*. London: Penguin.

Cabinet Office (2011) Big Society, London: www.cabinetoffice.govuk/big-society

Committee on Student Fees and Funding (2010) *Securing a Sustainable Future for Higher Education* (Browne Report). London: www.independent.gov.uk/browne-report.

Crouch, C. (2011) *The Strange Non-Death of Neo-Liberalism*. Oxford: Polity Press.
Davie, G. (1981) *The Democratic Intellect: Scotland and Her Universities in the Nineteenth Century*. Edinburgh: Edinburgh University Press.
Davie, G. (1986) *The Crisis of the Democratic Intellect: The Problem of Generalism and Specialisation in Twentieth-Century Scotland*. Edinburgh: Polygon Press.
Department of Business, Innovation and Skills (2011) *Students at the Heart of the System*, (White Paper on Higher Education). London: Department of Business, Innovation and Skills, http://www.bis.gov.uk/assets/biscore/higher-education/docs/h/11-944-higher-education-students-at-heart-of-system.pdf
Ferlie, E., McLaughlin, K., and Osborne, S. (2001) *New Public Management: Current Trends and Future Prospects*. London: Routledge.
Hirsch, F. (1977) *Social Limits to Growth*. London: Taylor and Francis.
Power, M. (1999) *The Audit Society: Rituals of Verification*. Oxford: Oxford University Press.
Psacharopoulos, G. (2009) *Returns on Investment in Higher Education: A European Survey* (a contribution to the Higher Education Funding Reform Project CHEPS-led consortium for the European Commission). Brussels: European Commission, www.ec.europa.eu/education/higher-education/doc/funding/vol3_en.pdf
Reay, D., Crozier, G. and Clayton, J. (2009) 'Fitting In' or 'Standing Out': Working-Class Students in UK Higher Education. *British Educational Research Journal*, V. 36:1, 107–124.
Ridder-Symoens, D. H., and Rüegg, W. (eds). (1992) *A History of the University in Europe: Volume 1—Universities in the Middle Ages*. Cambridge: Cambridge University Press.
Scott, P. (1995) *The Meanings of Mass Higher Education*. Buckingham: Open University Press.
Shattock, M. (2012) *Making Policy in British Higher Education 1945–2011*. Maidenhead: McGraw Hill/Open University Press.
Stiglitz, J. (1999) Knowledge as a Public Good, in: Kaul, I., Grunberg I., and Stein, M. (eds). *Global Public Goods: International Cooperation in the 21st-Century*. New York: Oxford University Press.
Wilkinson, R., and Pickett, K. (2010, revised editor) *The Spirit Level: Why Equality is Better for Everyone*. London: Penguin.

V. Institutionalising the Public Good: Conceptual and Regulatory Challenges[1]

MALA SINGH

Introduction

The language of crisis is often used to depict trends and developments in contemporary higher education. Debates about higher education and the public good are premised on the view that one non-monetary aspect of the crisis stems from absent or weak public good dimensions in current transformations of the nature and terms of the 'social compact' between higher education and society. Such transformations, it could be argued, require the more strategic insertion of the normative claims and agendas of the public good, not only into the purposes and policies of higher education but also into its strategies and practices. The public good discourse signals a 'contest of purposes' (Clark, 1995) and competing expectations about the social dimensions of higher education. Both externally driven calls for greater higher education responsiveness as well as internally defined higher education goals and purposes are now routinely framed within the entrepreneurial demands of the 'knowledge economy' on the one hand and the broader 'social good' aspirations of the 'knowledge society' on the other (Sorlin and Vessuri, 2007). Multiplying demands for societal accountability also contend with the growing global power of competitive reputational systems as rankings and research assessment systems become increasingly 'naturalised' as definitive measures of academic worth and institutional 'excellence' in the reputational economy (Hazelkorn, 2011). In an era of globalisation and internationalisation, the above-mentioned trends themselves reflect the mediations of local, national and regional specificities of history, social need and aspiration as well as the disciplinary and professional interests of academe. Such mediations in themselves do not open up possibilities for public good interventions.

Competing expectations about the relationship between higher education and society can be grouped broadly under two opposing discourses about the purposes and value(s) of contemporary higher education. Despite many well-founded critiques of it, the still dominant discourse, especially in the policy world, is associated with what is familiarly described as a neo-liberal paradigm of higher education—the idea of higher education as an essential part of the 'knowledge economy', a producer of knowledge and skills for economic competitiveness and a facilitator of private interests. Debates about higher education and the public good, despite a growing presence in research and policy as an oppositional or supplementary frame of reference, are still very much part of a secondary discourse. These latter debates presume that higher education is a contributor to achieving broader public purposes which encompass but are not reducible to narrowly framed economic goals and private interests, and that higher education is to be viewed as part of a 'knowledge democracy' (Biesta, 2007 p. 467) and not only of a knowledge economy.

In reality, both of the previous discourses, despite their differing ideological orientations, are underpinned by some conception of higher education's contribution to 'societal good'. They are both grounded in the view that higher education institutions are socially implicated and publicly accountable institutions and therefore have to deliver social benefits through their core functions.[2] The two discourses have, however, quite different associated notions and assumptions about the roles of states and markets in higher education, the purposes and accountabilities of higher education, the weight of public and private interests in producing social benefits, and the obligations of citizenship. The dominance of knowledge economy notions, which have powerfully (and contradictorily) impacted on the values, identities and behaviours of higher education institutions, is evident in many higher education policy frameworks in different national and regional settings but also attested to in the proliferating critiques of neo-liberalism in higher education and reflected in counter-proposals for revalorising public good objectives in the ethos and work of higher education institutions.[3]

The public good discourse in higher education (as distinguishable from the knowledge economy discourse) is now enjoying greater visibility and attention in both analytical literatures and in the policy domain, and has become more substantively elaborated especially in the last decade. The current economic and social crises in neo-liberal policy regimes in higher education have heightened the search for alternative normative and organisational models, many of which have coalesced around the necessity to re-imagine, strengthen and defend the public missions of higher education as part of a larger restoration of public values and public interest in institutional life. In order to get beyond assertions of commitment to the public good in higher education, it becomes necessary to ask how real and realistic are espousals and exhortations about the importance of the public good in higher education. What are the possibilities and modalities to institutionalise the public good in the practices and operations of higher education? Dill is critical of much recent analysis of the public good in higher education[4], dismissing it as being 'largely rhetorical and qualitative rather than being empirical' (Chapter X). The emerging analytical literature is nevertheless, rich in value through providing much needed clarifications of the conceptual and theoretical foundations of public good approaches, marking out key constitutive elements of the notion of the public good, capturing explorations of public good possibilities in teaching,[5] research and third function activities, and providing examples of contextualisation and localisation of public good notions.[6]

Dill's critique is, however, not entirely unwarranted. Sustained attention to concrete practices aimed at institutionalising the public good, especially at the level of system and institutional design, and engagement with the public good as a field of 'strategic planning'[7] or of empirical research has been less substantial than expected. It is possible that a more strategic approach could help to insert public good goals into multiple levels of institutional design, strategy and action, beyond largely normative commitments to the issue or diverse ad hoc and 'scatter-shot' initiatives, often in the area of community engagement.[8] However, the process of institutionalising the public good could bring its own difficulties and contradictions. It is feasible, for example, that some forms of institutionalisation could close off the imaginative horizon for ongoing engagement with and enlargement of public good potential; produce a creeping fundamentalism and authoritarianism around preferred public good conceptualisations and approaches; curtail diversity in choice and agency in interpreting and acting on the public good; result in the bureaucratisation of 'official' public goods in higher education systems and institutions, etc. Many of these contradictions revolve around vanguardist or exclusionary claims to power and authority in interpreting and enacting the public good. Such dangers raise questions as to the balances needed within higher education between close steering and surveillance of public good goals and modalities on the one hand and creativity and diversity on the other in interpreting and acting on public good goals; between having some broad framework coherence on the one hand without the undue coercion of official models, templates and criteria on the other.

In this chapter, I focus on some of the conceptual and regulatory challenges which are likely to arise in seeking to institutionalise public good objectives in higher education. Despite the fact that the notion of the public good is increasingly invoked as an alternative normative or policy perspective in critiques of neo-liberal imperatives, there is often a high level of generality and even fuzziness around the conceptual and policy content of the notion and what its contextualised variants might look like. Despite some commonly raised concerns about public 'bads', the public good is not viewed as a homogeneous or singular alternative pathway or outcome (Calhoun, 1998; Marginson, 2007). In addition to raising some conceptual and definitional issues, I also take a brief look at some of the potential implications and difficulties of regulating and evaluating the public good in higher education as part of processes of institutionalisation. Given that the issue of the public accountability of higher education is not uniquely or exclusively a corollary of neo-liberal accountability demands, I reflect on the challenges of regulating the public good and calling higher education to public account within the context of concerns about the 'evaluative state' (Neave, 1988, 1998).

Conceptualising the Public Good

In both policy and research domains there appears to be a 'booming interest'[9] in higher education and the public good in the last decade and a half. The analytical literature on the subject is on the increase, with a growing number of books and articles elaborating on the normative, conceptual and empirical dimensions of the issue.[10] Signalling the importance of or expressing a commitment to the public good in higher education has also become more visible in the policy world in a variety of national, regional and international settings.[11] There are also several instances of structured policy, advocacy and research initiatives intended to increase understandings of and information about higher education and the public good.[12]

Despite its widespread, often polemical use, many analysts have pointed to the difficulties of defining the public good in an unequivocal way. And yet, some kinds of conceptual and definitional choices or assumptions are necessary to allow for the translation of public good intent into contextually apposite interventions. Persuasive arguments remind us that there is no single or fixed formula for stipulating the content of the public good, especially in abstraction from specific socio-political struggles, and that the notion requires ongoing contextualisation, negotiation and trade-offs. Even among those deeply committed to the public good in higher education, it is inevitable that the notion will be differently valued, conceptualised and translated into policies and strategies. Much depends on what configurations of 'public bads' are the targets of oppositional struggle as well as what spaces and agencies are potentially available or created for transformatory change, shaped by the prevailing balance of forces in each context.

A critical conceptual issue to which Calhoun drew attention in 1998 is the view that the public good is not a given, self-evident notion and that there is in fact a 'continuous reshaping of the identity of any public (and of communities within it) as well as of the goods which different actors pursue' (1998, p. 20). Calhoun's much quoted phrase 'which public? and whose good?' (1998, p. 20) represents an almost common sense starting point in thinking about the public good, reminding us that both 'public' and 'good' are fuzzy and shifting notions, contextually shaped, contested even within the same contexts, not homogenous, and therefore in need of ongoing interrogation, discursive engagement and constant negotiation. Analysts have argued that there are many publics rather than a public, that publics are not simply 'out there' but are constituted, enacted, summoned, called into existence, and that they could be overlapping in interest, time bound and contingent (Mahony et al., 2010; Benington and Moore, 2011, p. 30; Mahony and Clarke, 2013). To this increasing layering of complexity in the notion of 'public,' one can add analyses which make the point that publics are not self-evidently progressive and cannot be presumed automatically to have emancipatory interests in contradistinction to private constituencies. There are publics, for instance, which value a consumer approach to higher education (Rhoades, 1987).

Such conceptual ambiguities do not pertain only to the notion of the public good but also to how higher education is understood in its public good dimensions. So, for instance, there are arguments for and critical analyses[13] of the view of higher education itself as a public good. Debates here focus, for example, on the connection between public good and funding source and funding rationale—whether a condition of publicness is that the state should have the main responsibility for the resourcing of higher education; whether higher education should be funded only as a return on investment or also for its public good value; what the state's regulatory and oversight responsibilities should be even where state funding is not substantial; and what public accountabilities and contributions might be required of private higher education institutions. In this context, arguments have been advanced about the incoherence in the notion of the public university as a state funded and non-profit institution. Already in 1963, Kerr (2001) had maintained that the modern American university was as 'a new type of institution...not really private and... not really public' (1995, p. 1). Dill points to the fact that, increasingly, higher education resourcing tends to come from both public and private sources, and that entrepreneurialism characterises the approach of both public and private institutions (2005, p. 4). Given the increasing difficulties in distinguishing cleanly between public and private higher education, analysts like Dill and Calhoun (2011) argue that it is better to focus on the public accountability of all higher education institutions, irrespective of mode of funding.

Other debates in this strand reflect on the difficulties of viewing higher education as a pure public good in light of the fact that higher education avails a mix of both public and private benefits but also that higher education has the potential to reproduce inequalities as much as to undercut them through simultaneously operating exclusionary and inclusionary mechanisms (Jonathan, 2001; Marginson, 2007). In relation to the latter, analysts have pointed to trends towards massification and impressive growth in student participation rates which have resulted in the growth of both the private and public benefits of higher education (Altbach, 2000) but which have also been accompanied by increasing differentiation and stratification in higher education according to student socio-economic profile and quality (Shavit et al., 2007; Brennan and Naidoo, 2007). There are also arguments cautioning against viewing the public good as no more than an aggregation of private goods (Marginson, 2007, p. 301; Calhoun, 2009). In a related issue, concerns about the power of private interests in higher education have led to calls for rebalancing the weight of public and private interests in shaping the purposes and identities of higher education.

Attempts to conceptualise the public good have also encompassed normative concerns about changes in what is valued in higher education and about higher education in the current conjuncture. The regulatory emphasis on efficiency and effectiveness in the face of large-scale public expenditure cuts is argued to have downgraded the intrinsic and/or non-monetary value of education in favour of the economically instrumental and the commodifiable. There are many critiques of the absolutisation of the economic purposes of higher education (labour market and employability imperatives in teaching, industry imperatives in research) and a range of counter proposals valorising a number of non-economic purposes for higher education which hold greater possibilities for public good outcomes. The latter purposes include arguments that higher education should afford transformatory intellectual and cultural experiences for students, and opportunities for personal development (Barnett, 1994); ensure that there are spaces for the pursuit of knowledge which is not narrowly instrumental (Burawoy, 2011); promote public discourse (Calhoun, 2011, p. 13); contribute to the building of critical and civic capabilities for democratic citizenship (Bergan, 2005; Chambers and Gopaul, 2008); and provide a far-seeing intellectually imaginative leadership role not only in being responsive to 'the current aspirations of citizens' but also providing 'resources for deepening and modifying those aspirations as circumstances change' (Jonathan, 2001, p. 79).

Public good aspirations become even more complicated and diffuse in the context of the increasingly transnational settings within which many higher education institutions now operate. This links to a set of debates about global public goods (Kaul et al., 1999) and especially the argument that knowledge is a global public good (Stiglitz, 1999). How can a higher education institution conceptualise and operationalise its public good goals and responsibilities both in its local and global contexts? This is a challenge likely to entail ensuring some kind of normative and curricular coherence between the national public good claims of higher education institutions and the public purposes and benefits/beneficiaries of their transnational activities, in contexts where income generation for the home base and unequal power relations in transnational higher education relationships remain predominant.

The previous brief survey of a range of dimensions and a variety of approaches in conceptualising and defining higher education and the public good provides a compelling sense not only of a wide canvass of issues and standpoints from which to consider the public good but also of the complex, contingent, layered and contested nature of 'publics' and of the 'good'. There may well be risks of paralysis or continuing inertia in overstating considerations of complexity and contestation in the pursuit of public good-driven change. What such insights about complexity and ambiguity do enjoin are close theoretical and empirical analyses of 'publics' and 'goods', especially the particular kind of good(s) that higher education is or facilitates, for whom, under what conditions and with what limits in particular contexts. In this regard, it may be useful to consider the public good also as a set of tasks of analysis, debate and intervention for different actors in different layers of higher education systems and institutions in addition to the search for an overarching integrating conception of the public good in higher education.

Regulating the Public Good

Asserting the importance of the public good as a foundational principle in framing the defining purposes, goals and features of higher education is a crucial normative and policy step. However, it is the next consequential question which is decisive for the effective institutionalisation of the public good within higher education systems and institutions. What new policies and strategies, structures, resourcing levels, capabilities and partnerships are required to serve as concrete and sustainable platforms for the effective realisation of public good aspirations and goals beyond policy symbolism? The normative turn to the public good is necessary but not sufficient. More explicitly, it is the 'policies, procedures, relations (internal and external to the institution), and institutional cultures {which} speak to the level of commitment to the public good.'(Chambers and Gopaul, 2008, p. 84). Essentially, one would have to consider what national and institutional systems would look like if designed and steered from the perspective of advancing the public good. This step takes one beyond the normative to quite concrete strategic and pragmatic questions about how public good intent could be operationalised and by whom. Such questions will have to be addressed in the face of multiple, often contending local, national and global expectations, resource and capability constraints, and in contexts where the social hold of public bads remains tenaciously powerful. If one proceeded from the perspective that a public good approach required a variety of socio-political and educational goals (and not predominantly economic ones) to be planned for, resourced and monitored so that public and private interests are reasonably balanced, a number of system and institutional design questions would arise, with both general and contextual dimensions. These might, for example, relate to what the most enabling principles, models and sources are for the funding of higher education or to the kinds of capabilities that are deemed most suitable for those who govern and work in higher education. Certainly, one of these design questions would pertain to the types of regulatory systems and criteria for assessment/measurement through which higher education could be evaluated, monitored and held to public account in a public good paradigm.

One assumption of a shift to a public good dispensation might be that a different regulatory regime would need to be designed and put in place, given the concerns about the connections between current governance and accountability systems and neo-liberal imperatives in higher education.[14] This takes us to questions relating to the nature and modalities of state steering, regulation and governance in a reconceptualised higher education system which takes the public good as its primary reference point. Jonathan argues that higher education always remains the 'proper business of the democratic state' (2001, p. 41). This would apply even in contexts where there are serious limits to the availability of public funding for higher education or where private higher education is a significant part of the landscape. Jonathan, in making a strong argument for the role of higher education in advancing the public good, speaks of 'democratic regulation and accountability' (2001, p. 39), 'democratic oversight' (2001, pp. 76–77) and the necessity for the transformation of higher education to be 'steered and regulated by government' (2001, p. 76). What then would be the parameters and modalities of legitimate

Institutionalising the Public Good 67

state regulation? Bergan in seeking to clarify higher education as a public good and public responsibility (2005, pp. 16–17) provides examples of non-resourcing dimensions of the responsibility of public authorities for higher education, e.g. the provision of enabling policy frameworks and regulatory oversight in facilitating qualifications frameworks, quality assurance systems, equal access provision, and ensuring protections for institutional autonomy and academic freedom through legal frameworks. In these arguments, issues of state regulation and steering, even quality assurance systems are not seen as antithetical to public good orientations in higher education. But would a regulatory regime with a public good orientation in place of a private good one remove the most serious concerns of critics about the nature, terms and impact of regulation on the academic and social project?

Critics of performativity in neo-liberal paradigms of accountability have often focused on state regulation in the form of measurement and evaluation systems like audit and accreditation as well as on monitoring and reporting systems in higher education. These systems are seen as buttressing a narrow economically framed accountability to the private interests of students as consumers and of employers. Such systems are argued to have entrenched an 'audit culture' (Strathern, 2000) in higher education whose consequences are increased surveillance, compliance, homogenisation and threats to academic freedom. Are such negative consequences unlikely or more tolerable if regulatory systems have broader public good accountability to a wider variety of social partners, beneficiaries and stakeholders? One assumes that it would be desirable to have publicly available information and some kind of credible judgments about the efficacy and impact of public good strategies and initiatives. This would require generating and collecting information on what public good outcomes are being delivered in and through higher education measured against public good goals and aspirations, to which publics, how effectively and with what impact. In seeking to assess the effective insertion of public good goals into the operational strategies and activities of higher education institutions, the same external regulatory imperatives might apply, raising a number of thorny normative, policy and operational questions. What kind of measuring and evaluative systems and instruments would be appropriate for a public good frame of reference in higher education? How would one embark on a public good 'audit' of a higher education institution—what kind of metrics might serve to plan for, steer, judge and incentivise the institutionalisation of public good goals and what kinds of evidence would count as indicators of public good achievement? It might be an unpalatable notion to consider that one might have to draw on 'enemy tools' from new public management like performance indicators and associated measuring, evaluating and reporting instruments. Or alternatively, one would have to investigate whether it might be possible to frame or fashion alternative regulatory tools, drawing on other literatures and practices of radical planning (Friedmann, 1987).

It is clear that in the attempt to assess, evaluate and monitor a public good orientation in higher education in the name of democratic regulation, complex and challenging issues of regulatory values and cultures and regulatory system design and methodology arise. For democratic regulation not to tread too closely to the much critiqued audit cultures of new public management, the notion of democratic regulation would itself have to be clarified as well as the nature of the relationship between external regulation and academic self-regulation. It would be useful to explore what the relationship between state regulation and academic self-regulation would look like in a framework of democratic regulation[15] oriented to the public good. This could also shed light on whether in a reconfigured set of regulatory relations, the power of academe would change on Clark's triangle of co-ordination (1983). The emphasis on the dialogical and the deliberative in seeking to identify and institutionalise the public good could restore to academe a greater space to engage with relevant publics on what it takes to balance the relationship between what is valued in and deliverable through the academic project and what drives societal expectations of higher education, between the private or professional interests of academia and the public responsibilities and accountabilities of higher education.

One possible consequence is that the scope of public good accountability could be enlarged if a broader public good orientation (beyond the economic domain) translates into many more significant publics and many more public goods for higher education and academe to address and deliver and report on. This would have repercussions that could simultaneously enrich and burden higher education and bring us back to considerations about what, in different contexts, constitute the core tasks and social responsibilities of higher education, even when conceptualised with public good intent. One aspect of this question can be seen in the position that there are distinct limits and conditionalities to the contribution of higher education to the public good. This is clearly a question of resources and capacity in higher education, as societal demands continue to multiply. But the issue of limit and conditionality could also apply if higher education transformation is viewed as a political project separate from or unrelated to social reform of policy and changes to structural arrangements and practices in other social sectors (Jonathan, 2001).

Conclusion

The debates about higher education and the public good have gone a long way beyond normative exhortations. There has also been movement beyond the use of the notion of the public good as a foil, sometimes lazily counter-posed, to neo-liberal imperatives and impacts in higher education. The analytical platform for thinking about public good issues in higher education is now much clearer and stronger. However, a more widespread, systematic and substantial institutionalisation of public good values and orientations in higher education systems, structures and practices remains as a large and challenging set of tasks. Proponents of the public good in higher education have yet to give sustained, large-scale and integrated strategic attention to questions of system redesign and structural transformation. It may also be the case that more tenacious struggles to expose analytically and dislodge operationally a number of entrenched public bads may be a necessary corollary of attempts to define and negotiate pathways towards the public good.

There are analysts who are sceptical about the possibilities of achieving public good objectives in a sustained and widespread way within the current knowledge economy regime, seeing neo-liberalism in higher education as the 'antithesis of public good.' (Chambers and Gopaul, 2008, p. 61). Docherty, for instance, sees the university as being central to 'ideas of freedom and justice' (2011, p. 11) and the extending of democracy and opposes the idea that the public sphere (of which the university is a key institution) is a marketplace of ideas of all kinds. On the other hand, Calhoun reminds us that 'Public and private purposes are not always divided by a neat line' (2011, p. 3). Kezar et al speak of the need 'to create a new vision for higher education that respects a balance between market forces and the public good' (2005, p. 26). The absence in many countries of feasible alternative political projects to radically transform the neo-liberal market-friendly state into a public good state, begs the question as to whether public good initiatives in higher education must by and large await larger state transformations and framework changes as a condition for their sustained success or whether such initiatives can be inserted (bottom up and appropriately contextualised and negotiated) into the current conjuncture to begin to shift the balances from the privatising missions of higher education to more publicly oriented ones. The question would nevertheless remain, whether, in the 'long march' through higher education institution and systems, some key publics and public interests, some bottom-line public value principles as well as some clear limits on privatising interests have to be identified and agreed on.

In their reflections on public values, Benington and Moore speak of the need to address three sets of issues when embarking on public values transformations—clarity about definitional issues, having authorising environments in place (enabling policy, partnerships, alliances), and developing the appropriate capacities to move to the next step (2011, p. 4). Whose responsibility is it to give effect to the public good in higher education? Analysts have argued that the public good is a moral collective task not achievable by single effort (Calhoun, 2011, p. 2; Chambers and Gopaul 2009, pp. 60–73) and point to the necessary roles of both government (public authorities) and non-government actors in the provision of public good benefits. Both top-down elements (state provision of enabling policy, resources and incentives, framework oversight and regulation to safeguard public purposes) and bottom-up approaches within higher education (principled and strategic institutional leadership, curriculum and research innovativeness, community partnerships) are equally required. There are numerous public good initiatives and projects in different contexts undertaken by a range of role-players, including governments. These, however, need to be considerably more joined up in specific systems and within institutions to constitute a decisive new trajectory for public good-oriented higher education and to ensure that their cumulative effects are more than just trickle down. In this regard, a greater measure of engaged academic agency (Docherty, 2011; Dill, chapter X and alliances among internal role-players and external publics in mobilising on behalf of the public good become decisive.

Notes

1. This chapter is based on a more detailed article which will be published in a Special Edition of *Acta Academica*, Rethinking the Public(s), 46:1, 2014.
2. In contrast, for example, to a position articulated by someone like Stanley Fish (2008) who argues against the idea that universities and academics have social obligations of any kind which must be given effect through the core functions of higher education.
3. See, for example, Bailey and Freedman, 2011; Hind, 2010.
4. In this regard Dill exempts the work of economists.
5. See, for example, Melanie Walker (2012) on developing public good capabilities in professional education and training.
6. See Sall et al., 2003; B. Leibowitz (ed), 2012.
7. In relation to strategic planning for the public good, it may be possible to draw on other literatures and approaches to planning besides the New Public Management framing of planning. See, for example, John Friedmann (1987) on the notion of radical/oppositional planning.
8. Strong arguments have been put forward for not reducing public good possibilities to community engagement as an obvious area of higher education societal involvement

but to consider public good possibilities as integral to teaching and research functions as well (Jonathan, 2001; Chambers and Gopaul, 2008, pp. 78–82).
9. I am drawing on the language used by Edelstein and Nunner-Winkler (eds), 2005, p.1, in their question about the 'booming interest' in morality.
10. See, for example, Jonathan, 2001; Newman and Couturier, 2002; Weber and Bergan, 2005; Calhoun, 2006; Docherty, 2011; Nixon, 2011; Rhoten and Calhoun, 2011; Leibovitz, 2012.
11. See, for example, espousals of the importance of the connection between higher education and the 'public good' in the policy documents and declarations of UNESCO 2009 Communiqué from the World Congress on Higher Education, declaring higher education to *be* a public good and deserving of support from the public purse as well as a contributor to the public good (www.unesco.org); the 2001 Prague Communiqué in the Bologna Process where ministers supported the idea that 'higher education should be considered a public good and... a public responsibility' (www.ehea.info), the Association of African Universities 2004 Accra Declaration on GATS and the Internationalisation of Higher Education in Africa (www.aau.org); expressing the commitment to higher education as a 'public mandate', even the World Bank in the report of its Task Force on Higher Education and Society: Peril and Promise is argued to be putting public interest back into higher education (Post et al., 2004)); the Higher Education Funding Council for England 2009 call for micro-studies demonstrating the public benefits of UK universities (www.hefce.ac.uk)
12. See, for example, in the US, the National Forum on Higher Education and the Public Good at the University of Michigan (www.soe.umich.edu); in the UK the HEFCE project on the Public Engagement of Universities; the SSRC Public Sphere Forum (http://publicsphere.ssrc.org).
13. See, for example, Jonathan, 2001.
14. See for example critiques of quality assurance systems in Strathern, 2000; Morley, 2003.
15. See Jonathan's point that a new social compact would have to be developed between the state and academe (2001).

References

Altbach, P. G. (2000) What Higher Education Does Right, *International Higher Education*, http://www.bc.edu/bc_org/avp/soe/cihe/newsletter/News18/text1.html
Bailey, M., and Freedman (eds). (2011) *The Assault on Universities*: A Manifesto for Resistance. London: Pluto Press.
Barnett, R. (1994) *The Limits of Competence*: Knowledge, Higher Education and Society. Bristol: SRHE and Open University Press.
Benington, J., and Moore. M. H. (eds). (2011) *Public Value*: Theory and Practice. London: Palgrave.
Bergan, S. (2005) Higher education as a 'public good and public responsibility': what does it mean? in: L. Weber and S. Bergan (eds), The Public Responsibility for Higher Education and Research. Council of Europe Publishing, Strasbourg.
Biesta, G. 2007, Towards the knowledge democracy? Knowledge production and the civic role of the university, *Studies in the Philosophy of Education*, 26, 467–479.

Brennan, J., and Naidoo R. (2007) Higher Education and the Achievement (or Prevention) of Equity and Social Justice, in Higher Education Looking Forward: Relations between Higher Education and Society. European Science Foundation, pp. 25–38. Strasbourg: www.esf.org

Burawoy, M. (2011) Redefining the Public University, http://publicsphere.ssrc.org/burawoy

Calhoun, C. (1998) *The Public Good as a Social and Cultural Project*, in Private Action and the Public Good, edited by W. W. Powell and E. C. Clemens. New Haven, Yale University Press.

Calhoun, C. (2006) The University and the Public Good, *Thesis* 11: 84, p. 7–43.

Calhoun, C. (2009) Remaking America: *Public Institutions and the Public Good*, SSRC public sphere Forum http://publicsphere.ssrc.org/calhoun

Calhoun, C. (2011) The Public Mission of the Research University, in: Rhoten D. and Calhoun C. (eds), *Knowledge Matters: The Public Mission of the Research University*. New York, Columbia University Press.

Chambers, T., and Gopaul, B. (2009) Decoding the Public Good of Higher Education, *Journal of Higher Education Outreach and Engagement*, 12:4, 59–91.

Clark, B. R. (1983) The Higher Education System: Academic Organization in Cross-National Perspective. Berkeley: University of California Press.

Dill, D. (2005) *The Public Good, the Public Interest, and Public Higher Education*, Background Paper, Public Policy for Academic Quality Research Programme, University of North Carolina at Chapel Hill, www.unc.edu/ppag

Docherty, N. (2011) *For the University: Democracy and the Future of the Institution.* London: Bloomsbury.

Edelstein, W., and Nunner-Winkler, G. (eds), 2005:1, Morality in Context, Boston, Elsevier.

Fish, S. (2008) *Save the World on Your Own Time*. New York: Oxford University Press Inc.

Friedmann, J. (1987) *Planning in the Public Domain*. Princeton, Princeton: University Press.

Hazelkorn, E. (2011) *Rankings and the Reshaping of Higher Education: The Battle for World-Class Excellence*. Houndmills, UK: Palgrave Macmillan.

Hind, D. (2010) *The Return of the Public*. London: Verso.

Jonathan, R. (2001) *Higher Education Transformation and the Public Good*, Kagisano, Council on Higher Education Discussion Series, Pretoria, 36–89.

Kaul, I., Grunberg, G., and Stern, M. A. (1999) *Global Public Goods: International Co-operation in the 21st Century*. New York: Oxford University Press, Inc.

Kerr, C. (2001) *The Uses of the University*, (5th edn). Cambridge, MA: Harvard University Press.

Kezar, A. J., Chambers, T. C., and Burkhardt, J. C. (eds). (2005) *Higher Education for the Public Good*. San Francisco: Jossey-Bass.

Leibowitz, B. (ed). (2012) *Higher Education for the Public Good: Views from the South*, Stoke-on-Trent, Trentham Books Ltd.

Mahony, N., Newman, J., and Barnett, C. (eds). (2010) *Rethinking the Public: Innovations in Research, Theory and Politics Bristol*: Policy Press.

Mahony, N., and Clarke, (2013) Public Crises, Public Futures, *Cultural Studies*, 27:4.

Marginson, S. (2007) The Public/Private Divide in Higher Education: A Global Revision; *Higher Education*, 53, 307–333.

Morley, L. (2003) *Quality and Power in Higher Education*: Maidenhead. SRHE and Open University Press.
Neave, G. (1988) *On the Cultivation of Quality, Efficiency and Enterprise: an Overview of Recent Trends in Higher Education in Western Europe, 1986–1988*, European Journal of Education, 23:1/2, 7–23.
Neave, G. (1998) The Evaluative State Reconsidered, *European Journal of Education*, 33:3, 265–284.
Newman, F., and Couturier, L. K. 2002 January. *Trading Public Good in the Higher Education Market*, London. The Observatory on Borderless Higher Education, Report.
Nixon, J. (2011) *Higher Education and the Public Good: Imagining the University*. London, Continuum Books.
Post, D. et al., (2004) *World Bank okays Public Interest in Higher Education, Higher Education*, 48, 213–229.
Rhoades, G. (1987) Higher Education in a Consumer Society, *Journal of Higher Education*, 58:1.
Rhoten, D., and Calhoun, C. (eds). (2011) *Knowledge Matters: The Public Mission of the Research University*. New York. Columbia University Press.
Sall, E; Lebeau, Y., and Kassimir, (2003) The Public Dimensions of the University in Africa, JHEA/RESA, 1:1, 126–148.
Shattock, M. (ed). (2009) *Entrepreneurialism in Universities and the Knowledge Economy – Diversification and Organizational Change in European Higher Education*. Berkshire: SRHE/Open University Press.
Shavit, Y., Arum, R., and Gamoran, A. (eds). (2007) *Stratification in Higher Education: A Comparative Study*, Stanford. Stanford University Press.
Sorlin, S., and Vessuri, H. (eds). (2007) *Knowledge Society vs Knowledge Economy: Knowledge, Power and politics*. Paris: Palgrave Macmillan, UNESCO/IAU.
Stiglitz, J. E. (eds). (1999) Knowledge as a Global Public Good, in *Global Public Goods* Kaul et al., New York: Oxford University Press Inc.
Strathern, M. (2000) *Audit Cultures*. London: Routledge.
Walker, M. (2012) *Universities, Professional Capabilities and Contributions To The Public Good in South Africa, Compare: A Journal of Comparative and International Education*, 42:6, 819–838.
Weber, L., and Bergan, S. (eds). (2005) *The Public Responsibility for Higher Education and Research*. Strasbourg. Council of Europe Publishing.

VI. A Most Public Private Matter— Changing Ideas of Economists about the Public–Private Dimensions of Higher Education

PEDRO TEIXEIRA

Introduction[1]

In recent decades it has become increasingly popular among economists to apply economic tools to analyse an expanding array of topics one of which is (higher) education. The development of these interests has led to the progressive consolidation of a specialised community that has aimed at establishing an economic view about higher education, with particular attention to issues such as the individual and social costs and benefits, mechanisms of funding and their effects and the transition of graduates to the labour market (Teixeira, 2001; Winston, 1999). The development of an economic approach to higher education issues has been received with interest, but also with controversy and even resistance. Several social scientists and policy makers have regarded it as yet another example of economic imperialism with little potential to contribute to a better understanding of higher education systems and higher education institutions (see Fine and Milonakis, 2009). Despite such resistance, economic concepts and arguments have made their way and are nowadays often used in public debates about higher education, notably in aspects such as funding (Teixeira 2009a and 2009b).

One of the central aspects in the economic debate about higher education refers to the nature and specificity of higher education as a good and the extent to which it should be provided as a public service or a private commodity. The debate about this issue has a long history in economics and goes back to the early stages of the development of political economy as an autonomous field of analysis. Since the late eighteenth century, leading figures in economic thought have reflected about the economic nature and dimensions of education and about the benefits and shortcomings of government intervention in higher education vis-à-vis the market–private provision. In these old reflections we find the roots of most of the contemporary economic discourse about the degree of market and state regulation that is appropriate for education. The old debates have nurtured and shaped the views of contemporary economists about higher education and the nuances in the application of economic principles to educational issues.

In this chapter, we will reflect upon the way economists' views about the specificity of higher education evolved from the late eighteenth century to the late twentieth century. By doing so, we will analyse how their prevailing views about the potential role of government in this sector have oscillated between a straightforward application of economic theory and an assumption of higher education as a peculiar sector to which the application of economic principles and concepts poses significant problems. The adoption of an historical perspective will help us to understand how this ambivalence still frames many of the contemporary economic debates about higher education and also to understand better the role that issues such as marketisation, privatisation and competition have come to play in contemporary higher education policy debates.

Constructing the Canon

Adam Smith and the Case for Market Forces in Higher Education

Since the emergence of economics, or more precisely political economy, as an autonomous body of knowledge in the late eighteenth century, economists have been attracted to the atypical subject of education, and particularly to universities. Hence, throughout the last two and a half centuries several leading figures in economics have reflected about the proper role of education, and more interestingly for contemporary economists, about the economic nature and dimensions of (higher) education. In these reflections we find the roots of most of the contemporary economic discourse on the applicability of markets to (higher) education.

As a good disciple of the Scottish Enlightenment, Adam Smith had great confidence in the power of education to mould and improve human behaviour, and he played down the importance of factors such as abilities and natural influences in accounting for differences in human character (Smith, 1976, pp. 28–29). These differences, promoted by social intercourse and education, would become increasingly useful, since the greater the difference of talents, the greater the difference of professions, and necessarily of products. Combined with the disposition to truck, barter and exchange, this meant that the entire community would benefit from the productive outcome of these differences. For Adam Smith the price of labour had to provide a compensation for formal education, notably in those cases in which the individual underwent a long process of education before beginning working life (1978, p. 495). The use of metaphors like instruments or machines to denominate workers (especially the educated ones) was not merely rhetorical, since education was also an important source of society's total capital (1976, pp. 118–119) and the acquired abilities through education were part of the nation's capital (1976, p. 282).[2]

However, for Smith, education was also important because it provided what modern economists would call social benefits. Education improved moral standards, provided individuals with subjects of thought and speculation, promoted a more peaceful character (and thus a more stable society), and curbed youngsters to the authority of the parents (1978, p. 540). Education also promoted a better understanding and judgement of government policies and made the lower classes less vulnerable to political intrigue and conspiracy (1976, p. 788).

Despite this Smith clearly favoured the role of private initiative over public ones in the provision of education, by relying on the effectiveness of competition, which, by stimulating rivalry and emulation, promoted excellence in terms of educational provision (1976, p. 759). The learning of the basic and most essential skills—reading, writing and counting—were reasonably performed, in quantity and in quality, by private institutions:

> *Those parts of education, is to be observed, for the teaching of which there are no publick institutions, are generally the best taught* (Smith 1976, p. 764).[3]

On the contrary, public institutions, namely universities, were not only frequently ineffective in their teaching, but also highly resistant to the introduction of new advances in knowledge. The fact that these kinds of privileges were awarded to public institutions was not only harmful to those institutions, but also to private ones, since it promoted inefficiency and idleness in the former, and obstructed the development of the latter (see also 1977, pp. 173–179). Moreover, Adam Smith preferred processes of learning with a strong practical emphasis which, he thought, were normally overlooked by public institutions.

Despite the objections to public intervention, there were a few circumstances that required some state role in education, namely in the case of the working classes, due to its political and moral benefits (Smith, 1976, p. 788). Moreover, education provided another reason for state intervention in order to neutralise some of the effects of the extensive development of the division of labour. Although the division of labour was a major force for a greater accumulation of wealth, due to the enhanced productivity associated with specialisation, the development of this process meant that the tasks performed by each individual became simpler and this simplicity prevented individuals from using their overall intellectual capacities.

Hence, the government was called to play a role mainly in the case of the labouring classes. Public support would consist of the promotion of a network of parish or district elementary schools, with shared costs between public and private sources. The government would take charge of the fixed costs, namely by providing a building where the activities would take place, and a part of the current costs (a part of the teachers' wages); and parents would assume the running costs of the schools, especially the remuneration of the teachers. Since both government and workers benefited from education, and in order to promote both efficiency and enlightenment, both should participate in its costs, with additional support potentially coming from private donors (1976, p. 815). Although Smith did not propose compulsory basic education, he suggested instruments that would indirectly promote universal basic education, such as the requirement of an examination on those basic skills for every individual seeking to join a corporation or start any business (1976, p. 786). Thus, for Smith, and although he regarded education as mostly a private issue, it had important social and political implications that required some degree of government intervention.

John Stuart Mill and the Emergence of State Paternalism in Education

This Smithian emphasis on the virtues of competition and private initiative in education would set the tone for most economic thinking about education during the nineteenth century. However, the tone would start to change slightly by mid-nineteenth century with John Stuart Mill. Mill was arguably the classical political economist who wrote most extensively on education. For him, education had various benefits at the individual and the social levels, as well as moral, political and economic impacts. At the political level, this was related to the advantages of a progressive enlargement of political participation, which necessitated prior education. Although an elite was in general better educated, and more prepared for the exercise of power, the aim was to combine this better-educated elite with the more widespread judgment and participation of the people. A more educated population increased the accountability of the political powers, promoting a better convergence of interest between the rulers and the ruled (1977, p. 23). Education also improved society since it promoted a more effective and prosperous society through a better awareness of individual and social purposes. It also reduced the superstition, credulity or mistrust typically produced by ignorance, and since each educated individual influenced his fellow citizens by his example, this had an endemic effect of promoting good habits and a virtuous life.

Mill was important among other classical political economists in that he considered the benefits of education were also prominent in economic terms and therefore a part of educational expenditures could be regarded as an investment with an economic rationale underpinning it (Mill, 1965, pp. 106 and 413–415). Moreover, the benefits tended to be above the contribution to production which he saw as 'a natural monopoly in favour of the skilled labourers' (1965, p. 386). Thus, he was very critical of a situation that favoured educated workers' access to well-remunerated tasks while restricting un- or less-educated ones, with attendant issues of nepotism. Hence, he saw the need for broadening access to education, especially in the lower levels of society.

For Mill it was crucial to ensure a satisfactory quantity and quality of the education provided. In terms of quantity, it was important to promote a more efficient use of resources; thus his proposal to concentrate all the educational endowments of a district in one single fund devoted to the maintenance of fewer but larger establishments (Mill, 1984, p. 211). In terms of quality he was very critical of private institutions, in particular the endowed ones, which he considered had deviated from their original and relevant purposes (1988, XXVIII, p. 298). It was this poor quality of education that required governmental intervention. Although it was possible that parents would perform an effective supervision of these endowments, he nevertheless considered that this was only the case if parents were solicitous and qualified judges of the merits and quality of education. However, this was seldom the case; hence Mill's requirement that the state assume a supervisory role in education, even in the case of the private institutions (1988, XXI, p. 211). He drew on the criticisms of others, such as Adam Smith's contention that the establishment of public endowments to education did not promote any good but rather idleness and inefficiency: 'I conceive the practice of payment by fixed salaries to be almost fatal to the general usefulness of educational endowments, and quite sufficient in itself to account for the admitted fact of their extensive failure' (1988, XXI, p. 209). However, while Adam Smith saw this as an argument for less public intervention, Stuart Mill saw this as a reason for more public intervention and to justify the government's supervision of these endowments.

In general Mill thought that state intervention in education was undesirable because of several fundamental principles ruling the definition of the limits of interference by the government and the assurance of individual liberty. First, the compulsory character of the intervention or of the funds to provide it was a concern (1965, pp. 937–938). Second, the increase of government power and influence was not welcomed, since it could promote the rise of arbitrary power and the introduction of restriction on private liberties (1965, p. 939). Third, this increased the occupations and responsibilities of government, a body that was already overcharged with duties (the result being that those duties were ill performed or not performed at all). These problems were also exacerbated by the bad organisation of governments (1965, p. 940). Fourth, private agency was considered to be more efficient due to the effectiveness of private interests (self-interest). Even if one conceded that the knowledge and intelligence of the government was larger than each individual, it could not be larger than the sum of the whole country (1965, pp. 941–942).

However, education represented an important exception in this respect, with major shortcomings in the application of the principles of the market in terms of the consumer's ability to pay, ability to recognise its value and sufficient capacity of judgment on the subject. The first Mill seemed to regard as less controversial, due to the widespread acceptance of the principle that if the poor are unable to pay for education, they should not be prevented from access to it (1967, II, p. 622). The main problems of privately-provided education concerned the second and third aspects, due to the ignorance and selfishness of parents (1967, II, p. 623). Contrary to the common rule, the consumer was not the best judge in this case since: 'The uncultivated cannot be competent judges of cultivation. Those who most need to be made wiser and better, usually desire it least, and if they desired it, would be incapable of finding the way to it by their own lights' (1965, p. 947).

The fact that the consumers did not care enough was confirmed by the insufficient private demand for education. Thus, and despite several objections and inconveniences regarding this intervention, the state had an important role in education, especially in supplementing and stimulating private and individual initiative, namely by making it compulsory (1965, pp. 948–949). This did not necessarily mean that the state would provide it or that it would be free, let alone that the state would constitute a monopoly in terms of provision of education (1965, p. 950; 1991, p. 118). This would be very problematic, especially because it would reduce the diversity in education (and consequently among people, since all would be subject to the same influences), creating a sort of despotism over the mind. Thus, state provision of education, exclusively, should not be the rule, and certainly not in the case of non-elementary levels of education, which would be mostly left up to private demand (1967, II, p. 627).

The classical political economists' proposal of public support should not therefore be understood as the establishment of a public system of education. In fact, the annual grant established in 1832 by the state to fund elementary schools was regarded by some as the price to pay for the establishment of a publicly supported network of parish schools (Judges, 1952, pp. 19–20). Even Mill was very clear about his preference for competition and private provision of education (1967, II, p. 622).[4] Moreover, and in order to avoid the promotion of idleness and inefficiency among teachers by making their remuneration certain, he considered that 'the fees of pupils would always be a part, and should generally be the greatest part, of his remuneration' (1967, II, p. 624), and he supported the principle of payment by results (1984, p. 209), even in terms of public institutions. Hence, although with Mill education remained better if mostly organised around the private sector, the role of the state had been enlarged and the public dimension had been visibly extended when compared with Smith's views.

Alfred Marshall and the Problem of Market Failures in Education

Mill started emphasising the peculiarities of the educational sector and the need for some government regulation and this would be pursued more systematically by Alfred Marshall. Marshall was a crucial figure in the development of modern economics (Maloney, 1992) and the most prominent economist pre-1950 to devote significant attention to the subject of the economics of education. Marshall considered that education represented a source of important benefits for the individual. In several passages of his *Principles of Economics*, Marshall emphasised the importance of promoting general education. Although technical education was becoming increasingly important at that time, Marshall considered that too much specialisation could potentially reduce the flexibility of many workers to adjust to new tasks or occupations (1961, I, p. 718). Although the benefits of general education were less visible, they were important in contributing to the development of the individual's intelligence, readiness and trustworthiness. Education also had an important role in socialising the working classes, inculcating more elevated modes of behaviour (1919, p. 229). Even more important, the development of mass general education would have a major impact in terms of meritocracy, by promoting a better assessment of the pool of talents through increasing educational opportunities. This avoided the waste of talent that would occur if access to education remained restricted to a minority of the population:

> *It is true that there are many kinds of work which can be done as efficiently by an uneducated as by an educated workman: and that the higher branches of education are of little direct use except to employers and foremen and a comparatively small number of artisans. But a good education confers great indirect benefits even on the ordinary workman. It stimulates his mental activity; it fosters in him a habit of wise inquisitiveness; it makes him more intelligent, more ready, more trustworthy in his ordinary work; it raises the tone of his life in working hours and out of working hours; it is thus an important means towards the production of material wealth; at the same time that, regarded as an end in itself, it is inferior to none of those which the production of material wealth can be made to subserve.* (Marshall, 1916, p. 211)

In Alfred Marshall's writings there are several references to the economic role of education and training, notably their contribution to the industrial efficiency of workers. In *Industry and Trade* (1919), he pointed out several times the role of education in the economic progress of several of the leading industrial powers. For Marshall, modern times were characterised by increasing levels of education and standardised knowledge, meaning that education was no longer a privilege of an elite. This general moral and mental progress of the masses prepared them for more complex technical activities and made them more productive.

When it came to the analysis of the costs associated with the supply of labour, he mentioned at the forefront those costs associated with rearing, general, and specialised education (Marshall, 1961, I, p. 156). The costs to acquire specialised knowledge and ability were considered as a type of investment, more precisely a long-term one (Ibid. I, p. 377). In fact, estimates of incomes directly governed the supply of specific trades, though there was an element of rent in wages (Ibid. I, p. 421), often to compensate extraordinary natural abilities that were not 'the result of investment of human effort in an agent of production for the purpose of increasing its efficiency' (Ibid. I, p. 577). This posed the difficult question of separating what part of the remuneration was due to 'capital invested in special training', to 'rare natural gifts', and to matters of chance and opportunity. However, part of the exceptional success of some individuals had to be considered in the wider long-term context and vis-à-vis the failure of others, as a compensation for a risky investment decision or a quasi-rent due to peculiar and exceptional capacities. Hence, Marshall hesitated in equating the acquisition of education to a productive investment.

Nevertheless investment in education faced important obstacles, particularly due to its long-term nature. One of the most important ones was the potential lack of foresight of the parents. Although people were normally able to ascertain the present value of future benefits (Ibid. I, p. 120), Alfred Marshall doubted the capacity of the lower classes to anticipate the future benefits that would accrue to their children through better education (Ibid. pp. 216–217).

In this context, expenditure in education could correspond to a choice between the parents' and the children's interests (Ibid. I, p. 217). Marshall thought that amongst the lower classes it was the parents' interest that would be privileged. This was related to the fact that education was a peculiar type of investment in which the costs were largely dissociated from the benefits (Ibid. I, pp. 560–562). Even if the parents were willing to support their children's education through borrowing, they were most certainly prevented from doing so due to their poorer financial condition (in modern terms one would call this 'liquidity-constrained'). These combined forces promote a situation in which the lower levels would persist at a lower level of education, from generation to generation, unless society, particularly through government, would take a more active role in funding those activities.

The problems facing this peculiar type of expenditure were also due to the motivations underlying it. Marshall considered that the intellectual, moral and artistic faculties on which industrial efficiency depended were acquired not only as an instrument/investment, but also due to their intrinsic (consumption) benefits. The acquisition of education was therefore the product of a combination of various investment and consumption motivations, many of which were not linked to any economic purpose (Ibid. I, p. 247). This was enhanced by the difficulty in foreseeing the circumstances by which earnings were determined. Thus, in Marshall we continued to observe a growing emphasis on the public dimensions and implications of higher education. The risk of market failures was strongly emphasised and created much greater room for public intervention and for restraining the role of private initiative and market forces.

Milton Friedman and the Contemporary Revival of the Market in Educational Policy

The emphasis on the peculiar nature of higher education and on the role of government persisted during much of the twentieth century. The balance shifted towards a greater emphasis on the role of the government in higher education and a greater scepticism about the perfectibility of markets in this respect. Due to this emphasis on the potential failures of a market in higher education, economics as a discipline became during the twentieth century less inclined to apply a market framework to higher education. However, bearing in mind the centrality of the market concept in economic analysis and economists' reliance on individual economic rationality, the resistance to apply this framework to higher education inevitably produced some tensions. These tensions would be exacerbated in the last quarter of the twentieth century with the so-called crisis of the welfare state and the resurection of economic laissez-faire.

The person who has arguably been the main contributor in again placing markets at the forefront of the educational debate was Milton Friedman. Through the effective rhetoric of his *Capitalism and Freedom* (1962), he launched the contemporary debate on the role of markets and governments in (higher) education. Interestingly, Friedman does this by recovering some of the intellectual tradition of the founding fathers' economic analyses of higher education. Now that the context has changed significantly and the role of government in education is taken for granted by most people, Friedman tries again to place the burden of proof on the side of government in order to limit its role in higher education:

> Formal schooling is today paid for and almost entirely administered by government bodies. [...] This situation has developed gradually and is now taken so much for granted that little explicit attention is any longer directed to the reasons for the special treatment of schooling. [...] The result has been an indiscriminate extension of governmental responsibility (Friedman, 1962, p. 85).

Friedman starts by acknowledging the massive modern role of government in education, the result of an expansion that took place mostly in the late nineteenth and early twentieth century. According to Friedman, the contemporary role of the government in education was mostly taken for granted and led to what he calls a substantive nationalisation of the educational sector. However, he wanted to underline that this was not always the case, especially in countries such as the US and the UK that had previously resisted it. In the case of the US, there were three main reasons for expansion. First, education was mostly considered a technical monopoly. Second, it aimed at creating a core of common values that was particularly relevant due to the large and diverse inflows of migrant population. Finally, there was the lack of an efficient technical administration that could handle subsidising individuals directly, instead of through institutional funding.

Hence, Friedman tries to rationalise this governmental presence, which he does on the basis of education externalities and a paternalistic concern for children and other irresponsible individuals. According to Friedman, the role of government was mostly justified as an instrument of promoting a common set of values and basic citizenship through general and compulsory education. At the financial level, he claimed that those that could afford it should contribute significantly to the education of their children. Moreover, government's role would be largely unjustified in the types of education, more vocationally-oriented, that clearly enhanced the individual's productivity. In this case the individual would reap a major benefit through enhanced lifetime income and therefore should be called on to bear most of the costs. Altogether, Friedman's reflections point to a greatly reduced role for the government in education.

The reduction of the role of the government was even more critical in his analysis of higher education. In this case, Friedman believed that the case for nationalisation was even weaker. Moreover, it introduced some major distortions in the functioning of the higher education system:

The subsidization of institutions rather than of people has led to an indiscriminate subsidization of all activities appropriate for such institutions, rather than of the activities appropriate for the state to subsidize (Friedman, 1962, p. 100).

He therefore proposed, based on some externalities and arguments about national productivity, that most funding should be directed to the students themselves in a sort of voucher mechanism. The funding of this system should be mostly at the state and not at the federal level. Friedman believed that the shift from institutional to individual funding would enhance the competition between higher education institutions and encourage better use of resources. Moreover, it would promote a larger diversity of types of higher education, which he largely associates with private provision. Thus, although Friedman wanted to redress the public dimension of higher education, he did not question that it had an important public relevance and that should guarantee some degree of government regulation, even if not to the level of the existing in many Western countries.

These arguments have been persistently repeated in recent decades to justify the growing role of market competition and privatisation in higher education (Weisbrod et al., 2008; Rothschild and White, 1995). Contemporary economists tend to regard a market as a powerful mechanism of social choice that, through rational utility-maximising behaviour of individuals, as if by an invisible hand, will distribute goods in such a way that no one could be better-off without making anyone else worse-off. In many countries, governments have asked institutions to compete for students, staff and teaching and research funds tied to specific goals (Teixeira and Dill, 2011a; Teixeira et al., 2004). This competitive environment has triggered important developments within higher education institutions, especially since these developments have coincided in many countries with a strengthening of institutional autonomy. The goal was to reduce inefficiencies, to generate additional revenues and to create innovative organisational models. Some of these initiatives have led to new institutional dynamics, with significant impact on management practices (Amaral et al., 2003), internal resource allocation and evaluation procedures. Since most of these changes took place in a context of scarcer resources, this was necessarily a difficult process, stimulating some internal tensions.

However, economists are also aware that markets do not always produce the optimal outcome from a society's point of view. Some markets can persistently produce too much or too little of goods and services, challenging the self-regulating capacity that economists usually associate with a market mechanism, i.e. the capacity to adjust to situations of excessive or insufficient supply (or demand). This is a case of *market failures* (Johnes, 1993; Stiglitz, 2000). Following Mill's and Marshall's original insights, the development of public economics has led to greater attention to this issue of market failures. The main types that have been identified were those of public goods, the existence of externalities, information asymmetry and monopoly powers. The most important and arguably most controversial in higher education is the first one. Mainstream economists have expressed the view that higher education cannot be properly considered a public good according to the conditions defined by public economics—non-rivalry and non-exclusion of consumption (Barr, 2004).[5] Hence, most economists advocate calling higher education a merit good rather than a public good. By this they mean that governments should promote private consumption of this type of good because of its individual and social benefits, but need not be necessarily concerned with its public provision. This is also an attempt to establish a compromise between the public and private dimensions in higher education.

The critical issue for economists when discussing higher education does not seem to be so much a dispute between advocates of complete deregulation and advocates of a protected status, but rather regarding what type and degree of government regulations will maximise the social benefits of higher education systems increasingly subject to market forces. Identifying the appropriate balance between private and public dimensions in higher education becomes even more important as countries have persistently expanded their university systems, because this expansion dramatically increases public expenditures for higher education (Weisbrod et al., 2008; Geiger, 2004). Therefore, if the relationship between the public's share of university costs and predicted social benefits is difficult to justify in elite systems, questions as to the efficiency of such expenditures only rise with *massification* (Teixeira et al., 2006;

Johnstone and Marcucci, 2010). The adoption of market-based policies in many countries represents the application of a less direct form of regulation. The challenge confronting those experimenting with market-based policies in higher education is therefore to identify the institutional framework of rules and incentives that produces welfare-maximizing competition among (mainly) publicly subsidised, but increasingly institutionally autonomous, academic institutions. Underpinning this is the resurgence of a long-standing belief (at least since Adam Smith) that competition, even if simulated, can produce an improved outcome in terms of the quality and quantity of education supplied. One would be tempted to say that we have come full circle, though the current challenges are certainly different and arguably more significant to higher education.

Final Remarks—A Legacy of Ambivalence and Controversy

The reflections on higher education of the founding fathers of economics as a discipline have left an intellectual inheritance that is strikingly present in the contemporary debates on markets in higher education. Adam Smith imprinted on the debate the emphasis on the positive contribution that competition and private supply could have in the effectiveness and responsiveness of higher education institutions. This initial pro-market stance has been progressively tempered. John Stuart Mill, despite acknowledging the virtues of competition and the dangers of *statism*, opened the door to a greater public intervention, notably due to the ill-judgment of individual educational consumers, especially those from lower socio-economic backgrounds and lower formal qualifications. Alfred Marshall further developed the arguments about the market failure that might occur in higher education due to the divergence between social and private benefits and to consumers' lack of foresight. Altogether, this has contributed to move the burden of proof, in the regulation of the market, from the government to the market. Nevertheless, in recent decades the emphasis on the prominence of market forces in higher education has gained ground, following the revival of political and economic liberalism in western societies.

This preference for a market solution with government regulation has attracted significant controversy and criticism from non-economists. Several have voiced concerns over the marketisation of higher education, maintaining that it has contributed to organisational fragmentation, increased administrative bureaucracy, or even to a crisis of identity in higher education. Many critics have even attacked the appropriateness of applying economic theory to the reform of higher education around the world and questioned both its relevance as well as its possibly perverse effects on higher education. To these criticisms, economists have counter-argued that there have been significant achievements in terms of cost reductions, as well as increases in teaching and research output quantity and quality (thus fulfilling Adam Smith's prediction). Arguments have also been made about the equity implications of a greater emphasis on markets or in government regulation, with several economists pointing out that a significant government intervention (notably in terms of funding) could produce regressive effects that were damaging for the quality it was supposed to promote (Barr, 2004).

However, the main dissension seems to be about how public or how private and market-oriented higher education should be. Economists' acceptance of the possibility of a market solution in higher education has tended to create a rift with a public discourse that regards higher education as within the public sphere. Moreover, the analytical separation that economic analysis develops between the nature of higher education as a public or private good and its funding and provision is perceived among economists as analytical niceties developed to undermine the public role in higher education and to reduce the debate about higher education to an economic matter (thus hegemonizing the framework in which these debates are framed). Despite the caveats about the potential social benefits of higher education and the need for some degree of government regulation, the emphasis on a public dimension has not been sufficient to temper the fact that economics ultimately considers higher education to be a private good rather a public good.

Economics' founding fathers have left an inheritance of some ambivalence in the way economists approach higher education. Although they have tended to consider it as something that could be provided by the private sector and that benefited from the stimuli of competition and private initiative, like many other sectors they have also recognised the important social and political implications of higher education and therefore the relevance of a government role. If, on the one hand, they have tended to support the view that market mechanisms and private initiative would contribute to a higher level of efficiency, on the other hand, many have also forcefully argued that the peculiarities of higher education as a business and the other missions that (should) preside over the system made it difficult, or even inappropriate, to promote a dominant market regulation of higher education. Although these views have somehow been redressed through the pro-market efforts of people such as Friedman, the sceptical endorsement of some market regulation is indeed largely present in the moves towards the market that have characterised higher education policies in recent years. This has created an inherent tension and hybridism in the public–private balance in higher education that still runs in the contemporary debate. Nowadays, as markets are rapidly coming to be regarded as an important and viable instrument for steering higher education systems, we could benefit by taking their views more seriously than ever.

Notes

1. This text extends and refines previous work published in Teixeira et al. (2006) and Teixeira and Dill (2011b).
2. For more on the relationship between Smith's work and modern human capital theory see Teixeira (2007).
3. See also Correspondence, pp. 173–179.
4. In several insightful texts E. G. West focused on the role of the state for classical political economists, and he has to be credited for clarifying that the classical economists' proposal of public support should not be understood as the establishment of a public system of education. In fact, the annual grant established in 1832 by the state to fund elementary schools, was regarded by some as the price to pay for the establishment of a public supported network of parish schools (Judges, 1952, pp. 19–20). However, West has overdone the differences between the classics, especially in placing Smith and Stuart Mill as opposed poles (West, 1964a). Fortunately, West himself was aware of the shortcomings of this approach, and he recognised that not only had Smith endorsed some paternalism in order to justify some state assistance to education (West, 1964a p. 165), but also that 'despite his [Stuart Mill] doubts about the efficiency of the market mechanism in education, Mill in the end, like Smith, came down in favour of private schools' (West, 1964a, p. 171). Moreover, he asserted that Stuart Mill 'confined his proposals for state intervention to a law rendering only education (not schooling) compulsory' (West, 1964a, p. 172).
5. The former means that the quantity consumed by one individual does not reduce the amount available for the remaining ones. The latter condition means that there are no effective mechanisms to prevent individuals from enjoying that good. Goods that satisfy this condition will be unattractive for private providers.

References

Amaral, A., Meek V. L., and Larsen, I. (eds). (2003) *The Higher Education Managerial Revolution?* Dordrecht: Kluwer Academic Publishers.
Barr, N. (2004) *The Economics of the Welfare State* (4rd ed.). Oxford: Oxford University Press.
Fine, B., and Milonakis, D. (2009) *From Economics Imperialism to Freakonomics: The Shifting Boundaries between Economics and other Social Sciences (Economics as Social Theory)*, Abingdon, UK: Routledge.
Friedman, M. (1962) *Capitalism and Freedom*. Chicago: University of Chicago Press.
Geiger, R. (2004) *Knowledge and Money*, Stanford: Stanford University Press.
Johnes, G. (1993) *The Economics of Education*. London: MacMillan Press.
Johnstone, B., and P. Marcucci (2010) *Financing Higher Education Worldwide: Who Pays? Who Should Pay?* Baltimore, USA: The John Hopkins University Press.
Judges, A. V. (ed). (1952) Pioneers of English Education, London, Faber & Faber.

Marshall, A. (1919) *Industry and Trade*. London: MacMillan.
Marshall, A. (1961) *Principles of Economics* (9th ed. Variorum, 2 vols.), with annotations by C. W. Guillebaud. London: MacMillan.
Mill, J. S. (1965) *Principles of Political Economy with Some Applications to Social Philosophy* (Collected Works, vols. II and III). Toronto: University of Toronto Press and Routledge.
Mill, J. S. (1967) *Essays in Economics and Society*, vols. I and II (Collected Works, vols. IV–V). Toronto: University of Toronto Press and Routledge.
Mill, J. S. (1977) *Essays on Politics and Society*, vols. I and II (Collected Works, vols. XVIII–XIX). Toronto: University of Toronto Press and Routledge.
Mill, J. S. (1984) *Essays on Equality, Law and Education* (Collected Works, vol. XXI). Toronto: University of Toronto Press and Routledge.
Mill, J. S. (1988) Public and Parliamentary Speeches (Collected Works, vol. XXVIII–XXIX). Toronto: University of Toronto Press and Routledge.
Mill, J. S. (1991) *On Liberty and Other Essays*. Oxford: Oxford University Press.
Rothschild, R., and White, M. J. The Analytics of Pricing Higher Education and Other Services in Which the Customers are Inputs, *Journal of Political Economy*, 103:3.
Smith, A. (1776 [1976]) *An Inquiry into the Causes of the Wealth of Nations*, Glasgow Edition of the Works and Correspondence of Adam Smith. Oxford: Clarendon Press.
Smith, A. (1978) *Lectures on Jurisprudence*. Oxford: Clarendon Press.
Stiglitz, J. (2000) *Economics of the Public Sector*, W. W. Norton & Co.; 3rd Revised ed.
Teixeira, P. (2001) The Economics of Education: An Exploratory Portrait, *History of Political Economy, Annual Supplement*. Duke University Press; 257–287.
Teixeira, P. (2007) *Jacob Mincer—The Human Capital Labour Economist*, Oxford University Press.
Teixeira, P. (2009a) Economic Imperialism and the Ivory Tower: Economic Issues and Policy challenges in the Funding of Higher Education in the EHEA (2010–2020); in: J. Huisman, B. Stensaker and B. M. Kehm (eds), *The European Higher Education Area: Perspectives on a Moving Target*. Rotterdam, Sense Publishers.
Teixeira, P. (2009b) Markets in Higher Education: Can We Still Learn from Economics' Founding Fathers? Research and Occasional Papers Series, Center for Studies in Higher Education, UC Berkeley; CSHE 04-06.
Teixeira, P., and Dill, D. (ed). (2011a) *Public Vices, Private Virtues? Reflecting about the Effects of Marketization in Higher Education*. Rotterdam: Sense Publishers.
Teixeira, P., and Dill, D. (2011b) The Many Faces of Marketization in Higher Education, in: Teixeira, P. and Dill, D. *Public Vices, Private Virtues? Reflecting about the Effects of Marketization in Higher Education*. Rotterdam: Sense Publishers.
Teixeira, P., Dill D., Jongbloed, B., and Amaral, A. (eds). (2004) *Markets in Higher Education: Reality or* Rhetoric? Dordrecht: Kluwer Academic Publishers.
Teixeira, P., Johnstone, B., Vossensteyn, H., and Rosa, M. J. (eds). (2006) *Cost-Sharing and Accessibility in Higher Education—A Fairer Deal?* Springer, Dordrecht.
Weisbrod, B. A., Ballou, J. P., Asch, E. D. (2008). *Mission and Money: Understanding the University*. Cambridge: Cambridge University Press.
West, E. G. (1964a) The Role of Education in Nineteenth-Century Doctrines of Political Economy, *British Journal of Educational Studies*, 12:2, 161–72.
Williams, G. (1991). The Many Faces of Privatisation, *Higher Education Management*, 8, 39–56.

Winston, G. (1999) Subsidies, Hierarchy and Peers: The Awkward Economics of Higher Education, *Journal of Economic Perspectives*, 13:1, 13–36.

Wolf, C., Jr. (1993) *Markets or Governments: Choosing between Imperfect Alternatives*. Cambridge, MA: MIT Press.

Part Two
Models and Policies

In broad terms higher education has always served three social functions. It has enabled some individuals to develop their abilities and interests to a high level. It has provided well-educated people to serve and reproduce powerful groups in society, the emperor and his court in ancient China, the medieval church in Europe, the nation states which emerged in more recent centuries and, some would say, global capitalism today. Third, there has also always been a subsidiary public function which has grown in importance from the time of the eighteenth 'enlightenment', the capacity to act as well-informed and intelligent prophets, explorers and critics of existing societies. These functions are the core of the public and private roles of universities, the advancement of individuals and collective sustainability and progress.

Higher education institutions have been organised to perform these functions in a variety of ways at different times and in different parts of the world. Sometimes a powerful state has attempted to control closely how its most promising individuals are educated and trained, sometimes there has been an unwritten compact which allows universities a very considerable degree of freedom with an understanding that they will not embarrass or undermine the powerful groups too much. Sometimes these arrangements have been enforced through legal and administrative fiat, occasionally by military force, and in the past half century mainly through control of the terms on which universities receive financial resources necessary for their survival.

In this section a variety of approaches are analysed and appraised. In particular they explore trends of the past quarter century in which universities have been granted considerable autonomy and legal freedom but are constrained by financial conditionality and external quality regulation. The debate about public and private natures of higher education has become a matter of the extent to which higher education is and should be organised and regulated collectively with its nature and development through political and bureaucratic mechanisms or whether democratic control though individual decisions in a market is the best way to balance its public and private responsibilities.

It is apparent from several of the contributions that the debate is also in large part ideological and in particular about whether equality between individuals and groups should be the underlying constant and whether the evaluation of any system should be to a large extent about whether it promotes equity.

There is, however, also the issue of whether higher education can be treated as an issue separate from the education system and the wider society. To what extent should universities have responsibility to make good any deficiencies in education earlier on, or to help schools to do so? If they have a responsibility to serve the public good separate from their role in the advancement of individuals, who should pay for the performance of these functions and how?

There can be little doubt that the trend of the past half century has been for the private functions to become more dominant. Arguments based on notions of 'a common culture' for example are heard much less frequently. These have been replaced largely by a commitment to the promotion of economic growth as the mechanism by which poverty in all its forms can be overcome and hence equality achieved. Therefore universities are justified in receiving funds from taxpayers to the extent that they make special contributions to economic growth that do not simply result in higher incomes for those who acquire the skills and abilities needed by a growing economy. The debate has certainly entered a new phase and the question of whether the market can provide an appropriate or acceptable balance between public or private interests in higher education is central.

VII. The Paradoxical University and the Public Good

ANGELA BREW

Introduction

This chapter exposes some of the conflicts of values and current practices that act to limit the capacity of the university to contribute to the public good in the twenty-first century. The chapter is based on the premise that universities should be exemplars of how to live and work in open democratic societies. That they are not, cannot be wholly attributed to outside influences such as government agendas, or the demands of industry and the professions. Universities themselves must take responsibility for critical self-evaluation leading to change. Embedded in university life are some key contradictions which trap higher education in the past. These include the juxtaposition of equality and meritocracy, the pursuit of democracy in autocratic institutions, the desire for creativity trapped by positivistic thinking, the conflict between collaboration and competition and the respective positions of university members (academics, students and professional staff) within it. Using examples from innovative initiatives to break down hierarchies, develop inclusivity among staff and students and to involve students in the academic project of the university the chapter highlights ways in which higher education can and is taking a proactive stance to prepare students for an unknown future.

The complexity and ambiguity of twenty-first century society is nowhere more apparent than in the contemporary university. Higher education exists within a range of forces which pull it in contrary directions and which affect all aspects of its functioning. This includes, for example, policies and strategies for achieving institutional objectives, ideas about appropriate ways to educate students, quality assurance agendas and standards, the intellectual climate, the nature of scholarly work, the interrelationship between research and teaching, the nature of research and how it is judged, academic workload and conditions, the university as a community and as it relates to the wider community, its relationship to industry and the professions and the use of transitional and learning spaces. In this chapter I argue that higher education is subject to a number of paradoxical forces which present contradictory messages about aspects of its functioning and that institutions tend to be reactive rather than proactive in preparing for a future that is in many ways unknown and perplexing.

By paradoxical forces I refer to factors that push and pull higher education in different directions such that conflicts have to be resolved at every level in the ordinary decision-making process from day to day. To some degree these mirror and are a response to the super-complex society in which universities operate. In some ways these contradictions are of universities' own making. The complexity of these paradoxical forces, coming as they do from every direction—governmental, global, technological, societal, economic, intellectual, institutional and demographic—reflect the ambiguity and super-complexity of twenty-first century society, and lead to dilemmas in how to respond and what to respond to.

This chapter explores some of these forces and their resulting conflicts of values and current practices that affect, both positively and negatively, the capacity of universities to contribute to the public good at the present time, and to suggest what needs to happen if higher education is to contribute to the public good in the future. I am not concerned with which aspects of higher education, for example, teaching, research or service contribute most. What I am concerned with is the ways in which these operate in paradoxical ways within university structures, systems and ideas about appropriate practice to either constrain or enable universities to address serious questions facing the world today. Contradictions are not always self-evident. Practice in some areas may mask contradictory forces pulling in opposite directions. So in this chapter, my aim is to draw out some of the silences, aspects which are not obvious and which have perhaps received less attention in the academic press and the media. Resolving paradoxes could lead to change, but while I would like to think that transformation is on the horizon, it is much more likely that in the future, universities will continue to live in ambiguity reacting to governmental and societal forces. Finding a more proactive way to do this which enhances and does not diminish higher education and which contributes more effectively to building a better future would seem to be a worthy objective.

I first discuss a number of paradoxes by reference to my own research and practice in order to illustrate ways in which universities are reacting to change agendas, while being conscious of tradition and existing organisational structures. I then suggest, by way of examples, how they can and are being proactive in breaking down traditional hierarchies through research and inquiry and reclaiming scholarly work for all who work within them.

Public Good

However, first, it must be established what is meant by public good. One of the problems we have in specifying how higher education contributes to the public good is that notions of what that good is are tied to history and politics and depend upon the direction from which we do the looking. The 'public' is also a contested term. As Powell and Clemens (1998, p. xiv) ask 'which public and for whose good?' Nixon (2011, p. 2) sums up the view which underlies this chapter when he says: 'To claim higher education as a public good is … to claim for ourselves—and others—membership of an active and inclusive public: to claim not only that higher education is 'good' (i.e. valuable and worthwhile), but that its 'goodness' resides in it being valuable and worthwhile to a public for which we share responsibility'.

I take it as self-evident that a focus on the learning and growing of individual students and staff has benefits in society. Many private benefits of higher education are economic, including people's capacity for greater monetary gain in terms of future income and promotional opportunities (Zhang, 2009), as well as better health in the future and job satisfaction. Public benefits are said to include higher levels of industrial innovation and economic growth (CERI, 2010; Dill, 2011; Marginson and Considine, 2000). There is already a paradox here in that the more the focus is on individuals the more the community directly benefits. This includes the students but also individual academics working on research which interests them personally and which ultimately contributes benefits to society.

I have been working over the past twenty years or so to understand and to change the ways that people think about higher education learning, teaching and research. This has involved exploring the nature of research and how academics think about it, examining people's ideas about the relationship between research and teaching and how they are endeavouring to bring them together, and, more recently, developing ideas about the role of undergraduate research in higher education. Along the way, I have become cognisant of the ways in which higher education mirrors and responds to ambiguous messages about what kind of institution it should be, and how it should relate to society. I have noted the ways in which it has been challenged by societal expectations of universities and a university education when its unit of resource has been seriously under pressure. It has become clear to me that contributing to the public good is not a straightforward matter of listening to politicians, industrialists, economists or any particular group. Standish (2011) questions whether universities exist to serve society's needs or to show new possibilities for society. Universities are products of their past, but in responding to pressing present-day demands, they inevitably set up conditions for an unknown future and, can and I believe should, point to new possibilities.

In the twenty-first century pluralistic context, universities must be exemplars of how to live and work in complex democratic societies. In this sense, we need to ask not whether universities are currently contributing to the public good, but whether they are contributing to shaping the society of the future and are likely to contribute to the public good for future generations. That they are not, cannot be wholly attributed to outside influences such as government agendas, or the demands of industry and the professions. By being seduced by the loud voices of big business, economic rationalism, ideas about technology, and out-dated ideas about knowledge, and failing to listen to the softer demands of those with less power, universities are being reactive rather than proactive in shaping their future and hence their capacity to contribute to a particular kind of public good. Universities cannot afford to take a narrow economic or political view. There must be within society critical self-evaluation leading to change and this properly belongs in universities. But to do this they must build on their inherent ideas of the value of scholarly endeavour in more proactive ways.

I use the notion of universities and the idea of higher education interchangeably while recognising that they are not the same. For me as an academic working in Australia, higher education refers to a range of institutions, some of which are known as universities and others are colleges that engage in degree-level work. My own experience and research has been conducted within universities in Australia and the UK and these are the institutions with which I am most familiar. Therefore, in this chapter, 'higher education' describes the activity universities engage in, the type of education pursued and the subject which I study. 'University' describes the type of institution in which I work.

Tradition and Change

At the core of the controversy about higher education as a private or a public good are questions about its purposes. A neo-liberal view sees that purpose in terms of economic utility: educating a workforce, and carrying out research that contributes to business growth and economic prosperity (Olssen and Peters, 2005). It regards the contribution of higher education to the public good in terms of the economic gains that students and the rest of society derive from it. In such a context, anything that can be measured is measured and the value of higher education appears increasingly to be viewed in quantitative terms (Hajdarpasic, Brew and Popenici, in submission). Neo-liberalist or economic rationalist ideas, (see for example, Davies, Gottsche and Bansel, 2006), have led to performative views of teaching and research 'productivity' (Lucas, 2006). A New Growth view, on the other hand, regards the public good in terms of the contribution of higher education to the growth of knowledge both of the individual and of the society as a whole. Knowledge is viewed as the economic commodity in this theory (Olssen and Peters, 2005). Such a view places more emphasis on what the student knows and can do as a consequence of his or her university experience, possibly redressing the performative focus on academics' research. Even though they both draw on economic theory, these different discourses are in tension. They each have different ideas about what is needed to make universities more useful. Moreover, they challenge core ideas about the university, such as academic freedom, which asserts the right of academics to free speech and their right to run their own affairs (Russell, 1993). University leaders and rank and file academics live with these contradictory theories on a day-to-day basis. They all draw attention to what is produced, whether economic benefits, knowledge or intellectual freedom. Each has a different view about what would be of most benefit to society.

Some of the key contradictions trap higher education in the past even as it responds to contemporary issues. This is nowhere more evident than when academics endeavour to change their teaching to more inquiry-based pedagogies. How and whether they are able to act to change their teaching is dependent on structures and policies which either constrain or enable change to take place. For example, assessment policies at the university level frequently determine how student learning is to be evaluated. If these policies give a certain percentage of the mark for a subject to be determined by examinations, then opportunities for more innovative assessment strategies may be curtailed. In North America, faculty (lecturers, instructors, professors) are frequently evaluated on ratings criteria and these determine salary levels, promotion and tenure decisions. This acts to inhibit innovation and creativity in teaching because there is a belief that ratings will drop in innovative courses and faculty do not want to risk low ratings by experimenting with new pedagogies. Yet there are currently serious concerns about the need to enhance student engagement (Kuh, 2008) and a need to innovate. On the other hand, changed institutional policies and strategies, for example the introduction of a policy on expected graduate outcomes, may be constrained by out-dated ideas about the purpose of higher education being to convey disciplinary content to the students, or myths about what it takes to learn a subject. As far as those who work in universities are concerned, the focus on graduate attributes, and, by extension employability, may be viewed as a neo-liberal plot to focus attention on universities' economic purposes. Tradition and change are always in tension at the individual teacher level.

Buildings also give messages about tradition. The cloisters and quadrangles of Oxbridge colleges reverberate through universities across the world. They are a reminder of past learning and teaching strategies and the kind of students who studied in former centuries, for example, men preparing for the church. They embody old ideas even as the public interest requires students to have the capacity to work creatively to embrace complexity and ambiguity. Lecture theatres embody enlightenment conceptions of disembodied knowledge which can be passed from the authority figure on the podium to the novices sitting to listen. Despite enormous strides that have been taken in recent years to define new pedagogies for higher education which respect uncertainties in knowledge and a more democratic role for the teacher, the lecture still maintains a central position in many university courses; paradoxically, in courses designed to prepare students in the STEM (science, technology, engineering, mathematics) disciplines which are at the forefront of scientific knowledge and understanding. There appears to be some evidence that what is understood by a lecture is changing to include discussion and active participation by students. Nevertheless, attempts to introduce research-based approaches to teaching and learning require not just a tinkering with existing structures, but new ideas about what it is to educate students at the higher levels, and importantly, new spaces in which students can carry out their work (Temple and Filippakou, 2007).

In a world where we increasingly need people who can deal with complexity and ambiguity, there is pressure on universities to reduce the complexity. Increasingly universities are being run by corporations, bureaucrats, financiers and accountants; people, in other words who do not necessarily understand the nature of scholarly work as a critical endeavour. The consequence is that creativity is undermined by positivistic thinking in contexts where content is central and viewed as separate from knowers. University courses are still dominated by notions of transferring disembodied content. This idea is embedded in contemporary debates about the use of information and communications technology, the availability of huge international databases, debates about whether Massive Open Online Courses (MOOCs) will dominate higher learning, all of which give expression to the idea of the centrality of information within a university education. Some have questioned whether universities as we currently know them are needed. A recent report on the future of universities produced in Australia suggests that in the next 10–15 years there will no longer be a need for broad-based teaching and research universities (Boker, 2012). Information (which they call knowledge) will be 'delivered and accessed' in new ways through digital technologies. The report points to what is called the 'democratisation of knowledge and access' by saying: 'The massive increase in the availability of 'knowledge' online and the mass expansion of access to university education in developed and developing markets means a fundamental change in the role of universities as originators and keepers of knowledge' (Boker, 2012, p. 4). Paradoxically, the role of universities as originators and keepers of knowledge changed long ago with the break-down in positivist notion of knowledge and the ways in which scientific research is now pursued. Nowotny, Scott and Gibbons, (2001, p. 115) summed this up when they said: 'There is a high degree of uncertainty, there is no clear-cut direction but many competing ideas, theories and methods, and no one is in overall charge'. Their notion of the agora suggests that the future is already here. The agora is a 'transaction space' in which, as a consequence of democratisation, universal franchise and mass higher education, a variety of organisations, groups and knowledgeable members of society, including researchers, negotiate and re-negotiate their desires, interests, needs and preferences in the generation of knowledge.

Notions of knowledge as content, equating information gained online with knowledge gained within a course of higher learning, confusing the knowledge obtained by uncritically reading online material with the knowledge gained in the process of rigorous scientific research, all reduce higher education to a mechanistic process which denies the agency of the individual and groups. Yet when universities are trying to manage ever-diminishing budgets, such trends are seductive and appear to respond to the demands of stakeholders, particularly governments and industry. Such trends also ignore epistemological challenges which critical questioning of positivistic conceptions of knowledge have generated over the past century. Further, they neglect to consider the capacity of the university to engage in intellectual critique of its own societal practices, theories and assumptions. Paradoxically, by ignoring such critiques, people in universities become seduced by arguments which promise more certainty than they can deliver. Indeed, within the undergraduate curriculum there is evidence of reluctance to let go of knowledge content to enable students to experience the challenge of coping with ambiguity (Brew, 2006). A consequence of this is that increasingly academic work is being taken out of the university. This is evident in the number of new institutions that are being set up. For example, the Social Science Centre at Lincoln, UK, with 83 academics that has been set up to provide degree level qualifications which is occupying various places in the city but which has nothing whatever to do with the university. This initiative is not alone. Arising from the Occupy movement, a number of people are questioning the value of universities and colleges as places to obtain an education. See for example the UnCollege (http://www.uncollege.org; Stephens, 2013) which is providing independent study programmes for students in their gap year. Ad hoc organisations like this are taking academic study away from the university.

Contributing to the public good relies on developing the capacity of people to engage in critical evaluation, to being open to novel solutions, to being capable of working within ambiguous and pluralistic contexts. There are enormous global problems to be solved requiring multi-disciplinary solutions. There are global tensions caused by narrow-minded adherence to particular ideologies. Universities have an important contribution to make to teach people how to live and work in ways that contribute to global harmony, that help to solve problems of, for example, climate change, poverty and fear. But to do this is to take a more proactive stance in specifying a future role for higher education which is not based on the narrow ethic of economic rationalism nor dependent on out-dated ideas about knowledge.

Hierarchy and Democracy

Mass higher education is infused with an ethic of preparing citizens for democratic society in which all people contribute (see for example, Brookfield and Preskill, 1999). Yet mass higher education is what it says: education for the 'masses'; and, by implication, carried out by an intellectual elite. Privilege is thus built into the very fabric of universities. This affects debates about who should do research and who should not, about how teaching and research should be organised, about the kinds of learning support and resources that should be provided for students, and about how spaces are used. Students are rewarded for high levels of academic attainment from entry to graduation and at every level in between. Academics are rewarded for high levels of academic achievement by promotion from one level to another. Hierarchical structures are everywhere to be found, from levels of academic positions, to student year levels, to distinctions between academic and support or professional staff. These levels act to determine how people work, what they think of others, how they relate to each other, and what they aspire to. Hierarchies are maintained not only in procedures for promotion and reward of faculty, but also in the ways in which students are clustered into year groups. Equality is valued but decisions are ostensibly taken on merit such that a privileged class develops. There is no equality within a meritocracy. Yet, paradoxically, such a meritocracy survives and thrives within democratic society.

Given that in many countries there is at least a 50 percent participation rate in higher education and some countries have special programmes to encourage so-called 'widening participation', higher education has acquired a central role in creating an educated citizenry capable of making decisions within a democratic society. This is the aspiration within the Future of the University report (Boker, 2012) when they call the availability of knowledge online together with the mass expansion of access to university education 'democratisation'. There is no recognition here of the need to treat students as equal citizens where the principles of democratic discussion are adhered to. According to Brookfield and Preskill (1999), this means mutual receptiveness of new ideas and perspectives and a willingness to question even the most widely accepted assumptions, widespread participation, listening carefully to what others have to say, acting on the assumption that one's own ideas are limited and incomplete, caring about everyone's self-development as much as one's own, different points of view being aired and only abandoned in the light of compelling evidence, expressing appreciation for the contributions of others, recognising that people can work through problems in a supportive environment and the ability to take a stand and argue for it but to accept the challenges of changing ideas (Brookfield and Preskill, 1999, p. 7).

For when students become members of universities they have much to contribute to its academic life but they are more often than not treated as in second-class citizens. This is nowhere more apparent than in their role in research. Hierarchical organisational structures tend to define undergraduate students as 'other' and to construct them as deficient, lacking the necessary skills and abilities to undertake research. Research is only available in many instances to those who have already attained a degree and in some cases to those who have demonstrated a commitment to the academic community by engaging in a PhD. Research tends to be treated as a reward for hard work and high levels of attainment. There is a tendency in some subject areas to view knowledge in hierarchical ways and requiring a step-by-step process to accumulating it. This effectively excludes all but the most advanced students from doing research.

Meritocracy creates competition because rewards such as promotion and tenure tend to be at the individual level. Yet universities are dependent upon collaboration if institutional policies and strategies are to thrive. Indeed, the tension between collaboration and competition also operates at many different levels. The paradox is nowhere more stark than in high level scientific research.

This is dependent on collaboration, for example, where costly equipment is needed. It is also necessary where complex projects require different kinds of expertise. Yet each researcher and research team competes with others to be the first to discover new knowledge in a particular field. Ultimately, promotion depends on the efforts of individuals. Students learn together in the same classroom and may assist each other with learning the subject, but they are usually ranked in terms of their individual learning achievements expressed in grades. Collaboration stresses the collective effort and this is in contrast to the individualism needed to succeed as a student and also to generate creative ideas.

Hierarchical structures within a meritocratic system formerly existed within a much more hierarchically ordered society and may then have seemed appropriate. Small student numbers and generous funding made research and teaching possible without the high levels of intense competition seen today. Increased student numbers and reduced funding have intensified competition at every level. The level of competitiveness in universities is frequently masked through polite language, for example, 'peer review' which sounds benign yet can mask brutal critiques, 'promotions committees' which sound equitable but can mask cut-throat behaviour and favouritism, or 'managing change' which can destroy careers and lives. In some institutions, mild-mannered behaviour masks little short of a war zone. It can be argued that this situation comes about through the reactions of university leaders and managers to external pressures overlaid on historically derived structures and processes. However, as resources become even scarcer, questions arise as to how to make higher education institutions sustainable. There are some parallels here with the recognition that we live on a finite planet. It points to the need to share resources and facilities and to find ways of working more collaboratively and that means more harmoniously. In short, it means that universities need to take a more proactive stance in moving towards sustainable ways of working.

Becoming Proactive

We know from research into students' awareness of research at university that many of them are unaware of the research that is taking place even as they are studying for their degree (Jenkins, Blackman, Lindsay and Paton Saltzberg, 1998; Turner Wuetherick and Healey, 2008; Zamorski, 2002). They tend to be unaware of what their teachers do when they are not teaching them (Hajdarpasic, Brew and Popenici, in submission). Students' views of the university derive from their experiences. Many of these students go into industry, the professions, the media or politics where their ideas are coloured by their experiences. They make decisions and statements about the nature of higher education and these get fed into national policies. Some of the bureaucrats and accountants also end up in managerial positions in universities. So it is little wonder that when they occupy positions of power in society and in particular when they have responsibilities for funding and policy making about universities that they do so on the basis that all there is to universities is the teaching that takes place. The consequence of this is that teaching is funded but scholarly endeavour is not. It is being done on academics' own time and at home. In other words, it is being taken out of the university.

Increasingly, the media publicises scientific discoveries in various fields. Television programmes with titles such as 'Coast', 'The Normans', 'Discovery', 'Frontiers: The Future of Particle Physics', 'Making History', 'Science in Action', all draw from academic research. In this sense higher education is contributing to the education of a wider public. However, ideas about research which are making their ways into the media tend to be detached from the teaching that people have experienced as students and are not noticeably affecting societal attitudes towards university research. The role of universities in community education and engagement through, for example, their museums, libraries, concerts, plays, school outreach programmes, public lectures and conferences, etc., is little recognised in government policy. In these ways, universities directly contribute to the public good.

If universities are to enhance the extent to which they contribute to the public good then scholarly endeavour must be reclaimed. This means that students have to be differently educated. It makes engaging students in the academic project of the university an imperative. Students need to be engaged in research but they also need to be engaged in scholarly work in relation to curriculum and pedagogy. They need to have a say in their education not just at the end of the course in a short questionnaire, but they need to progressively learn to work to devise the courses with their teachers. This means carrying out research into their own and other students' learning. It means working with academics to design courses, it means more inquiry-based education of course, but it also means working alongside academics in carrying out scholarly work of various kinds. This might be doing disciplinary research. It might be doing scholarship of teaching and learning and it might be looking into (researching) problems, challenges and issues in the academic workplace. Students must be involved in doing this with the academics, not at arm's length from them. They need to come to understand the nature of scholarly work. A different kind of future for higher education is envisaged if they are proactive in establishing universities as places where scholarly work is shared and is truly valued.

Taking a Proactive Stance

Barnett (2008) argues that in universities more emphasis should be placed on the being of the student, what Heron (1992) calls 'personhood'. All too often people, both within and external to universities, are concerned with what students know and not with who they are. The emphases on employability and the development in students of a broad range of skills and attributes and whether they should be taught in special courses or alongside disciplinary content have led universities to define benchmark standards for generic and specific capabilities and this, it would seem, would be a step in that direction. Barrie (2006) has suggested that generic attributes are understood in different ways. However, none of these ways focuses on the student's being; the person they are and the emotional aspects of learning within a university environment. Indeed, the concept of skills tends to be detached from the person whose skills are to be developed. Paradoxically also, little if any attention has been paid to whether the academics involved in developing skills in students actually possess the skills themselves.

One of the ways in which higher education is taking a proactive stance is in regard to engaging undergraduates in research. For students who are the professionals of the future, developing the ability to investigate problems, make judgments on the basis of sound evidence, take decisions on a rational basis and understand what they are doing and why is vital. Developing understanding and practice in engaging undergraduates in learning through research and inquiry is important not just for those who choose to pursue an academic career. It is central to professional life in the twenty-first century.

The role of research as an activity only for the elite is seriously being challenged by the growing number of opportunities available to undergraduate students to engage in research. Critical in this are the attitudes and objectives of research funding bodies. In the US the National Science Foundation, for example, views undergraduate research as a vital part of the nation's research effort (National Science Foundation, 2001). Other research funding bodies in the US such as the Research Corporation for Science Advancement and the Howard Hughes Medical Institute, have long traditions of funding and supporting undergraduate research. Some Canadian research councils also fund undergraduate research, and in the UK the government's investment of some £40 million to develop 'research-informed teaching' together with the establishment from 2005 to 2010 of six Centres for Excellence in Teaching and Learning focused on undergraduate research and inquiry, led to many curricular and co-curricular research-based experiences for students. This is important because it begins to break down hierarchies and also it begins to change relationships between academics and students.

In my book *Research and Teaching: Beyond the Divide* (Brew, 2006), I argued that we need to develop universities as places where we work with students and professional and technical staff in inclusive scholarly knowledge-building communities, where inquiry is central to how we communicate, to how we critically reflect on everything we do. This, I argued, involves developing new forms of university education where academics and students can:

- Share learning and understanding;
- Research personal and professional issues together;
- Engage together in generating knowledge in partnership;
- Share in developing professionalism in an academic sense;
- Develop the university as an inclusive community of scholars; and
- Develop relationships that work towards equalising power through democratic discussion (Brew, 2006).

I suggested that universities need to set as goals the interrelationship of students as participating scholars and to break down barriers to this. Some of this is happening in the margins through engaging students in research, some through academic development which encourages critical questioning of the relationships between academics and students; some through the design of collaborative research projects with undergraduate and postgraduate students including research on teaching and learning projects; some through the setting up of undergraduate research scholarship schemes, undergraduate journals and conferences; some through the redesign of curricula to include more research-based learning; and some through the planning of new spaces within universities for intellectual collaboration and socializing of students and academics.

These developments bring to the surface underlying concerns about how higher education can prepare students and staff to cope with the uncertainties of an unknown future. They also bring academic critique into a central role in university functioning while at the same time critically questioning and thereby loosening rigid hierarchical structures. For students who become research associates when engaged in undergraduate research experience programmes are reported to feel part of the research community. They are treated as junior colleagues rather than just 'students' engaged in courses. Their relationship with academics changes to a more inclusive one (Brew and Jewell, 2012). Developing opportunities for students to undertake research depends on changed relationships between students and academics. Ironically, engaging undergraduate students in research is seen not only to benefit student learning, but also to benefit universities' research efforts and staff engagement. What I have argued here would have the capacity to alter understanding in the professions of what needs to be done to solve the world's problems and the contribution of the university to doing this. Widespread acceptance of such attitudes is a critical factor determining whether students are enabled to contribute to the academic project of the public university.

Conclusion

In this chapter I have focused on some of the paradoxes and contradictions lying within higher education and have suggested how higher education institutions are responding to societal pressures in endeavouring to contribute to the public good. I have suggested how they might be more proactive in developing a higher education which is appropriate to the demands of an unknown and unknowable future. A key question that arises is to what extent universities have the capacity to take a much longer term view; to prepare not simply the current generation, but future generations for the world that they will have to face and to view such generations in a global context even when they are experiencing limitations in government funding and views of their role. There is a tendency to focus on the near future, because that is all that can be deduced at present. However, the longer term future is likely to remain uncertain and it is this that future generations will need to be educated to face. In contributing to the public good in the future, universities will need to be more proactive in addressing critical questions that arise through the process of educating future professionals, industrialists, politicians and academics. It is only by being more proactive in addressing issues which are not, by and large, being addressed by outside bodies, that the university can make a contribution to leading the ways in which society addresses the challenges of future generations.

Acknowledgments

The ideas in this paper have been developed through conversations with many colleagues. In particular, I would like to thank my fellow panellists Gary Poole, Jennifer Meta-Robinson, Randall Bass and the audience at the 2012 Conference of the International Society for the Scholarship of Teaching and Learning in Hamilton, Ontario, as well as participants at the 2011 SRHE Symposium on Higher Education as a Public Good: Critical Perspectives, and my colleagues Stefan Popenici and David Boud.

References

Barnett, R. (2008) *A Will to Learn: Being a Student in an Age of Uncertainty*. Maidenhead, UK: Society for Research into Higher Education and the Open University Press.

Barrie, S. C. (2006) Understanding What We Mean by the Generic Attributes of Graduates. *Higher Education*, 51:2, 215–241.

Boker, J. (2012) *University of The Future: A Thousand Year Old Industry on the Cusp of Profound Change*. Sydney, Australia: Ernst & Young.

Brew, A. (2006) *Research and Teaching: Beyond the Divide*. London: Palgrave Macmillan.

Brew, A., and Jewell, E. (2012) Enhancing Quality Learning Through Experiences of Research-Based Learning: Implications for Academic Development. *International Journal for Academic Development*, 17:1, 47–58.

Brookfield, S., and Preskill, S. (1999) *Discussion as a Way of Teaching: Tools and Techniques for University Teachers*. Buckingham, UK: Society for Research into Higher Education and the Open University Press.

CERI (Centre for Educational Research and Innovation, Organisation for Economic Co-operation and Development) (2009) *Higher education to 2030: Vol. 2. Globalisation*. Paris: OECD Publishing.

Davies, B., Gottsche, M., and Bansel, P. (2006) The Rise and Fall of the Neo-Liberal University. *European Journal of Education*, 4:12, 305–319.

Dill, D. (2011) Assuring the Public Good in Higher Education: Essential Framework Conditions and Academic Values. Paper presented at *Higher education as a public good: Critical Perspectives, New College, Oxford., July 4–5*. London: Society for Research into Higher Education.

Hajdarpasic, A., Brew, A., and Popenici, S. (in submission) The Contribution of Academics' Engagement in Research to Undergraduate Education. Submitted July 28, 2012.

Heron, J. (1992) *Feeling and personhood*. London: Sage.

Jenkins, A., Blackman, T., Lindsay, R., and Paton-Saltzberg, R. (1998) Teaching and Research: Student Perspectives and Policy Implications. *Studies in Higher Education*, 23:2, 127.

Kuh, G. D. (2008) *High-Impact Educational Practices: What They Are, Who Has Access to Them, and Why They Matter*. Washington, DC: Association of American Colleges and Universities.

Lucas, L. (2006) *The Research Game in Academic Life*. Maidenhead, UK: Open University Press and the Society for Research into Higher Education.

Marginson, S., and Considine, M. (2000) *The Enterprise University: Power, Governance and Reinvention in Australia*. Cambridge, MA: Cambridge University Press.

National Science Foundation (2001) *GPRA Strategic Plan* [Web Page]. www.nsf.gov/publs/2001/nsf0104/strategy.htm [2004, October 5].

Nixon, J. (2011) Reclaiming Higher Education as a Public Good. Paper presented at *Higher Education as a Public Good: Critical Perspectives, New College, Oxford, July 4–5*. London: Society for Research into Higher Education.

Nowotny, H., Scott, P., and Gibbons, M. (2001) *Re-Thinking Science: Knowledge and the Public in an Age of Uncertainty*. Cambridge: Polity Press.

Olssen, M., and Peters, M. A. (2005) Neoliberalism, Higher Education and the Knowledge Economy: From the Free Market to Knowledge Capitalism. *Journal of Education Policy*, 20, 313–345.

Powell, W. W., and Clemens, E. S. (1998) *Private Action and the Public Good*. New Haven, CT: Yale University Press.

Russell, C. (1993) *Academic Freedom*. London: Routledge.

Standish, P. (2011) Transparency, Accountability and the Public Role of Higher Education. Paper presented at *Higher Education as a Public Good: Critical Perspectives*.

Stephens, D. J. (forthcoming) *Hacking Your Education: Ditch the Lectures, Save Tens of Thousands, and Learn More than your Peers Ever Will*. New York: Penguin.

Temple, P., and Filippakou, O. (2007). *Learning Spaces for the 21st Century: A Review of the Literature*. York, UK. Higher Education Academy. http://www.heacademy.ac.uk/projects/detail/litreview/lr_2007_temple

Turner, N., Wuetherick, B., & Healey, M. (2008) International Perspectives on Student Awareness, Experiences And Perceptions of Research: Implications For Academic Developers in Implementing Research-Based Teaching and Learning. *International Journal for Academic Development*, 13:3, 191–211.

Zamorski, B. (2002) Research-Led Teaching and Learning in Higher Education A Case. *Teaching in Higher Education*, 7:4, 411–427.

Zhang, L. (2009) A Value-Added Estimate of Higher Education Quality of US States. *Education Economics*, 17, 469–489.

VIII. Is Higher Education a Public Good? An Analysis of the English Debate

TED TAPPER

Defining the Issues

Although there has not been much explicit discussion of the issue the English universities for most of their history have been perceived as providing a public good, which is formally recognised by their charitable status. Contemporarily, however, considerable attention has been paid to the private benefits that higher education bestows. This chapter explores, in terms of policy, what is meant by the claims that higher education is either a public or private good. What are the precise ways in which those terms have been interpreted? How is the contemporary emphasis upon the private benefits of higher education to be explained? The answers emerge from those political struggles that have influenced the recent course of higher education policy, and above all the attempts to restructure its funding base. The current intrusion into the debate of the idea of higher education as a private good is therefore reflective of a broader battle about both its purposes and the trajectory of its development. This is an ideological struggle with concrete policy implications. The chapter will conclude with a reflective overview on how English universities are responding to the forceful emergence of the idea of higher education as a private good and interpret its impact upon the overall structure of the system.

A Public or a Private Good

Perhaps the clearest understanding of why higher education was perceived as a public good is to be gained by examining a little of the background as to why educational bodies should be accorded charitable status. In the United Kingdom charitable status is granted to those organisations that are deemed to provide a public benefit, and for pursuing that public good they are exempted from paying certain taxes. Until the mid-nineteenth century the responsibility for deciding such matters was the prerogative of the courts, but thereafter the Charity Commission was established to control the regulation of charities. Although what was understood by the promotion of education was interpreted broadly and within itself was seen as providing a public benefit, there were also restrictive guidelines for those seeking charitable status: the provider had to be a non-profit-making organisation which also offered its wares to the public at large rather than a narrowly defined segment of the population. Thus, a school that proposed to educate only the children of the workers of one employer would not be granted charitable status, although historically there was no denial of the status to schools that charged high fees. However, we now have political intrusion upon the regulation of charitable bodies in the form of government legislation (legislation on charities was enacted in 1992, 1993, 2006 and 2011) and, although the promotion of education is within itself still considered to be the provision of a public benefit, there is now some expectation that those schools with charitable status which charge fees will take into account the needs of prospective pupils from poorer families. There is a distinction drawn between what gives the school its charitable status and how it chooses to manage that status (Independent Schools Council, September 14, 2012).

However, in terms of higher education the issue of social bias in the undergraduate student population has been more entrapped in the politically driven (by governments of differing persuasions) 'widening participation' agenda rather than the need to concur with requirements that have to be fulfilled in order to secure charitable status. Indeed, higher education institutions were 'exempted charities' and as such were not subject to review by the charity commissioners because it was assumed that their functioning was overseen by other regulatory bodies. However, the 2006 Act lays down the requirement that there should be a principal regulator for higher education, and the Higher Education Funding Council for England assumed that role in June 2010 with the exception of the Oxford and Cambridge colleges which elected to register with the Charity Commissioners.

While some universities have been more socially exclusive than others, it would be very difficult to use this as grounds for arguing that they not do provide a public benefit and, therefore, should not be awarded charitable status. The alleged discrimination has not been dependent upon the imposition of exorbitant fees, which in any case from at least the 1960s until quite recently were paid for directly out of public funding. Secondly, universities can argue that they need to select on the basis of judgments that secure the entry of those who in their estimate are likely to complete most competently their selected programmes of study. Thirdly, since the arrival of variable fees—whose costs are underwritten predominantly by income-contingent loans—we have seen an explosion of fee-reduction and bursary programmes directed mainly (although not exclusively) at students from lower-income families. This is in addition to schemes designed to attract applicants from schools whose pupils have tended to shun applying for a place at one of the more prestigious universities. The targeted universities could pursue a number of avenues on this front in order to protect their charitable status.

The 2004 Higher Education Act created the Office for Fair Access (OFFA) with which the universities had to reach 'access agreements' if they wished to charge variable fees. However, this has been more about the need to charge variable fees in order to secure viable funding to cover the costs of teaching and learning rather than a step required to cement charitable status. It is, therefore, a formal response to economic and political pressure and not a measure that the university is acting in the public interest. The latter is a matter for the charity commissioners who interpret the guidelines laid down by the courts and the statutory legislation. Certainly there are those who would like definitive social targets built into the 'access agreements' with financial penalties imposed when the targets are missed. The argument is that to miss the target is a measure of the institution's failure to fulfil its obligation to provide a public benefit. But the pressures, whether they are from OFFA or the charity commissioners, do not operate in such a draconian manner. There are so many variables that impact upon how higher education institutions select candidates for degree programmes and why particular decisions are made, that it has been seen as preferable to provide guidelines rather than impose a straitjacket (for the current legal position regarding OFFA's authority see, Farrington and Palfreyman, 2012). Nonetheless, guidelines do imply that there is an obligation to take action, and also suggest that there could be legislative movement in the officially desired direction should that action not be forthcoming.

But we are still left pondering the question of why, albeit with a few constraints, the mere provision of higher education should be seen as in the public interest? There are three broad reasons. Firstly, the possession of knowledge is seen as a positive *cultural good* and for it to be valued is perceived as critical to the well-being of society. Thus, it is a hallmark of the civilised society that it does its best to ensure both the transmission and enhancement of knowledge. The pursuit of knowledge is, therefore, assumed to be of public benefit in its own right. Secondly, there are lots of positive *social values* that accrue to society at large through the enhancement of education because the educated citizen is supposedly more likely to contribute to building the good society than the uneducated citizen. Thirdly, it is *politically* astute to promote education because it helps to ensure positive personal development, which in turn is likely to increase individual loyalty towards the established order. There is, therefore, a two-way interactive process between encouraging individual development and building system support.

All of these reasons for seeing the promotion of education as a public benefit are in fact problematic. Knowledge is a complex cultural variable and it could be argued that support for its expansion and transmission best serves the public good if these conform to a particular understanding of what is knowledge. Indeed, it could be argued that some forms of education promote knowledge that has harmful societal consequences, that education is far from a neutral force that always works to enhance the good of society. For example, the potentially close association between the doctrinal messages of a religious organisation and its schools (or even higher education institutions in certain countries) may make some wonder whether a public benefit is being served. In England this is not a contemporary issue for higher education (although until at least the end of the nineteenth century there was a close association between the Anglican Church and the Universities of Oxford and Cambridge), but rather the focus has been upon the alleged cultural biases of higher education—for the humanities and against the applied sciences, for discourse rather than experimentation. The issue, therefore, is how broadly the definition of knowledge can be drawn for it to be seen as a cultural product that serves a public benefit.

To claim that there is a connection between the personal experience of education and the inculcation of positive social values and behaviour is only superficially attractive. What are positive social values and behaviour? How is the linkage established? If it could be demonstrated that the family environment exercises a greater influence upon shaping values and behaviour then perhaps the resources accruing from the charitable status of educational pursuits could be put to better use by increasing public support for the welfare of families? Furthermore, would it not make most sense to target such resources at those families whose experience of education has been limited or even negative? That citizens who feel positively about how their society has attempted to shape their lives will be broadly supportive of it seems a reasonable proposition but there may be more effective ways of building political support than enhancing individual opportunity through education. Moreover, there is no guarantee that broadening educational opportunities necessarily builds system support. There may be good reasons for the state to view education as prescribing a public benefit but there has to be a much broader and deeper relationship between the individual and society to create a positive symbiotic relationship between the two. Indeed the educated individual may well be the politically discontented citizen.

The argument, therefore, is that while it is possible to claim that higher education is both a private and public good, it is difficult to substantiate conclusively a relationship between the two outcomes. Hopefully the experience of higher education will add to the individual's possession of the knowledge of a particular field of study, improve the ability to work systematically, enhance social networks, open up opportunities to obtain a respectable occupation and positively shape personal social values and behaviour, but what impact this has upon society at large (and thus becoming a public benefit) is problematic. Even if a positive relationship could be demonstrated then it would be necessary to know how cost effective it was. Moreover, the key public benefit that higher education has provided is the maintenance of a particular understanding of what is to count as high status knowledge, that is both what is taught and what is researched, and it is difficult to measure how this has impacted upon its role in enhancing the personal benefits that it makes available. In fact part of the contemporary critique of English higher education is that its dominant traditional forms of organising knowledge often have not enhanced either personal or societal development.

The Changing Understanding of Higher Education As a Public Good

Historically, although the universities were entwined in English society, they were considered to be autonomous institutions that defined their own goals. Indeed this continued long after they had become overwhelmingly dependent upon state funding to secure their development. Post-1945 they were essentially publicly-funded bodies but politically unaccountable in terms of the goals they pursued, although in a broad sense it was understood that they would evolve along lines that were commensurate with the national interest. From its foundation in 1919 onwards the University Grants Committee, which was responsible for the distribution of the Treasury's annual grant to the universities, steered, if only haphazardly, the growth of the university system. In effect the interpretation of the public good that the universities were meant to foster was controlled by interests internal to the world of the university, as was the model which it should follow—the necessity to have a broad disciplinary spread, the increasing attachment to honours degrees and thus entry requirements that sought out well-qualified and motivated applicants, the university as a socio-cultural community as well as a formal academic setting, the need to undertake research as well as to teach, the mutually supportive interaction of teaching and research, and—perhaps above all—higher education as the pursuit of knowledge as a worthwhile end in itself.

Over time it is unsurprising that this elitist definition of the public good that universities supposedly served was steadily challenged. The size of the overall system expanded to incorporate a range of higher education institutions other than the universities, the costs grew to make it a financial commitment that inevitably attracted greater political intervention, and the question was increasingly raised as to why universities as publicly-funded bodies should not be driven by more specifically defined and publicly-determined policy imperatives? The issue was who had the right to determine the understanding of the public good that the universities should attempt to fulfil? Historically, operating within the framework of legislation, court decisions and the rulings of the charity commissioners, this was determined by the dominant interests in the world of higher education. However, the 1988 Education Reform Act, reinforced by the 1992 Further and Higher Education Act, formally ceded the control of higher education policy development to the state. The 1988 legislation spelled out the policy supremacy of the Secretary of State in terms that are both clear and straightforward. The Secretary of State could make grants 'to each of the Funding Councils of such amounts *and subject to such conditions as he may determine*' and 'confer or impose on either of the Funding Councils such supplementary functions he thinks fit' and 'in exercising their functions ... each of the Funding Councils *shall comply with any directions given to them by the Secretary of State*' (Education Reform Act, 1988, clauses 134.6, 134.1 and 134.8 respectively, as quoted in Tapper, 2007, p. 35, emphasis added). While higher education could still be seen as fulfilling a public good what that was to mean in concrete terms would be subject to the dictates of government policy.

However, English higher education is not subject to a straightforward centralised model of control in which the state defines the public purpose of the university and central government controls the policy development that gives concrete meaning to that public purpose. While higher education may still be seen—almost by definition—as a public good in its own right, it is also under pressure to demonstrate that it merits that accolade. Successive governments have argued that higher education institutions should be more attuned to the country's economic and social needs in order to show that they are pursuing a public good. Thus they encourage social mobility by granting access to students from socially disadvantaged families, they have programmes that transmit useful knowledge which enhance job prospects, and their research is geared to assisting the country's economic base to perform more effectively. If the university pursues a public good it does so through the practical ways in which it can aid personal and societal development, and not simply through the propagation of a particular understanding of knowledge.

The emerging ideological framework within which the English universities are increasingly embraced has been promoted by governments of differing political persuasions. Furthermore, the pattern of system control has been broadly consistent since the 1988/1992 legislation which saw the abolition of the UGC, the emergence of the national funding councils and the implementation of the new public management mode of governance. While policy control rests in national political hands, the steering of the development of the universities has for the most part been indirect. The state has created a regulated market in which higher education institutions are offered incentives to move towards the government's understanding of what is meant by fulfilling a public good. Thus, part of the evaluation of research (the Research Excellence Framework in which the universities compete for core public funding) will be based on the ability of the university to demonstrate the practical payoffs of its research output, while accepting students from socially disadvantaged families has carried with it a teaching premium. The universities are encouraged rather than required to move in certain directions.

Higher Education As a Private Good

As the chapter has noted higher education provides numerous opportunities—social, cultural and financial—for individuals to develop their personal capital, which is often seen as one of the ways in which it can also provide a public good. The argument being that the more personal development is enhanced the better will be society at large. Although this chapter has questioned the logic of this argument, nonetheless, it does have a superficial persuasiveness. However, even if you embrace the claim, it is a long way from maintaining that its promotion should be the driving force that shapes the character of English higher education.

The initial stress on higher education as a private good was closely entwined with the funding of the university. If higher education imparts a private good is it not reasonable to require that those who partake of its benefits should also meet at least part of its costs? The private good that has received particular attention is the increased financial rewards that accrue to individuals who receive a higher education over those whose education did not extend beyond secondary schooling. The assumption is that the receipt of higher education is largely responsible for the greater earning power of those who attended university. Significantly, the National Committee of Enquiry into Higher Education (the Dearing Report, 1997), which was established to take the issue of student fees out of the 1997 General Election campaign, accepted this argument:

> *There is widespread recognition of the need for new sources of funding for higher education. The costs of higher education should be shared among those who benefit from it. We have concluded that those with higher education qualifications are the major beneficiaries, through improved employment prospects and pay. As a consequence, we suggest that graduates in work should make a greater contribution of the costs of higher education in future* (Dearing, 1997, paragraph 90).

Subsequently this policy was enacted (although not in the form recommended by the Committee) by the Labour Government. The fee was a flat-rate charge of £1,000 per annum, which has subsequently become a variable fee capped first at £3,000 (Higher Education Act, 2004) and now (for entrants who commenced their studies in 2012) at £9,000. The fees are paid for by loans with income-contingent repayment terms, and there are still maintenance grants for students from low-income families. Furthermore, universities have to reach 'access agreements' with the Office of Fair Access (OFFA) to demonstrate the financial support that underwrites their commitment to the widening participation agenda, which is effectively a condition for the right to charge a high fee. Although this was essentially the product of political manoeuvring on the part of the then Labour Government, the 2004 legislation passed its second reading in the House of Commons by only five votes. The big political objection to variable fees was the contention that they would undermine access to higher education by causing a decline in the number of applicants from those located in the poorer socio-economic families. However, it does appear that there has been a serious attempt to mitigate that possibility, which ties into the ruling of the charity commissioners that fee-charging charities should be mindful that they do not exclude the poorer sections of society, although—as has been noted—this is not a precondition for education providers to be counted as charitable bodies.

The most consistent intellectual support for the introduction of variable fees paid for through an income-contingent loans scheme has been provided by Barr and Crawford (2005). At an earlier date Barr had argued the case for student fees as follows: 'This conclusion is not based on ideology, but on the deeply practical reason that large-scale higher education is vital but is too expensive to rely entirely on public funding' (Barr, 2001, p. 194). Nonetheless, for some time within the world of higher education it had been assumed by many that the pursuit of a public interest meant public funding. The question now was, as it had always been for those schools that charged fees, whether the universities could impose fees but still be seen as pursuing a public interest. And in both cases the answer has been that charging fees is not inconsistent with providing a public benefit if certain conditions are met.

Barr justified his policy position on economic grounds—the sheer expense of higher education—but it is clear that the shift towards variable fees has also been supported by strong political arguments. Even before the current economic crisis the political support for increasing the public funding of fees was very limited and it was often argued that it represented a subsidy paid to the better-off members of society by the less affluent. Increasingly the universities resolved their financial dilemma by increasing the fees of overseas students. (All government subsidy of the costs of tuition of students from outside the European Union was withdrawn in 1979.) Furthermore, there was a growing recognition that it was the overwhelming dependence upon public funding that made higher education so vulnerable to government policy pressure with the expectation that increasing non-public funding would enable the universities to exercise their nominal autonomy more effectively.

The publication of first the Browne Report (*Independent Review of Higher Education Funding and Student Finance*, October 2010), and then the Government's White Paper (*Higher Education: Students at the Heart of the System*, June 2011), raise the possibility that henceforth the development of English higher education will be driven by the differing ways in which institutions respond to the idea that higher education provides a private good. In other words, while there may be solid pragmatic grounds for advocating variable fees as a viable policy option, what in fact may be occurring is that the idea of higher education as a private good is being used as an ideological weapon to force the pace of change in English higher education.

Much of the current Coalition Government's higher education policy has been directed at attempting to create a market in the charging of fees. The effort to achieve this was through manipulation in the distribution of student numbers (reserving 20,000 places to institutions charging fees of less than £7,500 per annum, and permitting universities to admit as many students in their 2012 intake that they could accommodate who had high grades in the 'A' level school leaving certificate, which was a clear use of the state-regulated market to steer the development of higher education. On the one hand, therefore, the regulation of student access to higher education reflects a range of attempts by the state to reshape the university system in a way that manifests its own understanding of what would best serve the public interest. There is clearly a desire to encourage the emergence of greater diversity in institutional missions that will be reflected in differential fees. However, both the Browne Report and the White Paper recognise the need to move beyond the state regulated market to achieve this goal and turn to 'student choice' as one of the means to secure it.

The Browne Report argues that, what it calls its 'independent review' is based on certain principles of which the second is:

> No HEI can grow in the current system to respond to student demand. Many prospective students do not get adequate advice or information to help them choose a course of study. Our proposals will put students at the heart of the system. Popular HEIs will be able to expand to meet student demand. Students will be better informed about the range of options available to them. Their choices will shape the landscape of higher education (Browne Report, October 2010, p. 4).

In what appears to be at least a partial genuflection to the Browne Report, it should be noted that the White Paper has 'students at the heart of the system' as its subtitle.

For the White Paper central to putting 'students at the heart of the system' is dependent upon their having 'access to high quality information about different courses and institutions' (Department of Business, Innovation and Skills [BIS], 2011, p. 27). Moreover,

> Wider availability and better use of information for potential students is fundamental to the new system. ... It will be correspondingly harder for institutions to trade on their past reputations while offering a poor teaching experience in the present. Better informed students will take their custom to the places offering good value for money. In this way excellent teaching will be placed back at the heart of every student's experience (BIS, 2011, paragraph 2.24, p. 32).

Universities will be required to place on their websites a Key Information Set (KIS) presented in a form that will enable potential students to make comparisons on: course information (incorporating student satisfaction), costs and the employment records (including salaries) of graduates.

It would be difficult to argue with the proposition that potential students should be informed about the universities to which they are making an application, and generally speaking the more comparative information they have at their disposal the better. However, in the Foreword to the White Paper, the Secretary of State for the Department (Cable) and the Minister for Universities and Science (Willetts) state:

> Our university sector has a proud history and a world-class reputation, attracting students from across the world. Higher education is a successful public–private partnership: Government funding and institutional autonomy (BIS, 2011, Foreword).

If English higher education is so successful then one is entitled to ask whether the student experience can be significantly improved.

We have moved, therefore, in a comparatively short period of time through different perceptions of the public benefits that universities provide: as guardians of a tradition of education that perpetuates high status knowledge, as institutions that assist society in enhancing its social and economic well-being, and as providers of an experience of teaching that meets with the satisfaction of its customers—that is, the students. The precise interpretation of what exactly constitutes the public interest has been shaped by different protagonists: the academic lobby, the dominant political and economic interests, and now students as customers. Intrinsic, therefore, to the idea that higher education is a public benefit is the control of the different dimensions of what is to count as high status knowledge: its content and modes of transmission/expansion (the dominant input of the academic lobby), the ends it should serve (the pre-occupation of political and economic interests) and the extent to which it satisfies private needs (the concern of those who see students as customers).

These differing interpretations of higher education's provision of a public benefit could be said to form an uneasy alliance in the sense that they represent interactive rather than mutually exclusive purposes for higher education. For example, the provision of a high quality teaching experience was very much a traditional concern for the universities, and it was always recognised (see the quinquennial reports issued by the University Grants Committee up to 1990) that the university system should develop in ways that were broadly responsive to changing national needs. Moreover, that the universities, as autonomous bodies, were free to control their own academic development was integral to the English idea of the university, and even today governments pursue their policy goals through the operation of a regulated market rather than by fiat through the imposition of a planned straitjacket. But, while there may be differing interpretations of what is meant by providing a public benefit, undoubtedly a clear shift in the political view of what should determine the development of the English system of higher education has occurred. For successive governments the system should be geared to meeting politically defined economic and social goals and this was to be achieved through the operation of firstly, a state-regulated market, and now, by higher education institutions that are more responsive to the choices made by a better-informed student population.

Universities in the Marketplace: Blurring the Distinction Between Public and Private Providers

The move towards the founding of privately-funded universities in postwar Britain was led by the University of Buckingham. In view of the fact that it was a non-profit-making institution there was no problem about granting it charitable status and viewing it as providing a public benefit. More recently we have seen the emergence of for-profit providers and, although they have not so far been granted charitable status, certain of them have the right to award their own degrees and are edging towards the acquisition of the university title, both of which it is currently the prerogative of the Privy Council to grant. If the development of higher education is increasingly dominated by the idea that its provision of a public benefit is to be measured by how swiftly institutions respond to the demands of a better-informed student population, then there is no logical reason why for-profit institutions should not also be seen as providing a public benefit. This is especially so given that the publicly funded institutions are functioning within the confines of a state-regulated market in fees, and the students of privately financed institutions are also permitted to apply for publicly funded student loans. However, while for-profit institutions may be providing a public good (and no doubt they see themselves in these terms), it makes sense to deny them the financial benefits that go with charitable status because they are also trading companies that pay dividends to shareholders out of their profits. Thus, charitable status is in part about how a body conducts its affairs to undertake the provision of a public good and not simply dependent upon the provision of the public good itself. Presumably most profit-making companies would see themselves as providing a public benefit, while also recognising that this does not make them charitable bodies.

An examination of the accounts of those institutions of higher education that since 1945 have received the majority of their funding from the public purse reveals that across the board they have, since the mid-1980s, become increasingly reliant upon non-public funding to balance their books, and this includes charging commercially viable fees to overseas students. These universities, therefore, aim to make a surplus on many of their activities, although they remain non-profit making organisations pursuing a charitable purpose, unlike the for-profit providers that may pay dividends to shareholders. However, charitable status is increasingly less valued because it is a desired accolade, the recognition you are dedicated to fulfilling a public benefit, but valued because it is accompanied by a number of tax concessions, and thus is an important aid to institutional survival. Undoubtedly there was always a certain amount of truth in this claim, but with the financial pressures that higher education institutions have faced in recent years it carries more weight.

What has emerged is an increased concern with institutional survival, which has become the driving force for change in English higher education. The ends that universities attempt to achieve are driven by judgments that it is believed will best help them, if not to prosper, at least to sustain their viability.

Consequently, the pattern of academic development is heavily dependent upon projected student demand and thus it is difficult to sustain established programmes that experience a decline in the number of applicants. It is no surprise that the private providers have tended to focus their programmes upon professional fields of study (law, accountancy, management and business studies) or the fine arts (music, dance and theatre) which tend to have a narrow intellectual focus and clear links to the occupational structure. Arguably this may be a perfectly reasonable way of responding to the argument that universities can best-fulfil a public benefit by corresponding to the changing pattern of student demand, but it does have important ramifications for how we understand the idea of the university. Should the university label be extended to incorporate institutions that embrace only a very limited range of disciplinary fields—indeed, perhaps only one area of knowledge? Should a university be able to retain the label if it jettisons traditional areas of knowledge in the belief that this will aid institutional longevity? In the context of an increasingly diversified system of higher education what are the boundaries, if any, as to how the idea of the university is to be interpreted?

As the chapter has noted, the understanding of providing a public benefit is open to varying interpretations. What is likely to occur in the future is that, whilst not explicitly rejecting any one interpretation, higher education institutions will attempt to create specific identities. For example, most institutions will argue that their degree programmes are reflective of high academic standards based in part upon a commitment to sustaining a research ethos (an integral part of the traditional English idea of the university), all will maintain that their degree programmes overwhelmingly offer a very positive experience of teaching and learning and thus represent an excellent private investment for their students, and most will claim that they are responding positively to the social and economic agenda that has been established by successive governments. Almost universally, university mission statements make the same claims—or platitudes, as the more cynical may argue. But universities have different traditions, varying resources and contrasting positions in the marketplace, which will impact upon their particular interpretations of the public benefit they bestow. The English model of higher education is increasingly one of contrasting sectors and increasingly of institutions occupying niche markets.

References

Barr, N. (2001) *The Welfare State as Piggy Bank*. Oxford: Oxford University Press.
Barr, N., and Crawford, I. (2005) Financing Higher Education: *Answers From the UK*. Abingdon: Routledge.

Browne, J. (2010 October) *An Independent Review of Higher Education Funding and Student Finance* (www.independent.gov.uk/browne-report).

Dearing Report (1997) National Committee of Enquiry into Higher Education: Higher Education in the Learning Society (summary). Norwich: HMSO.

Department for Business, Innovation and Skills (2011 June) Higher Education: Students at the Heart of the System. London: BIS.

Farrington, D., and Palfreyman, D. (2012) Is the OFFA Guidance (03/11) to be Challenged by Judicial Review? OxCHEPS Paper 40, www.oxcheps.new.ox.ac.uk.

Independent Schools Council (September 14, 2012) ISC Responds to the Charity Commission's Consultation on Public Benefit, www.isc.co.uk.

Tapper, T. (2007) The Governance of British Higher Education: The Struggle for Policy Control. Dordrecht: Springer.

IX. A Cultural Value in Crisis: Education As Public Good in China

Kai-ming Cheng and Rui Yang

Introduction

The nature of higher education has seldom been under scrutiny in China. By China here we refer to the Chinese Mainland. Education in ancient China, represented almost solely by the imperial civil examination, was always designed and expected to serve the state, which was represented by the Emperor. This chapter observes that the modern higher education system, borrowed from the west, exists in that legacy, and was reinforced under the communist regime in its first decades. In a sense, education was always a public good. However, there is recent attention to a transformation whereby higher education would become a private good, which would have fundamental implications for the entire education system.

Culture and History

Francis Hsu (1985), in his study of the Chinese from a cultural psychological point of view, concluded that absolute 'self' in the western sense never existed in China. Individuals are always seen as part of a social structure, which is basically hierarchical in nature. There is therefore no absolute self. Everything about self is relative to the social rubric. He further explains that in the Chinese culture, there is always a relative importance of self at all levels: the 'smaller self' and the 'larger self'. Individual persons are smaller selves compared with the immediate family, which is the larger self. The immediate family has a similar relationship to the extended family, the family to the village community, and so forth, until it comes to the entire kingdom, 'all that are under the sky', which was taken to mean 'the world'.

Hsu's observations are well echoed in the Chinese language. There is the saying, as a virtue, that 'the smaller self should sacrifice itself for the perfection of the larger self'. In the Confucian classic *Great Learning*, the 'formation' (borrowing here from the notion of Catholic writers) of a gentleman (i.e. the perfect intellectual) should be following the rungs on a ladder: cultivating the self, organizing the family, governing the kingdom, harmonizing the world.

In this context, self was subordinate to a larger community and was situated somewhere in the social rubric. Throughout, education played a very proper function of socialisation, which trained individuals into a social role (Levine, 1982; Solomon, 1971). Central to 'education' in the Confucian convention is less about knowledge and skills, but rather, about *li* or rituals so that individuals would behave properly according to protocols when facing different parts of the social rubric: as son towards father, as wife to husband, as the young to the elderly, as subordinated to officials, etc. In other words, 'knowledge' in ancient China's education was about interpersonal relations, or about society, differing from the west, where knowledge is more about individuals' knowledge of the nature of the world (Gardner, 1984).

This was echoed in the education system in ancient China. Since the establishment of the Imperial Civil Examination system in 603 A.D.[1], the Examination was synonymous with 'education'. Learning of concrete knowledge and practical skills were seen as petty. Education was about reading books and writing essays ('scholarship'), in preparation for the Examination. The objective of such education was purely for selection and appointment to the officialdom, and that was the one and only path for social mobility. Hence, education always played a community function during the dynasties. Although there was no market economy as such during the ancient dynasties, we may still borrow the term 'public good' as a proxy to indicate the public nature of education.

There was a demonstrated dialectical interplay between individuals and the state, or the private and the public. On the one hand, education was a public good, in the sense that it served only purposes of the state, or 'all that are under the sky'. On the other hand, however, individuals engage in 'education' not as a sacrifice, but with the dreams of appointment to be a Minister, marriage to a princess, status and prosperity, glorification of the family and all those irresistible rewards as dramatised in novels, operas, dramas, and in folklore in general.

There were indeed plenty of stories about young scholars reading hard under very difficult conditions, but such 'sacrifices' were personal investments in a currency, in order to receive personal returns in the end. In a way, although the 'education' (Examination) system was designed as a public good, individuals engaged in education as a private investment.

However, the particular wisdom in such a system was that it incurred little financial cost in its running, both to the individuals and to the government. There was only the Examination, which was an annual event. Schools were rare and teachers were dispensable. The curriculum was simple and the textbooks (*Four Books and Five Classics*) were household collections. If there were anything called educational budget, it would be trivial. The only significant education 'expenditure' for an individual would be the financial means to travel to the capital, if he were lucky to win the local and provincial selections.

It is the nature and effective practice of the Civil Examination that led to all the well-known characteristics of China's education: the cultural values for education, the over-emphasis on examinations, the culture of hard-working and perseverance, the belief in efforts over innate ability, the prominence of extrinsic motivation over intrinsic motivation, the tendency of conformity, and all that (Cheng, 2011).

Therefore, it would be safe to say that the 'education' system in ancient China was basically one of self-study. Researchers in China (Liu and Hayhoe, 2011, pp. 182–190) observed that success in the local examination could be equivalent to a bachelor's degree of today, success at the provincial level to a master's degree and success at the imperial court as a doctoral degree. Liu is tacitly taking the ancient education system to mean higher education.

Nonetheless, there were institutes of higher learning in ancient China. There were the four major 'colleges' (*shuyuan*)[2] which were established for deeper understanding and interpretation of the classics. In a way, they are the counterparts of universities in the west. They were started, often with the support of the state, by academics who voluntarily took on serving the state as their mission. A type of its own, they were meant for study of theories to advise the Emperor in his governance of the state. It was consistent with the Civil Examinations which was to serve the Emperor.

The Contemporary System

The contemporary higher education system was established at the turn of the nineteenth–twentieth century as part of the 'Self-Strengthening Movement', which was a top-down campaign for modernisation. The essence of the movement was to learn from the western powers, which had been invading China with advanced technologies, so called 'strong warships and fierce canons'. Unlike the Meiji Restoration in Japan, which took place more or less at the same time, the Chinese reform did not bring about economic success, but it did give birth to some of the oldest Universities that still exist.

The Imperial Civil Examination was abolished in 1905, after a history of more than 1,400 years, as part of the Self-Strengthening Movement started by reformers among the officials. The Imperial University of Peking (now both Peking University and Beijing Normal University) was established even before that, in 1898, as part of the same movement, and as a major imperial establishment. It was the first state-run public university. The objective of the establishment was to prepare technical personnel for modernisation. Strengthening of the nation was always the underpinning philosophy at the establishments. Against that background, universities as public institutions did not charge tuition fees. The whole idea was that young people were to be trained for the nation. Despite the reform ideals, it is the continuation of the ancient legacy where intellectuals study for the state. In a way, the first universities belong to the 'public good' in the sense of the time.

The situation did not change much following the downfall of the Qing Dynasty and the establishment of the first Republic in 1911. All available evidence agrees that the national government was conscious of the contradiction of training experts in western technology on the one hand, yet avoiding the influence of western ideologies of democracy on the other. Within a few decades in 1937, there were no less than 47 universities and 35 efficiently-run and well-equipped colleges according to (Ding, 2011, quoting a special report for the University of Hong Kong at 1937). The more prominent ones were established by Christian missionaries. The Warlord period immediately after the downfall of the Dynasty caused chaos and instability all over the county, but had created space for the establishment of higher education institutions at competitive speeds.

The emergence of private institutions, such as St John's University in Shanghai (established 1879) and Lingnan in Canton (now Guangzhou, established 1888), which were started by missionaries, created opportunities alternative to purely technical training. There was therefore also a competition of ideologies. Graduates were no longer limited to engineers and scientists. Prominent philosophers and sociologists of diverse schools of thoughts also emerged. These private institutions admitted many young people from less-well-off families and provided scholarships. In a way, they replaced the ancient Civil Examination in enabling social mobility. Tuition was seldom an issue even in the private institutions. Hence the general pattern was that the newly born universities followed the legacy of supporting poor scholars for the betterment of society. In most of these institutions, there was a 'Western' stream which taught science and technology and a 'Chinese' stream which maintained the conventional study of classics and Chinese literature.

Peace was short for the new Republic, which was disrupted by the Japanese invasion in 1937. The eight-year Japanese occupation was disastrous for the whole nation. However, again ironically, the consolidated higher education system in the unoccupied 'rear west' achieved some academic prosperity. It was in the iconic Southwest Allied University, which was a consortium of leading universities who fled the occupation, that China produced the first graduates (and last until today) who became Nobel Laureates, notably in Physics. One explanation was that scholars took resurrection of the nation as their prime goal of study.

Socialist Public Good

It was in 1949, following the Communist takeover, that the state systematically developed higher education, which was termed a total public good. It was part of the planned economy, where higher education, and education in general, played an essential part in manpower planning.

China was not the first country to undertake qualified manpower planning in a planned economy. The Soviet Union practised manpower planning in the 1930s. However, the rigour in planning for individuals to contribute to national development in China was unprecedented. Typically, national development went by Five-year Plans, and all aspects of life followed. The plans set economic target goals (often by percentage growth in the output) five years ahead, which were translated into target goals in respective production sectors, which were in turn translated into output goals for individual production units (e.g. factories). The output goal in each unit then guided estimation of manpower needs (at all levels and departments) during the five-year period, taking into consideration all factors such as replacement for natural attrition. Such estimation informed plans of manpower needs over the five years; the aggregate of such over all units and all sectors constituted the manpower plan for the whole nation.

This is only half of the story. The other half of the story started with the plans of manpower needs, and translated that into expected manpower output from the education system, again classified by sectors, years and ranks. Such outputs are allocated among school and education institutions, higher education included, as their planned number of graduates by year, by discipline. That is, for example, if it were estimated that 2,000 chemical engineers were required for year t, then different universities with Chemical Engineering would be allocated target goals of graduates in year t. This would also be the admissions target for the year t-4 (given the four-year programmes), taking into consideration of dropouts (which were minimal) during their study.

With that system in place, the Chinese higher education, in its early socialist years, was modelled almost completely on the Soviet system. Curricula in higher education were structured with very detailed and fine sub-disciplines, which shadowed the industrial workplace and labour structure. Institutions were also classified into hierarchical tiers, again reflecting the tiers of workers they were expected to produce.

The planning mechanism did not stop with the plan. Its effective implementation entailed measures such as guaranteeing that all graduates ended up in the designated work positions (they were not called jobs in those days), hence state assignment of work positions. There were also measures to guarantee, at the other end, the right number of secondary school graduates taking up the places offered in the specific disciplines (Cheng, 1993). All these were implemented with strict and complicated administrative and organisational processes facilitated by ideological education, so that young people not only had to abide by national requirements, but they also felt proud of being part of the national plan.

The previous account illustrates how higher education was treated as a public good in the socialist system. Perhaps the term 'public good' has to be modified here. First, 'public' here meant the nation, or the state, which was seen as the largest community to which the individual self was supposed to submit. This was part of the ancient cultural heritage in a socialist context. Second, this 'good', which was public, was not shared by everyone in the nation. It was not quite available to anyone who wanted it, not even through competition. There was always a class bias, where children of the proletariat (meaning workers, peasants and soldiers) were given priority. Perhaps it could be coined as a 'class-oriented public good'.

In this period, higher education was all free, because it was part of the state machinery. Not only were there no tuition fees, but students were given subsidies for subsistence. Scholarships were available for families with possible financial difficulties (they were sometimes difficult to identify because of the egalitarian system). These were called 'People's Scholarships', to make sure that the scholarships would only benefit families that belong to the 'people', in contrast to those descendants of former capitalists or landlords (Zhang, 2001).

The entire idea was that students were part of the national asset. They were prepared through higher education for national development. Hence they were provided with all means to go through the higher education processes. In the end, they would be equipped to serve the nation and contribute to national development by working in the assigned work positions. All these of course were only part of a more complicated system of social engineering.

A Cultural Value in Crisis 133

Once a person was in the assigned work position, he or she would be 'owned' by that work unit. They were supposed to be there throughout their lives. All aspects of their lives would be taken care of by the unit. This would include numerous benefits to provide them with the daily necessities (including milk, newspaper, haircut, cold drinks, bicycle purchase, for example), and also interventions from the leaders to ensure harmonious marriage and family lives, just to mention a few aspects.

Hence, it would be far from the reality if one imagined that life in the socialist system was one of physical deprivation. It was quite the opposite. Individuals were well-fed by the state, otherwise they would not be able to serve the state well. Even at times of difficulties (such as the famine in 1959–1961), the sufferings were egalitarian. However, it was not a life of individual autonomy as aspired for in other societies.

The previous descriptions illustrate 'public good' of another kind. It was supposed to be for the good of the largest community, and hence absolutely it required no investment from individuals. However, individuals did not have the freedom to choose, although they incurred no cost in the process.

The situation was further dramatised during the Cultural Revolution (1966–1976) which went to extremes to denounce 'bourgeois rights' which extended to all kinds of private ownership. However, the real disaster in higher education was the 'revolution' against 'bourgeois education', which resulted in the destruction of the entire higher education system. Institutions were taken over by Revolutionary Committees comprising workers, peasants and soldiers. Curricula were overhauled to fit production and revolution. Conventional universities were replaced by adult learning 'Workers' Universities' under the ideology that 'truth comes only from practice'. Higher education institutions, if they were still seen as existing at that time, became political apparatus to achieve class-struggle goals, in order to fulfil Mao Zedong's doctrine of continuing revolution in the intellectual domains after the completion of revolution in the economic system. In a way, higher education was also pushed to the extreme in the sense of a 'public good'. Of course, that also casts doubts on the definition of a 'public good'.

Turning to the Market

A dramatic shift came after 1976, with the ending of the Cultural Revolution. Since 1978, the so-called 'socialist market economy' was introduced. The change proved to be far reaching and fundamental (Cheng, 1997).

The first step was to re-open the conventional universities in 1977. In 1977 and 1978, three admissions exercises were conducted to speed up the process of reviving the conventional higher education. The second step was to introduce degrees in the system, starting in 1980. During the first three decades of the People's Republic, there was no degree system. It was not seen as necessary because the transition from study to work was achieved by state assignment. Any work transfer (which was rare) was done by transfer of passive individuals. The degree has allowed individuals to carry portable qualifications with them. These were essential for a job market which was just emerging. The degree system was introduced with almost no difficulties.

The third step, abolition of the work-assignment system, took longer to achieve. In the early 1980s, when graduates intended to work in places outside the assignment system, they were seen as illegitimate. They could do so only with permission after very strict procedures. Then it came to a stage where graduates could move beyond assignment by paying a penalty, in the argument that they were wasting the state investment on them. This was the case when non-government companies were still a minority. It was only in the late 1980s when the market economy began to gain momentum that notions like 'jobs', 'employment', 'employer' and 'employees' began to make sense. This was partially because of re-organisation of the state-owned enterprises, but partially also because of emergence of the private sector in the economy.

Some leading universities, in the late 1980s, started practising 'two-way selection', where companies sent teams to institutions to select graduates, and, in cases of multiple offers, for students to choose the employer. These were a kind of job-market fair, where the two-way selection physically took place. The percentage of job-seeking graduates, as compared with the work assignment graduates, increased over time. This went on until 1997 when the practice of work assignment ended completely, a milestone that signified the end of manpower planning.

The fourth step was the introduction of tuition fees. Since the late 1980s, because of the unquenched thirst amongst aspiring candidates, higher education institutions were allowed to admit students over and above the state plan. This was the first deviation from planned admissions, another important part of manpower planning. These extra-plan students were supposed to be self-financing and pay fees. There were therefore two tracks of students at one point: those who were supported by the state, and those who paid for tuition.

A crucial step was taken in 1997 when the state decided to 'merge the two tracks', which virtually meant that every student had to pay a tuition fee. The implications were tremendous. For centuries, education in China, with the Civil Examination in place, basically did not incur a cost for individuals. The aspiration for education bore no price tag. The cultural assumption was that as long as you work hard, you would win the competition in the examination, and your life would be changed. This was taken for granted and deep-rooted in the culture. Money did not come into the formula.

Hence, 1997 was the critical year when the abolition of work assignment and the introduction of fees occurred at the same time. Regardless of the immediate rationale for such important changes, the two policy measures indeed marked the transition where individuals became the stake holders of higher education. It marked the fundamental change of the nature of higher education in China from a 'public good' to a 'private good'. It also marked the beginning of undermining a culture that had been there for more than 1,500 years.

Unexpected Impacts

Policy makers of the previously mentioned changes might not have foreseen the far-reaching impacts of the policies. The rationale was largely to move the state away from total financial liability, and to mobilise community resources to support education, higher education in particular. However, the impacts have been tremendous and comprehensive. The following are some of the more visible aspects.

First, parallel to the introduction of tuition fees and the removal of job assignments was the replacement of people's scholarships by student loans. Ever since the establishment of the People's Republic, students who were admitted to universities also received subsistence support, so that there were no private expenditures at all. On top of that, selected students would also receive People's Scholarships'. These were sizable sums of money, but granted only to students from 'good' families, meaning families of workers, peasants and soldiers. It was granted in a class-struggle framework, where descendants of the 'people' were deemed to deserve more support. They received financial subsidy on top of priority admissions. Other students were seen as coming from less favourable families, the bourgeois and petty-bourgeois, who deserved no extra financial help. In a way, this was a financial subsidy for political 'correctness'.

The student loan was introduced according to models borrowed from the west, where students received a loan in anticipation of repayment with interest. For technical as well as cultural reasons, the student loan scheme never had any real success. However, the scheme provides a contrast to the People's Scholarship. Zhang (2001) identifies a fundamental change from *yi* (correctness) to *li* (interests) in the difference between People's Scholarship and student loan. The former was granted because of the students' family background or political application, as part of the state development of its cadre. The latter assumes individual ownership of the credentials, and hence the expectation of repayment of the loans.

The student loan scheme gave money to individuals as a commercial transaction, in return for repayment with interest. It was established with the conceptual assumption that higher education is a 'private good', where individuals spend money on tuition in order to receive a return later on. The loan scheme provides students with the initial investment. Both the technical liability (who should pay what) and the conceptual legitimacy (why should the state support individuals) are grounded in the perception that higher education is a private investment.

The immediate impact has been that there were students who lost their access to higher education because they could not afford the tuition and other expenditures. This was exacerbated by the increasingly intensified process of commercialisation, on almost all expenditures related to higher education. Although there have been interventions from the state in order to regulate and control the prices of, for example, accommodation and meals, the overall expenditure has gone beyond the affordability of less-than-average income families. In the initial years of the reform, there were many stories where poorer families borrowed money from their neighbours for their children to be able to attend higher education. There have also been cases where a whole village collected donations for a child to attend higher education, following the ancient tradition in anticipation of a glorious return of the child one day in the future.

Second, the inability to attend higher education for financial reasons has filtered down the system. When financial contributions were not necessary, as was the case throughout most of Chinese history, families in economically deprived villages in particular, placed all their hope in the school performance of their children, regarding that as a difficult but viable route to change the status of the family. Now with the financial barrier in sight, families have to count their income to assess the opportunities for their children to attend higher education. Increasingly more have given up hope, in view of the huge financial commitment which is beyond their capability. The process was rather slow, very much because of the cultural heritage which was rather blind to the reality. However, across generations, disruption of the heritage value of education is already showing in the poorest parts of the nation.

The situation almost came to a rupture at the turn of the twenty-first century. The ever-growing disparity among schools, because of decentralised financial responsibilities, became a national crisis. The deteriorated school quality and the declining motives to attend schools came at the same time, reinforcing each other. The central government, in 2006, revised the *Law for Compulsory Education* which promised differential subsidy to areas of different financial capabilities. However, the state rescue perhaps came too late to stop the tendency of serious school dropouts. With no foreseeable benefits of pursuing schooling, children simply dropped out of schools. Thus, the rather spectacular higher enrolment ratios in the 1990s gradually degenerated into a myth in the poor areas of the country.

The deterioration has been exacerbated by two other factors. The first is the massive exodus of rural population to the urban cities where economic activities are flourishing. Large numbers of children migrated to cities with their parents, leaving large numbers of rural school places vacant. These migrant children have become a major headache for the hosting governments, and for various reasons, their future chances of attending higher education are slim. They become another group of disappointed students.

In both rural and urban schools, the expenditures on basic education have tremendously inflated. In the pre-market era, state subsidy made textbooks extremely cheap and in practice often free. They have now become expensive items. Tuition fees are not allowed in compulsory years, but all schools collect money with various excuses, and this has further deprived children from poor families of fair education opportunities. Hence, the change of higher education from 'public good' to 'private good' has not only undermined the egalitarian concepts in higher education, but has also undermined the faith in education throughout the entire system.

Third, the change in formal higher education has also infected the adult education or continuing education sector. China has long had a very comprehensive and sophisticated system of adult and continuing education. Individuals, as state workers, were provided with means to attend adult education programmes with almost no individual expense. Most of them were provided with duty-bound time slots to attend such programmes on the job. The underpinning idea was again that state workers needed to upgrade themselves in order to better serve the nation. They were attending these programmes for public good. Things changed with the introduction of the market economy. Adult education programmes now charge fees, and the fees are set for the market value of the programmes, rather than according to the costs. Most work units are now private enterprises, and even the remaining state enterprises practice human resource policies as if they were private enterprises. Upgrading activities are purely individual undertakings. They have to find their own time and pay their own fees as a matter of individual self-improvement.

This has caused barriers to those workers who are in the low-income brackets; they are badly in need of upgrading, but they lack the means to engage in such upgrading programmes. They are in a vicious cycle. They are likely to spiral down the social ladder in an ever-changing society, and are likely to become an enormous social problem in the not-too-distant future.

Looking Ahead

China's education, basic education in particular, has been the envy of many other cultures. The values for education were very much due to the highly competitive yet highly rewarding system of Civil Examination. The Civil Examination was replaced by equally competitive and rewarding system of higher education in the early twentieth century. The socialist state inherited such values and maintained a system which became an essential part of the planned economy. All the way, the individual zest for higher education and the state commitment to higher education were underpinned by the faith in higher education as a public good.

The reforms in China since the late 1980s have created a market economy 'of Chinese characteristics', which is undoubtedly the main cause for spectacular advancement in the economy. It is noticed, by both the government and the critics, that the prosperity brought about by the reform has been accompanied by very significant income and life chances disparities, which are becoming increasingly unbearable. However, in the realm of education, there is the additional crisis of the unnoticed change of education from a 'public good' to a 'private good', which undermines the very faith in education. Such a faith was part of the cultural belief which was essential to the maintenance of the education system. Such a crisis, discussion of which has just emerged, runs counter to a belief in strengthening higher education as a major strategy for national development.

If disparity is indeed a major issue in national development, then China perhaps faces a fundamental challenge. Education used to be seen as a path for social mobility because it provided equal opportunities. The loss of its 'public good' nature is now removing such a mechanism of social equilibrium, and education will soon become the culprit for social disparity. Disparity now starts with education.

Notes

1. A very good account of the Imperial Civil Examination could be found in Benjamin (2000) or in Chinese in Liu (2005).
2. A good introduction to the ancient college in China could be found in Li and Hayhoe (2011).

References

Benjamin, A. E. (2000) *A Cultural History of Civil Examinations in Late Imperial China*. Berkeley: University of California Press.

Cheng, K. M. (1993) 'Changing Legitimacy in a Decentralizing System: The Changing Role of The State in China', *International Journal of Educational Development*, 14:3, 265–269. Also collected in J. D. Turner (1994) *The Reform of Educational Systems to Meet Local and National Needs*. Manchester: University of Manchester.

Cheng, K. M. (1997) 'Markets in a Socialist System: Reform of Higher Education in China'. In: K. Watson, S. Modgil and C. Modgil (eds), *Educational Dilemmas: Debate and Diversity, Vol 2: Higher Education*. London: Cassell.

Cheng, K. M. (2011) 'Education in Confucius Society'. In: J. Banks (ed), *Encyclopaedia of Diversity in Education*. Thousand Oaks: Sage.

Ding, S. P. (2011) *A History of the University of Hong Kong*. Paper Prepared for the Impact Study at the Centenary of the University of Hong Kong.

Gardner, H. (1984) 'The Development of Competence in Culturally Defined Domains: A Preliminary Framework', In: R. A. Shweder and R.A. LeVine (eds), *Culture Theory: Essays on Mind, Self, and Emotion*. Cambridge: Cambridge University Press.

Hsu, F. L. K. (1985) 'The Self in Cross-Cultural Perspective', In: A. J. Marsella, G. DeVos and F. L. K. Hus (eds), *Culture and Self: Asian and Western Perspectives*. New York: Tavistock Publications.

LeVine, R. A. (1982) *Culture, Behavior and Personality* (2nd ed.). New York: Aldine. Chapter 4. 'Concepts of socialization'. 61–68.

Li, J., and Hayhoe, R. (2011) 'Confucianism and Higher Education', in: In J. Banks (ed), *Encyclopaedia of Diversity in Education*. Thousand Oaks: Sage.

Liu, J. (2005) *Study of Imperial Examination*. Wuhan: Huazhong Normal University Press. *In Chinese*.

Solomon, R. H. (1971) 'Confucianism and the Chinese life cycle', In *Mao's Revolution and the Chinese Political Culture*. Berkeley: University of California Press.

Zhang, M. (2001) *Concepts of Equity and Policies for University Student Financial Support: Chinese Reforms in an International Context*. PhD Thesis, Hong Kong: University of Hong Kong.

X. Assuring the Public Good in Higher Education: Essential Framework Conditions and Academic Values

David D. Dill

Introduction

An important concern in contemporary debates about higher education policy is the 'public good'. Economists have long distinguished 'public' from 'private' goods. Private goods are excludable; those who own the good can exercise private property rights, preventing those who have not paid for the good from using it or consuming its benefits. Private goods are also rivalrous; consumption by one consumer prevents simultaneous consumption by other consumers. In contrast a 'public good' or service is neither rivalrous in consumption, nor excludable in ownership, and is available to all. Such goods—national defense being the classic example—will thus either not be provided or provided in insufficient quantities by the private (market) sector and therefore must be provided or subsidised by the state.

Traditionally education, particularly higher education, has been considered by economists to provide both private and public benefits and goods (OECD, 2008; McMahon, 2009). The private benefits of higher education, which many students are willing to pay for, include postgraduate employment opportunities, higher wages and increased income over a lifetime. Even when one calculates the private internal rate of return, which considers the opportunity costs of a university degree including earnings foregone during the time used to obtain it, higher education is financially beneficial. In addition to monetary benefits, higher education produces non-monetary private benefits: direct benefits experienced in the process of consuming higher education, and over time better health, improved cognitive development for one's children, higher returns on financial assets and greater job satisfaction. In addition to these private benefits there are clearly social benefits provided by university graduates: higher taxes paid, less frequent incidence of smoking/poverty/incarceration (and therefore also less consumption by university graduates of public support), as well as more frequent participation by university graduates in volunteer activities, blood donations and voting. In addition, investments in higher education are positively associated with social benefits such as industrial innovation and economic growth. It is worth noting that these private and social benefits exist in all OECD countries and with the recent massification and expansion of access to higher education in many countries, including the UK[1], the levels of these benefits have generally been enhanced (OECD, 2008).

In contrast to this economic research, recent writings on the public good in higher education by sociologists, political scientists and educationists have been largely critical (Calhoun, 2006; Tierney, 2006; Marginson, 2007; Brown, 2010; Rhoten and Calhoun, 2011). This literature suggests the policy reforms of the last several decades, which have introduced greater 'privatisation' and market competition into higher education systems (i.e. so-called 'neo-liberal reforms'), have also lessened the 'public goods' provided by higher education institutions and are compromising academic activity within universities. This literature, written primarily by those who work within higher education institutions, makes valuable contributions, but has several limitations. First, it is largely rhetorical and qualitative, rather than empirical. When this literature is empirical, it is often focused on the views of academics themselves rather than on indicators of the outputs or outcomes of universities. Furthermore, in critiquing the impacts of current policies, many of these studies do not cite or assess the economic research on the increasing private and public returns produced by higher education noted earlier. While the impacts upon those actively involved in the production of higher education should certainly be included in any calculation of the public good and/or the social benefits derived from higher education, focusing primarily on the impacts upon producers may not provide a totally objective assessment of the public good. An important question policy researchers must confront is 'which public' and 'for whose good' (Powell and Clemens, 1998).

Concerns also have been raised that studies based primarily upon the views of academic staff may be biased by their private interests. Gläser, Spurling and Butler (2004), commenting on interview studies of the impacts of the UK Research Assessment Exercise (RAE)[2], noted such studies were often not scrupulous about reporting sampling procedures, investigating bias due to nonresponse, or constructing questions carefully to avoid passing on negative assumptions about the RAE to the respondents. Processes like the RAE that reduce researcher autonomy may create in respondents a negative bias in answering questions regarding the effect of the policy on research performance. Nor do these studies always systematically control for factors possibly influencing respondents' replies such as type of university, field, gender or seniority. With regard to the study of the public good in higher education the sociologist Craig Calhoun (2006, pp. 34–36), while largely critical of recent higher education policy reforms, nevertheless clearly articulates the challenge for academic researchers:

> *Professors tend to think universities exist naturally, or as a gift of history, in order to employ them.... Most academics in other words, believe they deserve their university jobs on the basis of their previously demonstrated merit.... [But academic] ... productivity... depends on the larger social institutions, not simply the brilliance or other merits of individuals. It depends on a variety of support systems, of course, and also on collaboration.... My point is not to castigate professors for the self-interested misrecognition common in their understanding of academic institutions. Nor is it to support all the claims of those who think universities should exist mainly to support only marginally intellectual ends from economic development to narrow job-skills training. Rather what I want to suggest is that the academic self-understanding—the class consciousness of professors—has inhibited adequate recognition of major transformations in universities, higher education, and the production of knowledge, and has stood in the way of focusing attention on the public purposes of universities.*

Nonetheless, the recent literature on the public good in higher education has raised some important and challenging questions regarding the potential impacts of national policies on the academic integrity of universities. In the sections that follow these issues will be explored.

Concerns regarding the negative impacts of market-based higher education policies on the 'public good' have been particularly acute in the UK, where enrolments in the university system have substantially increased over the last thirty years (i.e. 'massification') and public funding per student has been substantially reduced (OECD, 2011). However, research on 'nonprofits'[3] in every sector and society (Powell and Clemens, 1998) suggests as the non-profit sector expands there are strong pressures to become more like governmental and for-profit organisations, inevitably challenging traditional social goals. While issues of institutional control have predictably absorbed much of the oxygen in current UK debates about higher education, the research on non-profit organisations (Schlesinger, 1998) also suggests that the public good is less impacted by questions of ownership and more influenced by the institutional framework affecting non-profit, governmental and for-profit institutions alike. The primary focus of this chapter therefore is how best to regulate universities to assure the public good.

In contrast to the UK the institutional framework for colleges and universities in the US has long been characterised by a market-based approach. Contemporary 'neo-liberal' or market-based university reforms in other countries have therefore sometimes been described—unflatteringly—as the 'Americanisation' of higher education. However, US policies on higher education still differ markedly from those currently guiding universities in the UK and in other OECD countries (Barr, 2012a). Furthermore, despite the envious glances of EU policy makers towards the 'world-class' reputation of many American research universities, recent research has raised questions about possible distortions in the current market-based US system of higher education (Dill, 2010). For example, there is concern the efficiency of the overall US academic research enterprise is declining, the proportion of the relevant age group graduating from colleges and universities is shrinking rather than increasing and now has been surpassed by a number of other nations including the UK and the per-student costs of higher education—already the highest in the world—are continually increasing, outpacing inflation. Indeed, in contrast to this latter cost curve, a recent and much discussed study of a national sample of US college and university students suggests American academic standards are deteriorating (Arum and Roksa, 2011).

The economist Nicholas Barr has provided one of the more systematic efforts to define the public good of higher education and articulated a national framework of policies and/or regulation to assure the public interest (Barr, 2009, 2012a). While acknowledging the impacts or social benefits of higher education mentioned earlier, Barr suggests our understanding of these impacts is necessarily limited or uncertain because of the nature of the measures employed. Therefore he bases his suggested higher education framework not on policies designed to measure or estimate the social benefits of higher education, but on an analysis of the information assumptions necessary for a truly efficient and competitive market to function in higher education. I consequently begin my analysis with a discussion of a number of the policies suggested by Barr. But given the focus of much of the public debate about higher education, Barr understandably limits his analysis to the educational mission of universities. Recent national policies for higher education, however, also have included efforts to influence or steer university research and public service as illustrated by the Research Assessment Exercise and the '3rd Sector' programme in the UK (Dill and Van Vught, 2010). Therefore my analysis will examine the institutional framework for maximizing the public good of university education, research and public service.

Education Policy

My reading of the research in higher education policy is largely supportive of Barr's institutional framework for assuring the public good in higher education. However, with regard to education there are some debatable issues regarding the design of UK policy on variable fees and tuition caps, on information provided to potential university students, as well as on regulations for academic quality assurance.

Variable Fees and Tuition Caps

As part of a needed regulatory framework Barr has supported variable fees as well as a government cap on university tuition and fees. However under the tuition caps adopted in 2004–2011 most UK universities charged the maximum permitted fees, thus undercutting the supposed efficiency and diversity of a competitive market.[4] UK public support for higher education is below the OECD (2011) average and, as noted earlier, public funding per student has been cut substantially over the last decade. Therefore it may be argued the need to sustain academic quality provides a rationale for nearly all institutions to charge the maximum permitted under the national fees cap.

But the observed lack of fee—and institutional—diversity may also be due to market distortions encouraged by the current institutional framework for universities in the UK. First, all universities try to increase their expenditures for research, since it is a primary determinant of university reputation and helps attract the best scholars and students. Therefore a major dynamic driving all universities is an increasingly costly and inefficient 'reputation race' (Van Vught, 2008), which prompts a permanent hunger for financial revenues (and higher fees). In this sense Bowen's famous law of higher education still holds:

> in quest of excellence, reputation and influence... each institution raises all the money it can... [and] spends all it raises (Bowen, 1980, p. 20).

Second, universities offer an 'associative good' in which potential students choose their university based in part upon the intellectual aptitudes, previous accomplishments, wealth and family connections of the university's other students (Hansmann, 1999). The potential student understands that these and other attributes of future classmates have a strong influence on the quality of one's education and social experiences as well as on one's future personal and professional reputation. When non-profit firms produce 'associative goods' there is a strong tendency for customers to become 'stratified' across firms according to their individual characteristics. Moreover, this stratification provides market power to all competing universities. That is when the top-ranked university has secured all the best students and is charging them a monopoly price the second best university has every incentive to charge its students the same price without fear of losing students to the best institution. And so on down the line.[5]

For these reasons a fixed tuition cap for all universities is unlikely to promote effective price competition and provide an incentive for socially beneficial institutional diversity. Economists have therefore suggested a number of alternative university fee regulations to tuition caps (Douglass and Keeling, 2008). One approach, proposed by the US Carnegie Commission in 1973, is for government to estimate the proportion of public and private benefits generated by universities and to finance universities on this basis. The Commission proposed a division of costs among students and their families, state government and institutional sources, including federal financial aid support. At the time of this proposal in 1973 around 15 percent of all operating expenses at US four-year public institutions were covered by fees, while today it is around 20 percent. As Barr notes, measuring effectively the proportion of public and private benefits of higher education is challenging and uncertain, but McMahon (2009) has suggested a systematic method for addressing this problem.[6]

A second approach attempts to peg university tuition to the economy by setting fees as a percentage of a general economic index such as the consumer price index (CPI) or gross domestic product (GDP) per capita. Fees would therefore rise only in relation to what people could afford. However such percentage limits ignore both Baumol's (1996) 'relative price effect', whereby the price of labor intensive commodities such as higher education may rise more rapidly than prices generally, as well as the effects of significant declines in state subsidies.

My own view is that an effective regulatory framework would control fees, not as now by institutional category or title, but rather by recognizing existing differences in the market contexts of universities. For example those universities that are successfully competing in the global market (e.g. as indicated by their ranking in a designated world league table, or by valid measures of their research capability such as research with international impact, high-quality research doctoral education and attracting significant numbers of competitive research grants) would be awarded the autonomy to set their own tuition and fees.[7] As in UK soccer leagues, access to this level of autonomy would be permeable, based upon public measures of current performance (i.e. universities could be 'promoted' and 'relegated') and therefore over time other institutions could become eligible for this authority. This type of fee differential is more equitable as students attending 'world-class' universities generally gain higher lifetime earnings than those attending institutions of a more local reputation.[8] Furthermore, as in the UK, universities awarded the autonomy to set fees could be assigned target proportions of admitted students from lower-class backgrounds and/or, as in the US, required to fund a certain proportion of need-based aid for admitted students.

A framework for regulating fees could be retained for the more teaching-oriented universities that do not initially qualify for the fee autonomy outlined previously. As suggested this framework might be based upon estimates of the public and private benefits generated by higher education and/or guided by economic indicators such as the rate of inflation.

'Perfect' Information for Student Choice

A standard assumption for an efficient market is that both consumers and producers have 'perfect' information—rational choice requires that economic agents are well-informed about both price *and* quality (Teixeira et al., 2004). Therefore Barr (2012a) argues because university applicants are more mature and (and along with their parents) better informed than those making school education decisions, relying on market competition in the higher education sector is a feasible national policy. Similarly UK policy makers believe if student consumers have sufficient information on the quality of university academic programmes their choices will provide a powerful incentive for universities to continually improve those programmes, thereby increasing the human capital that benefits society.[9]

However the many university guides and league tables that have proliferated around the world do not effectively address the expected information deficiencies in the higher education market (Dill and Soo, 2005). Information provision is likely to positively influence academic standards only if quality rankings utilise measures linked with societally-valued educational outcomes, students use this information in their choice of subjects and institutions respond to student choices by improving relevant academic programmes (Gormley and Weimer, 1999). But the cost and complexity of developing valid indicators of academic programme quality to inform student choice are significant. Furthermore, for-profit publications already enjoy substantial sales and influence among opinion leaders, higher achieving students and even university personnel by producing *institutional* rankings utilizing indicators of academic prestige, which have questionable validity as predictors of effective student learning (Pascarella and Terenzini, 2005). This focus on institutional prestige in many league tables distorts the assumed constructive link between information on academic quality and university efforts to improve academic programmes. Influenced by institutional rankings many universities, including those in the UK (Rolfe, 2003; Dill, 2007), have responded to market competition primarily by emphasizing admissions marketing, 'cream skimming' of high achieving student applicants[10] and investing more in student amenities as well as research reputation. Some UK universities have been motivated by academic quality rankings to improve their internal data gathering (Locke et al., 2008), but since the commercial league tables are not based on any testable theory or model of university educational performance it is not clear this investment in information leads to institutional actions that actually improve the educational quality of academic programmes.

While many first degree students are 'myopic consumers', whose university choices are unlikely to provide strong incentives for the assurance and improvement of academic standards, there is evidence in the US (Romer, 2000) and some other developed countries of a significant market failure in student choice. Students are choosing in societally insufficient numbers demanding academic fields such as the sciences and engineering that clearly provide substantial private and social benefits. Therefore, independent of its impacts on academic quality, there may be a public interest in a policy requiring the provision of valid information to guide student choice, similar to that now being implemented in the UK. Such a policy likely should be designed to require publication of data on student retention, student progression and graduate outcomes (i.e. including the nature of graduates' employment, their average salaries and their further education) *by subject field* for all institutions of higher education (OECD, 2008).[11]

Quality Assurance Policy

Barr also supports the need for academic quality regulation, but suggests past efforts in the UK have been overly intrusive and bureaucratic (Barr, 2009). The term quality assurance in higher education is used increasingly to denote the practices whereby university academic standards, i.e. the level of academic achievement attained by higher education graduates, are maintained and improved (Brennan and Shah, 2000). This definition of academic quality is consistent with a human capital perspective on the efficiency of universities, which combines estimates of university costs with assessments of learning outcomes, particularly the specific levels of knowledge, skills and attributes that students achieve as a consequence of their engagement in a particular education programme (McMahon, 2009).

Much of the critical literature on the public good in higher education addresses academic quality assurance. Neo-liberal reforms are perceived as 'privatizing' academic life, altering in a negative manner the academic relationship between students and academic staff and lowering academic standards (Calhoun, 2006; Barnett, 2011). The greater commitment to research by members of academic staff and institutions may be driven more by the desire to enjoy additional individual career benefits and advance the prestige of the university than by the desire to benefit students and society. But as noted this increased investment in research and academic specialisation comes at a cost, which includes less time by academic staff to devote to improving student learning in their individual teaching, and less time and inclination to collectively assure and improve academic standards in subject programmes. Furthermore the academic processes often accompanying massification—modular teaching, continuous assessment, student surveys of instruction, programme funding based upon enrollment and university funding based upon student graduation—all provide greater incentives for the inflation of grades or marks as well as the relaxation of academic standards. In this new context of increased privatisation for both academic staff and students, better balance is needed between professorial/programme autonomy and the collective actions controlling academic work. As Calhoun (2006, p. 35) concludes regarding the public good in higher education:

> *Not least of all the productivity of academe depends upon the extent to which it is internally organized as a public sphere—with a set of nested and sometimes overlapping public discussions providing for the continual critique and correction of new arguments and tentatively stabilized truths.... The answer must lie in the organization of academic institutions and academic work in fields which provide plausible boundaries to these critical debates, but boundaries which never allow for more than partial autonomy. There must also be boundary-crossing: physicists must sometimes question chemists, sociologists must sometimes question economists.*

Our analyses of national academic quality assurance processes provide some support for this concern (Dill and Beerkens, 2010; Dill and Beerkens, 2012). First, developing a stronger culture of quality for teaching and student learning and creating conditions for the continual assurance and improvement of academic standards within universities will require actively engaging both the collegial leadership of an institution as well as academic staff in departments and programmes. The positive impacts of studied subject assessments, accreditations and academic audits were most clearly visible in the increased discussions about academic quality as well as changes in curricula organisation, student assessment and modes of instruction that took place within academic programmes. But an effective external quality assurance process also must create conditions in which the collective university assumes ongoing responsibility for maintaining academic standards and implements rigorous and effective collegial processes for assuring and improving academic quality in all the institution's academic programmes. For this to occur, the university's core academic processes for assuring academic standards must be externally evaluated by competent peer reviewers and the effectiveness of these processes must be confirmed by assessing their influence and impact on the quality of teaching and student learning in a representative sample of study programmes within each institution.[12]

A second design principle is the core academic processes that must be evaluated. As in the Hong Kong Academic Audit process (Massy, 2010), this requires a laser-like focus on the essential processes universities employ for assuring academic standards: the design and approval of new course modules and programmes of study; procedures for reviewing academic programmes; procedures governing the validity of grading and marking standards; procedures influencing the evaluation of teaching; procedures affecting student assessments; as well as the university's processes for identifying and sharing best practices in assuring academic standards among its academic programmes. The design of some academic audit or subject assessment processes attempt to cast such a wide net or are so heavy handed that they may deflect academic staff from needed efforts to improve student learning outcomes.

A third design consideration is the administration of these external reviews. The most effective and legitimate instruments in the views of academic staff possess characteristics similar to those exhibited by the Teacher Education Accreditation Council (TEAC) in the USA (El-Khawas, 2010), the accreditation and quality processes of the General Medical Council in the UK (Harvey, 2010) and the ABET international accreditation process in applied science, computing, engineering and technology (Prados, Peterson and Lattuca, 2005). These external reviews all strongly emphasise a culture of evidence-based decision-making within institutions directly applied to the improvement of teaching, student learning and academic programmes. Accordingly they place much weight on assessing the validity and reliability of institutional measures and mechanisms for assuring academic standards. Peer reviewers are trained, supported during the review process by professional staff and employ systematic, standardised procedures and protocols.

A final problem with academic quality assurance regulation is accountability and the typical policy response to this question is to require a public evaluation of the academic quality agency as a means of protecting the public interest in effective regulation. However, the adopted process for actually evaluating national academic quality assurance agencies provides evidence of 'regulatory capture' in which those whose interests are affected by the relevant regulation gain influence over the regulatory agency and promote their private interests over those of the public (Dill, 2011). The design and conduct of quality assurance agency evaluations are often controlled by the agencies themselves in cooperation with associations of agency professionals and/or selected representatives of those regulated. Such evaluations lack independence, often fail to employ a suitably relevant and robust method of validation and generally ignore the critical issue of value for money (Blackmur, 2008). This type of evaluation may provide inadequate evidence for improving the efficiency of external quality assurance regulations. The public interest is therefore better served if the effectiveness and efficiency of academic quality assurance agencies are evaluated by established, respected and independent national evaluation or audit agencies similar to the Government Accountability Office in the US and the United Kingdom National Audit Office.

University Research Policy

The policies recently implemented by national governments including the UK also have had direct effects on the research behaviour of universities (Dill and Van Vught, 2010). The combination of new financial policies for research and research evaluation instruments such as the RAE are leading universities to develop more specific institutional strategies, towards 'focus and mass,' towards increased specialisation and concentration in research. The new policies also appear to be making universities in nearly all OECD countries more productive in their output of publications, research doctoral graduates, as well as their patenting and licensing activities. Marked improvements in the organisation and management of university research activities and programmes were also reported in most of our OECD cases (Dill and Van Vught, 2010). However, it is likely that these organisational improvements are due not only to the recently implemented policy instruments mentioned earlier, but also to the general reductions in funding for publicly supported universities that have occurred in conjunction with the massification and expansion of higher education in many countries including the UK (Williams, 2004). As a consequence, universities in some of our case-study countries have necessarily become highly motivated to pursue alternative sources of revenue for their research programmes and therefore have been required to develop the research centres and internal research management processes necessary to survive in this more competitive market.

Several of our case studies (Dill and Van Vught, 2010) noted that the increased incentives for applied research and knowledge transfer may reduce the amount of basic research and over the longer run actually retard or diminish innovation by reducing the number of significant discoveries in fundamental knowledge. However studies in both the United States and the United Kingdom, where national research funding has become increasingly competitive, do not yet indicate a reduction in the proportion of basic research being conducted (Dill, 2010; Henkel and Kogan, 2010).

Finally, the policy of allocating the majority of academic research monies through competitive government research proposals, which is the current practice in the US, requires the investment of time by researchers applying for and administering these research grants. US academic scientists now report spending 42 percent of their research time filling out forms and in meetings required for pre- and post-grant work (Kean, 2006). This suggests that an appropriately balanced dual funding model for universities may still be most efficient for society.

Research Doctoral Programme Policy

In contrast to the national markets for first degree-level education where the 'myopic' choices of student consumers may limit the potential for user information to improve academic programmes, the international market for research doctoral students appears to behave in accordance with classic economic assumptions. Many universities now provide full financial support to the best doctoral applicants in an effort to compete aggressively for the most able international students. Doctoral applicants are an older, more educationally experienced set of consumers, who are pursuing advanced degrees primarily for vocational reasons. Doctoral applicants therefore are less likely to be swayed by consumption benefits, social factors, geographical considerations and institutional reputation in their choice of academic programmes and more likely to be influenced by valid information on doctoral programme quality (Van Bouwel and Veugelers, 2009).

In this more perfectly competitive market the research doctoral rankings of the National Research Council, which are in fact the only government supported university rankings in the United States, appear to have been highly influential on student choice and also motivated demonstrable improvements in US PhD programmes in a number of the leading universities (Dill, 2009). With the support of the National Science Foundation and the National Institutes of Health these research doctoral rankings have been designed by leading US social scientists and in international comparison are noteworthy for their attention to the validity and reliability of measures. Given the acknowledged positive influence of research-doctoral graduates on economic growth in the developed countries (Aghion, 2006), government support for doctoral quality rankings appears to be a particularly well-justified policy.

Technology Transfer Policy

A much debated issue is national policy on intellectual property rights (IPR). The original changes in the IPR legislation in the United States—the

Bayh-Dole Act—were motivated by a desire to speed knowledge to market. Patent and licensing rights were reallocated to universities through new laws designed to increase university incentives for knowledge transfer. The policy was not promoted as a major new source of funding for universities. However, with the growing international competition for academic research monies, many universities are now more aggressively seeking research revenues from other sources and, in many instances, have interpreted new IPR legislation as an exhortation to 'cash in' on their research outcomes. The evidence suggests (Dill and Van Vught, 2010) that the majority of universities in the OECD countries are at best breaking even and many are suffering net losses from their investments in technology transfer offices and affiliated activities. While many universities see their technology transfer expenses as a necessary investment they expect to bear significant fruit over time, research in the United States (Geiger and Sa, 2009) suggests that over the longer term the institutions that do reap some financial benefit from patenting and licensing are the most highly ranked and best-known research universities. But even in these institutions, there tends to be a natural 'ceiling' or limit to the amount of such revenue that can be earned, because patents and licenses are influential on innovation and profits in a relatively small number of industries and technical fields, biotech being the most prominent example (Cohen, Nelson and Walsh, 2002).

One unintended impact of public policies that emphasise IPR as a means of stimulating academic knowledge transfer is their influence upon the core processes of academic science (Geiger and Sa, 2009). Because of increased incentives for universities to patent and license their discoveries as a means of raising revenues, some theoretical results and research tools that have traditionally been freely available to other scholars and researchers are now being restricted. This constriction of open science may in fact lessen the economically beneficial 'spillovers' that are a primary rationale for the public support of basic academic research. Policy instruments intended to provide incentives for knowledge transfer, therefore, have to be designed with particular care to maintain the benefits of open science.

Research Evaluations

Performance-based funding of research has increasingly been emphasised in many OECD countries including the UK both by increasing the proportion of research monies allocated competitively by research councils and by basing institutional funding of research on evaluations of research quality including measures such as publications and citations. The most prominent example of the latter approach is the Research Assessment Exercise (RAE)[13] in the UK. The evidence suggests that performance-based funding of UK research has increased the productivity of the academic research enterprise and possibly also its quality, stimulating latent capacities for research that had not been previously effectively mobilised (Henkel and Kogan, 2010; Hicks, 2008). UK universities are also reported as adopting a more strategic approach to their research efforts with marked improvements in the internal organisation and management of research programmes and activities.

However, performance-based funding has other impacts on university research (Hicks, 2008). There is concern that the focus on peer-reviewed publications may suppress excellence, inducing a certain homogenisation of research at the upper levels. Furthermore the emphasis on publication counts encourages some researchers to become more calculating in their publication patterns, slicing their research into smaller topics and more numerous articles. The benefits of performance-based funding also appear to be discontinuous creating a one-time shock to the overall system, which initially motivates increased research productivity in all universities eligible for the funding, but tends to dissipate over time (Crespi and Geuna, 2004). Performance funding also further contributes to the stratification of universities, concentrating research in those institutions with richer resources, larger numbers of internationally recognised academic staff and established reputations.[14]

The challenges of effectively applying an assessment instrument such as the RAE to university research also reveal a number of complications predicted by the principal–agent model (Weimer and Vining, 1996). These include the need to continually adjust the output indicators in order to address the complexities of academic research, the high costs of monitoring university research performance and the difficulties of controlling cross-subsidies in an organisation like the university, which possesses the multiple outputs of teaching, research and public service.

In addition the attention awarded to the UK RAE has distracted policy makers and analysts from alternative research assessment approaches. For example the Netherlands has implemented a research assessment system for its universities, but it is not focused primarily on indicators of research publication and is not tied to university funding. Instead, every six years each university conducts an external peer review of its research programmes involving internationally respected researchers (Jongbloed, 2010). These reviews follow a Standard Evaluation Protocol (SEP) designed by the universities themselves in concert with national research organisations. The SEPs focus on the academic quality, scientific productivity and long-term vitality of each research programme and utilise a variety of information sources including on site interviews, university self-reports and bibliometric evidence. The evaluations are made public, but do not inform government funding.

Research suggests that these more formative evaluations have had similar positive impacts on research productivity, research quality and improvements in each university's strategic management of research as the much more highly publicised summative performance funding system in the UK (Westerheijden, 2007). But the more qualitative and collegial research evaluation process developed in the Netherlands has not produced the same amount of rancor and divisiveness among the members of the academic profession, nor contributed to the same degree of research stratification as in the UK.[15] Furthermore, in contrast to the RAE, the system in the Netherlands has been more stable in design, likely less costly to run and potentially provides more nuanced and useful information to each university on means of improving its research activities. As such these research evaluations can continue to make over time an effective contribution to improving the academic research enterprise.

Public Service

National policies increasing the incentives for university technology transfer are also reshaping the public service role of universities. There are legitimate concerns that this emphasis on technical innovation may reduce the important but difficult to measure role universities have traditionally played in enriching their regions socially and culturally. But research also suggests that a 'one size fits all' national technology transfer policy may in fact diminish the contribution universities have traditionally made to fostering regional economic development (Lester, 2007).

Comparative research on a number of OECD countries, including the United Kingdom, has revealed that the knowledge transfer processes—patenting, licensing and new business formation—favoured by national innovation policies were often not the most important contributors to local and regional development (Lester, 2007). While some 'global' universities produce technology artifacts that are transferable worldwide, effective knowledge transfer for most universities is a more local process and depends upon the nature of industrial development occurring in the regional economy. Universities do in fact contribute to the creation of new businesses, but much more commonly they help to upgrade mature industries, support the diversification of existing businesses into new fields and assist in the transplantation of industries. In these roles traditional publications, the provision of skilled S&T graduates for the regional economy, and technical problem-solving with local business and industry through consulting and contract research, are much more significant channels for influencing technical innovation than are patents and licenses (Cohen, Nelson and Walsh, 2002). Universities also play a crucial role by providing a 'public space' (Lester, 2007) in which, through meetings, research conferences and industrial liaison programmes, local business practitioners can discuss the future direction of technologies, markets and regional industrial development in a non-collusive manner.

This contribution to regional development is potentially a role all universities with scientific and/or technical faculties, not just 'world class' institutions, can perform. National policies encouraging this type of local and regional focus would therefore also help promote the development of socially beneficial diversity in higher education systems. Such policies should provide incentives for universities to focus less on their possibly inefficient investments in conventional technology transfer and more on developing a strategy for encouraging innovation in their region. This approach would encourage universities to systematically assess the circumstances and development of local industry, the research strengths of the institution and the most appropriate channels for aligning the university's capabilities with the needs of the local economy (Lester, 2007). The Finnish National Centres of Expertise Programme provides one well-regarded national model for developing universities as nodal points in regional networks of innovation by helping them better integrate their research expertise with local industry and business along the lines suggested here (Dill and Van Vught, 2010).

Conclusion

Barr (2012a) has consistently argued that the welfare state will endure and adapt to social change because it not only offers poverty relief but also provides means of addressing the intractable economic problems of imperfect information, risk and uncertainty. Similarly I conclude that the self-regulating aspects of universities will endure and adapt to social change because, as noted earlier, the complexity and uncertainty of academic work distort the efficiency of higher education markets and, consistent with principal–agent theory (Weimer and Vining, 1996), compromise direct government efforts to assure the public good in higher education.

One danger of inadequately regulated market competition in higher education appears to be in providing incentives for the privatisation of academic work, understood as the pursuit of autonomy for individual teaching and research, for programme development and for institutional prestige, less to better serve the public and more to maximise private benefit. The most effective institutional framework for assuring the public good in higher education appears to be one that provides incentives to reform and reinforce the collegial mechanisms by which the members of the academic profession monitor, socialise and support the values essential to effective university teaching, research and public service. The form of these collegial mechanisms must change over time in response to new circumstances and new technologies. But one reason the university, which first emerged in the twelfth century, has continued to be a vital institution for society, and if anything is of greater importance today, is that it has the capacity as a collective community to assure the integrity of its core processes. Contemporary examples such as the academic audit process in Hong Kong, the research assessment process in the Netherlands, the research doctoral rankings in the US and the regional development initiative in Finland suggest how well-designed public policies can provide incentives for universities to improve and strengthen the collegial processes necessary for assuring the public good in the changing environment of higher education.

Notes

1. Throughout I refer to the UK and UK policy, but there has been increasing divergence in higher education policy among England, Scotland, Wales and Northern Ireland (Bruce, 2011). While I discuss Parliamentary actions, the UK Quality Assurance Agency (QAA) and the 2011 UK government White Paper, the primary focus of my analysis is on policy and research relevant to England as well as to the activities of the Higher Education Funding Council for England (HEFCE).
2. The UK RAE has now been renamed the Research Excellence Framework (REF) and is being redesigned. My comments are based upon the previous administrations of research assessment in the UK and their reported impacts.
3. While UK universities now receive the majority of their funding from the national government, they are autonomous, property-owning institutions whose independence is guaranteed by Royal Charter or by Parliamentary Statute (Williams, 2004). Therefore their governance is more similar to non-profit, private universities in the US than to the state-controlled universities of many other countries including the US.
4. Parliament has now raised the cap to £9,000 in 'exceptional cases' and the vast majority of universities—'unexpectedly'—have raised their tuition and fees to this new level.
5. In the market-based US system the average increase in tuition fees for all institutions over the last thirty years has exceeded the general rate of inflation and independent colleges and universities particularly exhibit market power. For example, in 2011–2012 Harvard University in Massachusetts, the top-ranked private university in the US, charged $39,849 for tuition and fees, while private Hampshire College, also in Massachusetts and ranked 110th among nationally known selective liberal arts colleges, charged $42,900 (http://www.usnews.com/education).
6. Based upon his analysis of public and private benefits in OECD nations McMahon (2009) estimates 52 percent of total investment in universities (including institutional support and some student foregone earnings) should be supported by government

funding and institutional endowments, while 48 percent should be covered privately by tuition, fees, and some foregone earnings (in the US he estimates the latter as roughly equivalent to student expenses for room and board).
7. The adoption of differential fees based upon global markets has already been endorsed in England for MBA programmes at Oxford, Cambridge and the London Business School (Douglass and Keeling, 2008).
8. Barr (2012b) has also recommended a categorical differentiation among UK universities based upon market performance. However in contrast to my suggested award of greater fee autonomy for true 'world class' universities, Barr has suggested continuation of T-Grant subsidies for teaching in the humanities and social sciences for all universities save those charging higher fees and possessing low price elasticity (e.g. Oxbridge). Both categorical approaches would likely lead to a similar differentiation of the university sector.
9. Following the Government's Higher Education White Paper (BIS, 2011), the HEFCE now requires all universities subject to the QAA to develop and publish Key Information Sets (KIS) on undergraduate programmes in order to assist students in making better informed decisions about what and where to study.
10. The Government's White Paper (BIS, 2011) also proposed allowing unrestrained recruitment of high-achieving applicants (those achieving grades AAB or above at A-level or equivalent), which could also increase existing incentives for a costly 'amenities arms race' (Barr, 2012b) among universities designed to better attract these students.
11. This argument supports some of the 'key information' required by the HEFCE, but there are a number of important methodological issues that need to be addressed for any such policy to be effective (Dill and Soo, 2005). For example, assuring the validity and reliability of student performance information reported by institutions as well as the graduate outcomes reported in alumni surveys, addressing the limitations of possible differential response rates by academic fields in student surveys, the fact that graduate salaries may reflect regional differences more than university differences, etc.
12. The issue of evaluating academic subjects as part of academic audits has been a particularly contentious issue in England, but the failure to do so undermines the effectiveness of external audits. Logically the only effective means for assessing the effectiveness of teaching or instruction is to evaluate their impact upon student learning. Similarly, the only feasible means of evaluating the effectiveness of a university's processes for assuring academic standards is to investigate their impact upon and the responses by a sample of academic subjects or programmes.
13. Now (2014) Research Excellence Framework (REF).
14. Many of the academic critics of the RAE perceive research stratification in negative terms. But in mass systems of higher education greater concentration of the limited public resources available for academic research may be more efficient for society and necessary to better serve the public good. As in other areas of regulation, the issue then is the legitimacy and effectiveness of a research assessment system.
15. However, unlike the UK the Netherlands has retained a binary system of higher education featuring polytechnic institutions, which offer bachelor programmes closely tied to professional fields and businesses in the local region and which are not permitted to engage in research doctoral education. This binary line lessens the need for

stratification within the university system. The Netherlands also has a smaller system of higher education and possibly a more consensual culture than the UK.

References

Aghion, P. (2006). A Primer on Innovation and Growth. *Bruegel Policy Brief*, 6, 1–8.
Arum, R., and Roksa, J. (2011) *Academically Adrift: Limited Learning on College Campuses*. Chicago: University of Chicago Press.
Barnett, R. (2011) The Marketised University: Defending the Indefensible, in: M. Molesworth, R. Scullion, and E. Nixon (eds), *The Marketisation of Higher Education and the Student as Consumer*, London: Routledge.
Barr, N. (2009) Financing Higher Education: Lessons from Economic Theory and Reform in England. *Higher Education in Europe*, 34:2, 201–209.
Barr, N. (2012a) *The Economics of the Welfare State*, (5th ed). New York: Oxford University Press.
Barr, N. (2012b) The Higher Education White Paper: The Good, the Bad, the Unspeakable—and the Next White Paper, *Social Policy & Administration*: doi: 10.1111/j.1467-9515.2012.00852.x
Baumol, W. J. (1996) Children of Performing Arts, the Economic Dilemma: The Climbing Costs of Health Care and Education, *Journal of Cultural Economics*, 20:3, 183–206.
Blackmur, D. (2008) Quis custodiet ipsos custodes?: The Review of the Australian Universities Quality Agency, *Quality in Higher Education*, 14:3, 249–64.
Bowen, H. R. (1980) *The Costs of Higher Education*. San Francisco: Jossey-Bass.
Brennan, J., and Shah, T. (2000) *Managing Quality in Higher Education: An International Perspective on Institutional Assessment and Change*. Buckingham, UK: OECD, SRHE & Open University Press.
Brown, R. (2010) *Higher Education and the Market*. London: Routledge.
Bruce, T. (2011) *Universities and Constitutional Change in the UK: The Impact of Devolution on the Higher Education Sector*. Oxford, Higher Education Policy Institute: http://www.hepi.ac.uk/466-2053/Universities-and-constitutional-change-in-the-UK--the-impact-of-devolution-on-the-higher-education-sector.html
Calhoun, C. (2006) The University and the Public Good, *Thesis Eleven*, 84:1, 7–43.
Cohen, W. M., Nelson, R. R., and Walsh, J. P. (2002) Links and Impacts: The Influence of Public Research on Industrial R&D, *Management Science* 48:1, 1–23.
Crespi, G., and Geuna, A. (2004) *The Productivity of Science*. Science and Technology Policy Research Unit (SPRU), University of Sussex, UK: www.sussex.ac.uk/spru/documents/crespiost2.pdf
Department for Business, Innovation and Skills (BIS) (2011) *Higher Education: Students at the Heart of the System*. London: The Stationery Office Limited: http://www.official-documents.gov.uk/document/cm81/8122/8122.pdf

Dill, D. D. (2007) Will Market Competition Assure Academic Quality?: An Analysis of the UK and US experience, in: D. F. Westerheijden, B. Stensaker, and M. J. Rosa (eds), *Quality Assurance in Higher Education: Trends in Regulation, Translation and Transformation*. Dordrecht, the Netherlands: Springer.

Dill, D. D. (2009) Convergence and Diversity: The Role and Influence of University Rankings, in: B. M. Kehm and B. Stensaker, *University Rankings, Diversity, and the New Landscape of Higher Education*. Rotterdam: Sense Publishers.

Dill, D. D. (2010) The United States, in: D. D. Dill and F. A. Van Vught, (eds), *National Innovation and the Academic Research Enterprise: Public Policy in Global Perspective*. Baltimore: The Johns Hopkins University Press.

Dill, D. D. (2011) Governing Quality. in R. King, S. Marginson, and R. Naidoo (eds), *A Handbook on Globalization and Higher Education*. Cheltenham, UK: Edward Elgar.

Dill, D. D., and Beerkens, M. (2010) *Public Policy for Academic Quality: Analyses of Innovative Policy Instruments*. Dordrecht, The Netherlands: Springer.

Dill, D. D., and Beerkens, M. (2012) Designing the Framework Conditions for Assuring Academic Standards: Lessons Learned About Professional, Market, and Government Regulation of Academic Quality, *Higher Education*: doi 10.1007/s10734-012-9548-x

Dill, D. D., and Soo, M. (2005) Academic Quality, League Tables, and Public Policy: A Cross-National Analysis of University Ranking Systems. *Higher Education*, 49:4, 495–533.

Dill, D. D., and Van Vught, F. A. (2010) *National Innovation and the Academic Research Enterprise: Public Policy in Global Perspective*. Baltimore: The Johns Hopkins University Press.

Douglass, J. A., and Keeling, R. (2008) The Big Curve: Trends in University Fees and Financing in the EU and US. Center for Studies in Higher Education, University of California, Berkeley. Research & Occasional Paper Series, CSHE.19.08: http://cshe.berkeley.edu/publications/docs/ROPS-2-Douglass-BigCurve-11-12-08.pdf

El-Khawas, E. (2010) The Teacher Education Accreditation Council (TEAC) in the USA, in: D. D. Dill and M. Beerkens (eds), *Public Policy for Academic Quality: Analyses of Innovative Policy Instruments*. Dordrecht, The Netherlands: Springer.

Geiger, R. L., and Sa, C. M. (2009) Technology Transfer Offices and the Commercialization of University Research in the United States, in: P. Clancy and D. D. Dill, (eds), *The Research Mission of the University: Policy Reforms and Institutional Responses*. Rotterdam: Sense Publishers.

Gläser, J., Spurling, T. H., and Butler, L. (2004) Intraorganisational Evaluation: Are There 'Least Evaluable Units'? *Research Evaluation*, 13:1, 19–32.

Gormley, W., and Weimer, D. (1999) *Organizational Report Cards*. Cambridge, MA: Harvard University Press.

Hansmann, H. (1999) Higher Education as an Associative Good. Yale Law and Economics Working Paper No. 231: http://papers.ssrn.com/sol3/cf_dev/AbsByAuth.cfm?per_id=110510

Harvey, L. (2010) The Accreditation and Quality Processes of the General Medical Council in the UK, in: D. D. Dill and M. Beerkens (eds), *Public Policy for Academic Quality: Analyses of Innovative Policy Instruments*. Dordrecht, The Netherlands: Springer.

Henkel, M., and Kogan, M. (2010) The United Kingdom, in: D. D. Dill and F. A. Van Vught (eds), *National Innovation and the Academic Research Enterprise: Public Policy in Global Perspective*. Baltimore: The Johns Hopkins University Press.

Hicks, D. (2008) Evolving Regimes of Multi-university Research Evaluation. Georgia Institute of Technology, School of Public Policy Working Papers #27: http://smartech.gatech.edu/bitstream/handle/1853/23496/wp27.pdf?sequence=1

Jongbloed, B. (2010) The Netherlands, in: D. D. Dill and F. A. Van Vught (eds), *National Innovation and the Academic Research Enterprise: Public Policy in Global Perspective*. Baltimore: The Johns Hopkins University Press.

Kean, S. (2006) Scientists Spend Nearly Half Their Time on Administrative Tasks, Survey Finds. *Chronicle of Higher Education*, July 7.

Lester, R. K. (2007) Universities, Innovation, and the Competitiveness of Local Economies: An Overview, in: R. K. Lester and M. Sotarauta (eds), *Innovation, Universities, and the Competitiveness of Regions*. Helsinki: TEKES.

Locke, W., Verbik, L., Richardson, J., and King, R. (2008) *Counting What is Measured or Measuring What Counts?: League Tables and Their Impact on Higher Education Institutions in England*. Bristol, UK: Higher Education Funding Council for England.

Marginson, S. (2007) *Prospects of Higher Education: Globalization, Market Competition, Public Goods and the Future of the University*. Rotterdam: Sense Publishers.

Massy, W. F. (2010) Academic Quality Audit as Applied in Hong Kong, in: D. D. Dill and M. Beerkens (eds), *Public Policy for Academic Quality: Analyses of Innovative Policy Instruments*. Dordrecht, The Netherlands: Springer.

McMahon, W. W. (2009) *Higher Learning, Greater Good: The Private and Social Benefits of Higher Education*. Baltimore: The Johns Hopkins University Press.

OECD (2008) Tertiary Education for the Knowledge Society, Volume 1: *Special Features: Governance, Funding, Quality*; Volume 2: *Special Features: Equity, Innovation, Labour Market, Internationalisation*. Paris: OECD.

OECD (2011) *Education at a Glance: OECD Indicators*. Paris: OECD.

Pascarella, E. T., and Terenzeni, P. T. (2005). *How College Affects Students, vol. 2. A Third Decade of Research*. San Francisco, CA: Jossey-Bass.

Powell, W. W., and Clemens, E. S. (1998) Introduction, in: W. W. Powell and E. S. Clemens (eds), *Private Action and the Public Good*. New Haven: Yale University Press.

Prados, J. W., Peterson, G. D., and Lattuca, L. R. (2005) Quality Assurance of Engineering Education through Accreditation: The Impact of Engineering Criteria 2000 and Its Global Influence, *Journal of Engineering Education*, 94:1, 165–184.

Rhoten, D., and Calhoun, C. (2011) *Knowledge Matters: The Public Mission of the Research University*. New York: Columbia University Press.

Rolfe, H. (2003) University Strategy in an Age of Uncertainty: The Effect of Higher Education Funding on Old and New Universities, *Higher Education Quarterly,* 57:1, 24–47.

Romer, P. M. (2000) Should the Government Subsidize Supply or Demand in the Market for Scientists and Engineers? in A. B. Jaffe, J. Lerner, and S. Stern (eds), *Innovation Policy and the Economy.* Chicago: University of Chicago Press.

Schlesinger, M. (1998) Mismeasuring the Consequences of Ownership: External Influences and the Comprehensive Performance of Public, For-profit, and Private Nonprofit Organizations, in: W. W. Powell and E. S. Clemens (eds), *Private Action and the Public Good.* New Haven: Yale University Press, 1998.

Teixeira, P., Jongbloed, B., Dill, D., and Amaral, A. (2004) *Markets in Higher Education: Rhetoric or Reality?* Dordrecht, the Netherlands: Kluwer.

Tierney, W. G. (2006) *Governance and the Public Good.* Albany, NY: State University of New York Press.

Van Bouwel, L., and Veugelers, R. (2009) *The Determinants of Student Mobility in Europe: The Quality Dimension. Department of Managerial Economics, Strategy & Innovation,* Katholieke Universiteit Leuven: https://lirias.kuleuven.be/bitstream/123456789/256921/3/MSI_0912

Van Vught, F. A. (2008) Mission Diversity and Reputation in Higher Education, *Higher Education Policy* 21:2, 151–174.

Weimer, D. L., and Vining, A. R. (1996) Economics, in: D. F. Kettl and H. B. Milward (eds), *The State of Public Management.* Baltimore: The Johns Hopkins University Press.

Williams, G. L. (2004) The Higher Education Market in the United Kingdom, in: P. Teixeira, B. Jongbloed, D. Dill and A. Amaral (eds), *Markets in Higher Education: Rhetoric or Reality?* Dordrecht, the Netherlands: Kluwer.

XI. Inequality and the Erosion of the Public Good

JON NIXON

Introduction

Strong democratic societies require educated and informed publics that are both inclusive and questioning. Within such societies, knowledge is the most public of all public goods—and education, therefore, is an indispensable resource, the benefits of which cut across a range of public interests and concerns. The more complex the society, the wider that range becomes; and the wider the range of public interests and concerns, the greater the need for public goods generally and for the public good of education in particular. From this perspective, higher education is a public good because it contributes to the development of an educated public with the capabilities necessary to fulfil the human potential of each of its members and of society as a whole. In so doing it also contributes—both directly and indirectly—to economic stability which might be seen as a public good in its own right.

That was the rationale for the massive post-WWII expansion of higher education in many countries—an expansion premised on the notion of higher education as a public good. Within the UK seven new universities—East Anglia, Essex, Kent Lancaster, Sussex, Warwick and York—were announced in 1961; two years later, in 1963, the Robbins report recommended further rapid expansion of the higher education sector; and, in 1971, the newly established Open University enrolled its first cohort of students. Tony Judt (2010, p. 394) highlights both the rapidity and the extent of this expansion across post-WWII Europe: 'by the end of the 1960s, one young person in seven in Italy was attending university (compared to one in twenty ten years before). In Belgium the figure was one in six. In West Germany, where there had been 108,000 students in 1950, there were nearly 400,000 by the end of the Sixties. In France, by 1967, there were as many university students as there had been *lycéen* in 1956'. As he concludes, 'all over Europe there were vastly more students than ever before'.

The argument for higher education as a public good found its logical expression in this vast global expansion of student numbers. The expansion continued through most of the second half of the twentieth century. As N.V. Varghese (2013, p. 36) notes, 'enrolment in higher education totalled 152 million in 2007, and has doubled every 15 years starting from 1970'. However, it was—and is increasingly—the cost implications of this logic that have generated controversy: if education is deemed to be a public good, is the argument for its cost being borne either by individuals or by for-profit providers diminished? Should public goods incur private costs? If public goods are privately purchased, do those goods thereby lose their public value? Indeed, can they continue to be categorised as public goods? Having accepted, in the boom years, the irresistible logic of the argument for expansion and widening participation, we are left in these more austere times with its unavoidable legacy: the paradox of a privately funded public good. In the face of that paradox, the economic question assumes overriding importance.

A Privatised Public

Economists advance a definition of public goods as products or services of which anyone can consume as much as desired without reducing the amount available for others. Multiple individuals can consume such products or services without diminishing their value and an individual cannot be prevented from consuming them whether or not the individual pays for them. These textbook distinctions hinge on what are referred to as the 'non-rivalry' and 'non-excludability' criteria: public goods are 'non-rivalrous' in the sense that they are accessible to all (without my consumption reducing your consumption) and 'non-excludable' in the sense that we all have access to them (regardless of our ability to pay for them).

These distinctions—relating to what is and is not designated a public good—make better sense when historically located. That is because the idea of 'the public' is itself shaped by history and epoch: within an unrestrained monarchy, 'the public' is little more than a body of office holders dependent on the Crown for status and courtly prestige; within a republic, on the other hand, 'the public' is an expanded 'body politic' of republican citizens endowed with political will and purpose; and within a modern late-capitalist democratic state 'the public' is literate and reasonable, critical in the defence and promotion of its own vested interests, external to the direct exercise of political power and deeply committed to the ideal of individual freedom.

The latter comprises a more or less informed electorate, for whom property, private ownership and the assumption of merit become the prime *raison d'être*. This modern construction of 'the public' is, as Dan Hind (2010, p. 44) puts it, a 'public of private interests' that has produced 'the paradox of modern power, the fact of a secret public'. What holds this public together is its shared commitment to private gain: the public interest becomes an aggregate of private interests. This is a privatised—and a privatising—public, for whom, as Judt (2012) puts it, 'what is private, what is paid for, is somehow better for just that reason' (p. 362). 'This', Judt points out, 'is an inversion of a common assumption in the first two thirds of the [twentieth] century, certainly the middle fifty years from the 1930s to the 1980s: that certain goods could only be properly provided on a collective or public basis and were all the better for it' (p. 362).

The 'public of private interests' judges all questions of dispensability and indispensability according to the criterion of private interest. Its default position has been neatly satirised by Will Hutton (2010, p. 183): 'my property is my own because I and I alone have sweated my brow to get it; I have autonomy over it and no claim to share it, especially by the state, is legitimate'. Short-term individual gain wins over the long-term public good—with consequences which, as Dambisa Moyo (2011, p. 90) has argued, may have negative consequences for society as a whole: 'Western society has spent thirty years attracting the best and the brightest into consulting, financial services and banking—but now that these businesses have imploded in the 2008 crisis, what will these people do?'

The answer to Moyo's question depends to some extent on who 'these people' are and where they are located. If they are between 16 and 21 years of age then their chances of being employed or in full-time education or training are greatly reduced. In the UK for example,

> *we have identified youth unemployment "hotspots" in 152 local authority areas around the country, where the proportion of young people claiming unemployment benefit is twice the national average, where we estimate at least 1 in 4 young people are NEET (not in education, employment or training), and where we need emergency action to turn things round* (ACEVO, 2012, p. 4); see also, Lee and Wright, 2011).

A concerted and sustained effort to meet that need would require some serious consideration to be given to the arguments for 'active government' (Chuka Umunna, 2012), 'big government' (Jeff Madrick, 2009), 'good capitalism' (Will Hutton, 2012), and 'the social investment state' (Howard Reed and Neal Lawson, 2011). But the idea of 'active' or 'big' government—or a state committed to 'good' capitalism and 'social investment'—is not deemed to be in the best interests of a 'public of private interests': a public whose atomised members remain quietly but determinedly protective of the inequalities that support and perpetuate their own vested interests.

The supposedly classless society on which the idea of the 'public of private interests' is premised is in fact riddled with inequality: 'at the top', suggests Erik Olin Wright (2009, p. 114), is 'an extremely rich capitalist class and corporate managerial class, living at extraordinarily high consumption standards, with relatively weak constraints on their exercise of economic power'; at the bottom is 'a pattern of interaction between race and class in which the working poor and the marginalised population are disproportionately made up of racial minorities'. It is a public without a vibrant polity, a polity without a vibrant citizenry: a public the economic sustainability of which is based not only on pre-existing levels of inequality, but on escalating inequality.

'Inequality', as Richard Sennett (2006, p. 54) puts it, 'has become the Achilles' heel of the modern economy'—the defining characteristic of 'the culture of the new capitalism'. The victory of freedom (as embodied in the free market) carried with it immense costs. David Harvey (2003), in his depiction of the 1990s as a decade of 'corporate corruption' and 'scams and fraudulent schemes', spells out the cost to society exacted by the 'new capitalism': 'society seemed to be fragmenting and flying apart at an alarming rate. It seemed ... in the process of collapsing back into the aimless, senseless chaos of private interests' (pp. 16–17). The extreme inequalities that characterise 'the new capitalism' impoverish everyone through their relentless erosion of the democratic space of civil society.

The gap between rich and poor is, as Polly Toynbee and David Walker (2009) point out, particularly marked within the UK: 'the UK was and remains far less equitable than in other European Union countries. While the top 10% of income earners get 27.3% of the cake, the bottom 19% get just 2.6%. Twenty years ago the average chief executive of one of the top hundred companies on the FTSE index earned 17 times the average employee's pay. By 2008, the typical FTSE boss earned 75.5 times the average' (Ibid, pp. 6–7). Toynbee and Walker estimate that as a group the wealthiest pay less in tax than the tax payers in the lowest income bracket: 'take the 1,000 people who appeared in the *Sunday Times* Rich List for 2007 ... If in 2007 Her Majesty's Revenue and Customs had secured the 10% of their capital gains and 40% of their higher-bracket income as Parliament ordained, the Treasury would have been better off by £12 billion, simply by collecting what is avoided'

(p. 18). (See also Hannah Aldridge et. al., 2012; John Hills et.al., 2010; Richard Wilkinson and Kate Pickett, 2010.)

In spite of continuing calls—from Andre Gorz (1989) to Andrew Glyn (2006) and, more recently, Richard Swift (2012)—for some form of 'basic income guarantee', the economic inequalities within the UK have increased and their social consequences become graver. Insofar as the post-WWII expansion of higher education pointed towards the ideal of a more just and equal society, then the last three decades undoubtedly mark a collective failure. We have become accustomed to injustice and inequality: 'we have', as Judt (2009, p. 88) puts it, 'adapted all too well and in consensual silence'.

What can account for this silence? Judt (2009) argues that a large part of the reason is to be found in the process of privatisation, whereby the public interest is re-categorised as the aggregate of private interests and the public good as the aggregate of private gains: 'in the last thirty years, a cult of privatisation has mesmerised Western (and many non-Western) governments' (p. 88) Like any cult, the 'cult of privatisation' presents itself as an enlightenment project: an exit route from the dark cave of unknowing. In this case the dark cave is budgetary constraint and privatisation is the exit route. Privatisation appears to save money: 'if the state owns an inefficient public program or an expensive public service—a waterworks, a car factory, a railway—it seeks to offload it onto private buyers' (p. 88). Not only will the private buyers reduce public expenditure, but they will also manage the expensive public service—the energy utility, the public transport system, and, increasingly, higher education—with (so the argument goes) much more efficiency than their public sector counterparts. From within the 'cult of privatisation', privatisation is just plain common sense. There is (to evoke a famous phrase of UK prime minister Margaret Thatcher) no alternative.

Inequalities of Access and Outcomes in Higher Education

That is the supposed rationale by which 'the public of private interests' justifies the increasing privatisation of higher education and the increasing disparity of institutions across the higher education sector. Privatisation, however, leads to marketisation which in turn leads to competition. In England this has resulted in the current situation whereby the older universities have almost permanent and undisputed occupancy of the premier league, the post-1992 universities are well represented across the broad span of second league institutions, and the bottom league is occupied almost entirely by institutions that have gained university status in the twenty-first century. League tables are a self-fulfilling prophesy whereby those institutions located at the top recruit high profile academic staff, attract the bulk of available research funding, and select students from a small and highly privileged pool of often privately educated applicants.

This situation has given rise to gross *inequalities of access*. In an analysis covering over one million university student admissions during the period 2002–2006, the Sutton Trust (2008) documented for the first time the extent to which a few individual schools supply the majority of students to the UK's leading research universities—and with lower academic qualifications. 'Basically put', as the Chairman of the Sutton Trust claims in his foreword to the report, 'a student in a state school is as likely to go on to a leading university as a student from the independent sector who gets two grades lower at A+ level' (p. 1). The social capital—or cachet—of the public school entrant outbids the academic achievements of the state school entrant. Private interest—and privilege—wins over the common good.

The analysis, based on admissions figures for 3,700 schools with sixth forms, sixth form colleges, and further education colleges across the UK during the period from 2002 to 2006, provides disturbing evidence of extreme inequalities across the system. Focusing on a group of thirteen leading research-led institutions whose degree courses generally have the most stringent entry requirements, the report showed that the feeder schools supplying most of the entrants to these universities are attended almost exclusively by children from privileged backgrounds: 'independent schools—representing just 7% of schools and 15% of A-level entrants—dominate the university rankings. These schools are available for the most part to children whose parents can afford fees. The remaining places are taken up by state schools that are themselves socially selective—either as a consequence of academic selection or by being situated in a middle class area' (ibid p. 18).

Moreover, of these elite feeder schools, those with the highest admission rates to the 13 leading universities are *socially* selective. The top 100 schools are, for example, composed of 83 independent (fee-paying) schools, 16 (state-funded, selective) grammar schools and one (state funded) comprehensive school, while the top 30 schools are composed of 13 independent (fee paying) schools, 16 (state-funded, selective) grammar schools and one (state-funded) comprehensive school. Figures relating to student admissions to Cambridge and Oxford Universities present a similarly bleak picture of social selection and systemic inequality. Here the top 100 hundred schools with the highest admission rates are composed of 78 independent (fee paying) schools, 21 grammar (state-funded, selective) schools, and one (state-funded) comprehensive school, while the top 30 schools are composed of

29 independent (fee paying) schools and one (state-funded, selective) grammar school—and not a single state-funded comprehensive school.

The inequalities evident in patterns of entry to institutions of higher education as documented previously are reflected in the entry patterns to the older professions. The funnel effect whereby the privately educated gain a disproportionate share of places at the leading universities has the further effect of ensuring that they fill not only a disproportionate number of posts within the older professions but also a disproportionate number of top posts within those same professions. The deep codes of chronic structural inequality remain: institutional stratification across the higher education sector, the reproduction of privilege through the selective mechanisms of higher education and the consolidation of private and professional elites.

Inequalities of access are thus reproduced at the point of exit as *inequalities of outcome*. So, for example, the legal profession is top heavy with those who have been independently educated. Again the Sutton Trust (2005) highlights inequalities inherent in and reproduced by the system: 'our findings show that in both samples [1989 and 2004] over two thirds of barristers at the top commercial chambers went to fee-paying schools and over 80 per cent were educated at Oxford or Cambridge, while very few went to universities outside the top 12—just seven per cent in 2004' (ibid., p. 5). A similar pattern emerges from a Sutton Trust (2006) study of the educational backgrounds of leading journalists: 'over half (54%) of the country's leading news journalists were educated in private schools, which accounts for 7% of the school population as a whole' (ibid., p. 4). To argue that such individuals are appointed on merit is to miss the point: merit in such cases is, in part at least, a consequence of gross inequality.

The UK National Equality Panel has provided further evidence in its independent report of the cumulative effect of inequality across the life cycle: 'we see this before children enter school, through the school years, through entry into the labour market, and on to retirement, wealth and resources for retirement, and mortality rates for later life. Economic advantage and disadvantage reinforce themselves across the life cycle, and often on to the next generation' (John Hills et.al., 2010, p. 386). This cross-generational reproduction of inequality is evident in the pattern of student achievement within higher education: 'two thirds of those with professional parents received firsts or upper seconds, but only half of those with unskilled parents. White students were the most likely to get firsts or upper seconds, and Black and Pakistani/Bangladeshi students the least likely' (p. 366).

Yet—to return to Judt's point—we consent, in the main silently, to a system that perpetuates these inequalities of access and inequalities of outcome:

inequalities that have a hugely detrimental effect on the life chances of a significant proportion of young people in particular. Moreover, those inequalities are compounded by inequalities in the quality of provision—the *inequalities of quality*. Addressing the totality of inequalities is not, therefore, simply a matter of providing more public resources for higher education—important though that may be—but a matter of distributing those resources in such a way as to ensure equality of provision across the sector.

Inequalities of Quality

The impact cuts in public expenditure on higher education—and an increased reliance on private funding through the marketisation of higher education—is double-edged. On the one hand, such policy changes clearly reduce access to higher education: a reduction which, given contributory factors such as the rise in student fees and institutional variations across the sector, hits prospective students from disadvantaged backgrounds with the greatest severity. Hence, inequalities of access and outcome such as those documented earlier. On the other hand, they undoubtedly reduce the quality of higher education provision for the majority of students in the majority of institutions, with the result that those students who rely most heavily on state support have an impoverished experience of higher education: more mass lectures, less one-to-one tuition, fewer opportunities for seminar discussions, shorter courses. These have a massive impact on universities in general and on teaching in particular. They introduce into a system already characterised by *inequalities of access* and *inequalities of outcome* a new level of inequality: *inequalities of quality*.

Reduction in public funding puts at risk, then, not only the quantity of higher education on offer, but also quality of higher education overall. 'Under pressure to cut costs', argues Martha Nussbaum (2010, p. 142), 'we prune away just those parts of the educational endeavour that are crucial to preserving a healthy society'. Within the UK, the government's 2011 White Paper *Higher Education: Students at the Heart of the System* reproduces the rhetoric of 'market entry'—thereby opening the gate to the privatisation of higher education, both through the establishment of new institutions and the increased involvement and possible take-over of existing 'not for profit' institutions (Department for Business, Innovation and Skills, 2011). These legislative changes are proposed in the interests of developing 'a diverse and responsive sector': 'diverse', in this context, means 'differentiated'—but differentiated in respect not of need but of affordability; similarly, 'responsive' means 'responsive to the market'—with the emphasis on competitive edge. The result, as Peter Wilby (2011, p. 35) anticipated, is 'two tiers of unfairness':

> *students from prosperous homes will get an expensive education, with the taxpayer bearing not only the upfront cost but also the risks that students drop out, fail their degrees, or wind up in a monastic retreat, making it impossible to repay their loans.*

This will, in turn, impact on the quality of provision for the most disadvantaged elements within society:

> *the poor will get a cheaper version at one of those universities that you've never heard of. Cheaper means larger teaching groups, less contact with academic staff, more ill-paid, part-time and temporary tutors, less well-stocked libraries, more obsolete science and engineering labs.*

There is, therefore, as Stefan Collini (2011, p. 14) makes clear, a need to ensure that those entering universities

> *are not cheated of their entitlement to an education, not palmed off, in the name of "meeting the needs of employers", with a narrow training that is thought by right-wing policy-formers to be "good enough for the likes of them", while the children of the privileged classes continue to attend properly resourced universities that can continue to boast their standing in global league tables.*

The decline in staff–student ratios in the past three decades (from an estimated high of 1:8 to the current 1:22) has, claims Collini (2012), resulted in 'an alarming reduction in the number of "contact" hours and amount of personal attention each student receives' (p. 31) He adds that 'nearly all parents with children at university hear disturbing reports of overcrowded "seminars" and minimal contact hours or attention to written work' (p. 179). The massive reduction in university funding undertaken by a Tory government in 1981—of the order of 11 percent across the system and with some institutions suffering sudden funding cuts of around 20 percent—did much to normalise reduced 'contact' hours, overcrowded 'seminars', and lack of detailed 'feedback' on written work (p. 33).

The introduction of the Research Assessment Exercise in 1986 exacerbated this problem by fostering a culture within higher education that rewards research disproportionately more than it does teaching. A survey conducted by the Open University Centre for Higher Education Research and Information found that between 1992 and 2007 there had been a decline in the number of hours academics reported spending on teaching and an increase in the amount of time UK academics reported spending on research. The proportion of academics that reported a primary interest in teaching had also decreased since 1992, while the percentage of staff claiming a primary interest in research rose by 9 percent. Moreover, far fewer UK academics in the UK reported a primary interest in teaching compared with their international counterparts, with the UK lagging far behind China, South Africa and the US (Universities UK, 2008). Clearly, the research agenda—the terms of which were set by the Research Assessment Exercise and carried forward into the Research Excellence Framework—is impacting more forcefully on the professional identity of academics than the widening participation agenda with its implicit emphasis on closing the social class gap through a renewed focus on teaching and learning and on curriculum innovation.

There is a need to critically examine some of those aspects of the US system that the UK system seems so eager to emulate. The US Ivy League system, as Howard Hotson (2011) has shown, is in fact less egalitarian and less successful than the UK system once population is taken into account: the most selective universities within the US admit only 3 percent of their students from the lowest socio-economic quartile (mostly African-American), while admitting 74 percent from the highest. Moreover, 'market competition in the United States has driven up tuition fees in the private universities and thereby sucked out the resources needed to sustain good public universities' (p. 22). The idea that market forces will simultaneously drive up standards and drive down prices does not bear critical scrutiny. Yet, this is precisely the idea that the UK government advances in its promotion of what it terms 'a diverse and responsive sector' (Department for Business, Innovation and Skills, 2011, pp. 46–53).

What is at risk is the quality of provision offered by the higher education sector as a whole. The extent to which the supposedly elite universities have imposed their own narrowly defined standards of excellence on the broad swathe of institutions comprising that sector has had a profoundly deleterious effect on many of those institutions. The search for excellence, as Nelly Stromquist (2012, p. 179) puts it, 'has become an exclusionary project due to narrowing definition'. Far from promoting institutional diversity, the competitive culture within which 'league tables' and 'rankings' play such a prominent part encourages academic conformity and institutional homogeneity. Moreover, as Tero Erkkila (2013) argues, these influential global ranking exercises—such as the *Times Higher* exercise—are subject to no formal mechanisms of public accountability or public scrutiny. While institutions struggle to define a particular niche in the market, the vast majority of them inevitably lose out to those who occupy the only niche that really matters—the niche located at the top end of the global rankings. The result is institutional inertia across the higher education sector.

A Hard Choice

Higher education faces a hard choice: either it continues to acquiesce in the reproduction of inequality or it challenges its own role in that reproductive cycle. The choice is between two sharply contrasting visions of society and the place of higher education within it. The first is of a society that lacks cohesion and is politically disengaged. It relies on subjects who know their place in society and are punctilious in the protection of their own private interests. It focuses on the past and views inequality as inevitable. At the bottom of this society are, as Joseph Stiglitz (2012, p. 289) shows, 'millions of young people alienated and without hope'. Within this vision of society, higher education contributes to the private gain of those individuals who are in the fortunate position of being able to afford it.

The second vision is of a society that embraces difference and is economically resilient and democratically purposeful. It requires citizens who demand their place within the polity and consider their own interests to be inextricably entwined with the public interest. It focuses on alternative futures and challenges the legacy of inequality. It is a society where, as Stiglitz again puts it, 'the gap between the haves and the have-nots has been narrowed, where there is a sense of shared destiny, [and] a common commitment to opportunity and fairness' (p. 289). Within this vision, higher education contributes to the public good of society as a whole and is accessible to anyone able to benefit from it regardless of whether they can pay for it.

Those involved in higher education—as researchers, teachers and scholars—bear a particular responsibility for keeping alive this vision of the good society. No such society can exist without an open and accessible system of mass higher education that reaches out to the needs of an increasingly diverse and internationalised public. Higher education cannot resolve all the ills of society. But it can begin to realign itself in such a way as to resist its own role in the reproduction of those ills—and, in doing so, open up new possibilities and opportunities. How, then, might those with responsibility for higher education—those, that is, comprising the authorship and readership of this book—set about this task of realignment?

We might start by acknowledging that higher education is not synonymous with the university. Higher education is conducted in most university settings, but is also conducted in a range of other educational settings: the workplace, further education colleges, public libraries, the home, internet cafes, etc. Realignment requires, among other things, valuing those other places of learning as contributing to the public space of higher education. That is not to devalue the university, but simply to speak to the assumption that the university has a monopoly on higher education. Universities must reach out, render themselves more permeable and accessible and re-orient themselves beyond their own institutional interests. More specifically, higher education needs to re-imagine its institutional connectivity with further education, secondary schooling, primary schooling and early-years provision.

Higher education should focus on the recognition of student achievement. Currently, students who do not complete a course of undergraduate study are deemed to have failed. Such students are given no public recognition for the work they have undertaken or indeed for the hard and difficult decision they may have taken in discontinuing their study. Their experience of higher education is one of failure and a source of continuing blockage rather than enablement. Universities that cater predominantly to first-generation students and students from economically disadvantaged backgrounds have a disproportionate number of such students. Far from helping these students to become confident members of society—and active citizens within the polity—the higher education system brands them as 'failures', 'drop-outs', 'non-completers'.

Higher education should also help redefine new forms of civic engagement. The gains of the post-1945 settlement were, across the UK, of huge democratic importance. But we cannot simply loop back to that earlier social democratic settlement. Nor can we wholly reject it. In moving forward we need a vision of higher education that will help students develop as resilient and assertive citizens who look to the future for the reconstitution of the public good. Higher education still has to find a voice within this debate on what constitutes citizenship within the twenty-first century. The crucial issue then, as now, is how to move beyond a system that has manifestly failed to deliver on the basic requirements of a fair and equal society.

Finally, the public good now has to be defined with reference to a pluralist world society. The internationalisation of higher education has become so marketised and commercialised that there is a possibility of losing sight of the broader vision of global governance, cosmopolitan learning and global citizenship. Higher education must be about helping ourselves to live together in a world of incommensurable difference and uncompromising contingency. All occurrences are both local and global and as such have both unforeseen and unforeseeable consequences. The world is not going to stop being like this. On the contrary, it will become increasingly super-complex in its interconnectivity and will make ever increasing demands on our human capacity to understand.

I am not here arguing for a particular programme of reform or a particular framework of curriculum and pedagogical change—although, of course, my argument has implications for programmatic reform and change at the level of curriculum and pedagogic practice.[1] What I am arguing is that policy makers in higher education must decide whether they wish to pursue the great and hugely ambitious social democratic enterprise of widening access and participation to higher education as a public good—or whether they prefer a risk-averse system of higher education that sustains and reproduces inequalities inherent in society. Do we continue to drift into that hopeless cul-de-sac? Or can we acknowledge that we have come to the place where roads meet—and divide—and where hard choices must be made?

Notes

1. My thinking on these matters is outlined in greater detail in *Interpretive Pedagogies for Higher Education* (2012), *Higher Education and the Public Good* (2011) and *Towards the Virtuous University* (2008).

References

ACEVO (2012) *Youth Unemployment: The Crisis We Cannot Afford* (The ACEVO Commission on Youth Employment) London: ACEVO.
Aldridge, H., Kenway, P., MacInnes, T., and Parekh, A. (2012) *Monitoring Poverty and Social Exclusion 2012*. York: Joseph Rowntree Foundation and New Policy Institute.
Collini, S. (2011) From Robbins to McKinsey, *London Review of Books*, 33:16, 9–14.
Collini, S. (2012) *What Are Universities For?* London: Penguin.
Department for Business, Innovation and Skills (2011) *Higher Education: Students at the Heart of the System*. London: Department for Business, Innovation and Skills.
Erkkila, T. (ed). (2013) *Global University Rankings: Challenges for European Higher Education*. London and New York: Palgrave.
Glyn, A. (2006) *Capitalism Unleashed: Finance, Globalization, and Welfare*. Oxford and New York: Oxford University Press.
Gorz, A. (1989) *Critique of Economic Reason*. London and New York: Verso.
Harvey, D. (2003) *The New Imperialism*. Oxford: Oxford University Press.
Hills, J. et.al (2010) *An Anatomy of Economic Inequality in the UK: Report of the National Equality Panel*. CASE Report 60 London: Government Equalities Office/CASE The London School of Economics and Political Science (January).
Hind, D. (2010) *The Return of the Political*. London and New York: Verso.
Hotson, H. (2011) Don't look to the Ivy League, *London Review of Books*, 33:10, 20–22.
Hutton, W. (2010) The Financial Crisis and the Need of the Hunter Gatherer, in: R. Williams and L. Elliott (eds), *Crisis and Recovery: Ethics, Economics and Justice*. Houndmills and New York: Palgrave Macmillan.
Hutton, W. (2012) Enlightened Labour, in J. Denham (ed), *The Shape of Things to Come*. London: Fabian Society and Foundation for European Progressive Studies.

Judt, T. (2009) What is Living and What is Dead in Social Democracy? *The New York Review of Books*, LVI, 20 December 17, 2009—January 13, 2010, 86–96.
Judt, T. (2010) *Postwar: A History of Europe Since 1945*. London: Vintage.
Judt, T. and Snyder, T., (2012) *Thinking the Twentieth Century: Intellectuals and Politics in the Twentieth Century*. Heinemann: New Hampshire.
Lee, N., and Wright, J. (2011) *The Geography of NEETs: A Snapshot Analysis for the Private Equity Foundation*. London: Private Equity Foundation.
Madrick, J. (2009) *The Case for Big Government*. Princeton and Oxford: Princeton University Press.
Moyo, D. (2011) *How the West Was Lost: Fifty Years of Economic Folly—And the Stark Choices Ahead*. London: Allen Lane.
Nixon, J. (2008) *Towards the Virtuous University: the Moral Bases of Academic Practice*. London and New York: Routledge/Taylor and Francis Group.
Nixon, J. (2011) *Higher Education and the Public Good: Imagining the University*. London and New York Continuum.
Nixon, J. (2012) *Interpretive Pedagogies for Higher Education: Arendt, Berger, Said, Nussbaum and their Legacies*. London and New York: Continuum.
Nixon, J. (2013) The Drift to Conformity: the Myth of Institutional Diversity, in: Erkkila, T. (ed), *Global University Rankings: Challenges for European Higher Education*. London and New York: Palgrave.
Nussbaum, M. C. (2010) *Not for Profit: Why Democracy Needs the Humanities*. Princeton and Oxford: Princeton University Press.
Reed, H., and Lawson, N. (eds). (2011) *Plan B: A Good Economy for a Good Society*. London: Compass.
Sennett, R. (2006) *The Culture of the New Capitalism*. New Haven and London: Yale University Press.
Stiglitz, J. E. (2012) *The Price of Inequality*. London: Allen Lane.
Stromquist, N. P. (2012) Higher education and the Search for Excellence in US Universities, in: B., Adamson, J. Nixon, and F. Su, (eds), *The Reorientation of Higher Education: Challenging the East–West Dichotomy*. Hong Kong: Springer with CERC.
Sutton Trust (2005) *Sutton Trust Briefing Note: The Educational Backgrounds of The UKs Top Solicitors, Barristers and Judges*. London: The Sutton Trust (June).
Sutton Trust (2006) *The Educational Background of Leading Journalists*. London: The Sutton Trust (June).
Sutton Trust (2008) *University Admissions by Individual Schools*. London: The Sutton Trust.
Swift, R. (2012) Preparing the ground: Left Strategy Beyond the Apocalypse, *New Internationalist*, 453 (June), 29–35.
Toynbee, P., and Walker, D. (2009) *Unjust Rewards: Ending the Greed that is Bankrupting Britain*. London: Granta Books.
Umunna, C. (2012) Stepping up, not stepping back, in: J. Denham (ed), *The Shape of Things to Come*. London: Fabian Society and Foundation for European Progressive Studies.
Universities UK (2008) *The Changing Academic Profession in the UK and Beyond*. London: Universities UK.

Varghese, N. V. (2013) Drivers of Reforms in Higher Education, in: B. Adamson, J. Nixon, and F. Su, (eds). *The Reorientation of Higher Education: Challenging the East–West Dichotomy*. Hong Kong: Springer with CERC pp. 36–49.
Wilby, P. (2011) This Half-Baked Ivy League Spells Two Tiers of Unfairness. *The Guardian* (June 30), 35.
Wilkinson, R., and Pickett, K. (2010) *The Spirit Level: Why More Equal Societies Almost Always Do Better* (Revised ed). London: Penguin.
Wright, E. O. (2009) Understanding Class: Towards an Integrated Analytical Approach, *New Left Review*, 60 (Nov/Dec), 101–116.

Coda

XII. Reflections on the Debate

Gareth Williams

Introduction

The extent to which higher education can be considered as public or private depends in large part on what it is. Paul Standish (Chapter III) quotes the philosopher MacIntyre who is unequivocal:

> *when it is demanded of a university community that it justify itself by specifying what its peculiar or essential function is, that function which, were it not to exist, no other institution could discharge, the response of the community ought to be that universities are places where conceptions of and standards of rational justification are elaborated, put to work in the detailed practices of enquiry, and themselves rationally evaluated, so that only from the university can the wider society learn how to conduct its own debates, practical or theoretical, in a rationally defensible way* (MacIntyre, 1990, p. 222).

This places universities firmly in the public sphere. They serve the public by being bastions of reason and the pursuit of truth, which they make available to a wider population. That this view has some resonance beyond the citadel of philosophy is shown by the frequency with which professors are called in to radio and television debates to be the voice of reason and truth and to explain new advances in understanding the natural or social world. However, Standish judges MacIntyre's answer to be condescending to a wider public, many of whom like to think they are also rational and truthful, and also that it focusses on only a part of what actually happens in modern universities.

As several of the authors in this book have pointed out 'public good' and 'higher education' are both slippery terms. They have meant different things in different periods of history and in different countries, and they now mean different things to different people. There are, as Barnett (Chapter II) among others points out, many publics: and Singh (Chapter V) adds the cautionary note to those who equate 'public' with 'equitable':

> to this increasing layering of complexity in the notion of 'public,' one can add analyses which make the point that publics are not self-evidently progressive and cannot be presumed automatically to have emancipatory interests in contradistinction to private constituencies.

Nixon also (Chapter XI), echoing Margaret Thatcher's widely quoted agnostic comments about the existence of 'society', raises the question of whether 'the public' is anything more than a public of private interests.

'Higher education' too is beset by many conceptual problems. For many commentators it is synonymous with 'university', itself becoming a rather elastic term especially in England. For others it is an all-embracing concept covering virtually all education and training and re-education and retraining of people above the legal age of majority.

The clash between Simon Blackburn and Ron Barnett in *Times Higher Education* in the early months of 2013 exemplifies some of the ambiguities. Blackburn has a clear view, similar to Macintyre of what universities are for:

> 'universities are about educating a new generation into procedures of understanding, reason, analysis and explanation ….. (Blackburn, 2013, p. 47).

For Barnett the idea of a university is much broader:

> A university will always be an amalgam of ideas and not necessarily coherent at that.' (Barnett, 2013, p. 147).

At a less abstract level today's higher education must provide challenging learning experiences for the most intellectually able young people of each generation and worthwhile learning experiences (and there are many disagreements over what is considered worthwhile) for a very broad cross section of the population prior to their entry into full adult life. In addition in recent years higher education institutions have laid claim over a large part of the lifelong learning and renewal of the professional skills of older people. They also expect to be in the forefront of the pursuit of new knowledge which can be used to make technological, economic and social progress. For many of the authors in this volume higher education is a public activity because its institutions are expected to do all these things equitably and ethically. However, equity and ethics are also words with a variety of interpretations.

Scholarship has always been at the heart of the university and from the early nineteenth century onwards this has overlapped with empirical research and over the course of the last 200 years there has come to be a correlation between a university's research success and its reputation as a place where students will acquire learning of lasting value. Universities have always been custodians and architects of knowledge and their function has been to ensure that the most up-to-date and most reliable knowledge is passed on to each new generation. As the Robbins Committee put it in 1963, the function of higher education institutions was as creators, disseminators and stores of knowledge. However, as knowledge has increased in leaps and bounds and the number of people deemed able to benefit from some form of it has grown almost equally rapidly what was once a rather narrowly constrained range of activity has become very large and very diverse and the boundaries of what universities do have become very indistinct. Furthermore the internet is proving to be at least as good a place to store and disseminate knowledge as many universities.

The question of whether higher education is public or a private good is both positive and normative and there can be no simple answer to either 'what is?' or 'what ought to be?' because there are many publics and many higher education activities. Which of its many different aspects contribute primarily to individual and which to collective well-being? Even those who believe that higher education like virtue or health or knowing how to read and count is an end in itself, cannot avoid coming to terms with its diversity. Paul Standish wrestles with this problem in the present volume. He distinguishes 'functional' and 'transformative' drives that run through various conceptions of the nature and purposes of higher education. As I read him the former refers to the multiple roles of higher education as a means of meeting the various needs of a wider society (getting near to the traditional Chinese view as set out by Cheng and Yang in Chapter IX) while the latter is nearer to the claim that higher education is an important end in itself enriching the lives of those who receive it. Standish endorses Derrida who

> *sets out what he claims is 'less a thesis' or even a hypothesis, than a declarative engagement, an appeal in the form of a declaration of faith: faith in the university and, within the university faith in the Humanities of tomorrow.* (Chapter III).

Public good conveys even more ambiguities. 'A public good' signifies something different from '*the* public good'. The latter is a rather general term used to signify almost anything that is not clearly private and of which the writer or speaker approves—a 'hurrah' word as Standish has put it. A public good is a term coined originally by economists to signify a good or service, whose use cannot be easily limited to any particular individual or group.

For some of our authors the purpose of contributing to a volume on higher education as a public good is to help redeem the idea of higher education as a service that contributes to the public good at least as much as it demands in resources from taxpayers over and above the increases in the private earning capacities and wider benefits accruing to its immediate beneficiaries. Equity looms large in most of these arguments. For Jon Nixon for example,

> *higher education is a public good because it contributes to the development of an educated public with the capabilities necessary to fulfil the human potential of each of its members and of society as a whole* (Chapter XI).

For Nixon equality is at the heart of the issue. In his opinion higher education serves the public good if it helps to promote a more equal society and he regrets that most present day higher education systems are helping to perpetuate inequality. This leaves open the question of whether higher education could ever be a public service in the sense in which Nixon understands the word. As Angela Brew points out, there is an intrinsic tension between meritocracy and equality. Developing the full potential of every individual person inevitably results in heterogeneity and there is a fine (but indistinct) line before this becomes inequity and inequality. It seems to me that the only way of achieving equality in the sense that Nixon desires would be to remove children from parental control as soon as they are born. This has been tried in some communities and societies from ancient Sparta to Maoist China but it is not a practical proposition for democratic societies, and in any case it has always led to new elites being formed. Meanwhile we must recognise with Singh (Chapter V) that publics cannot be presumed automatically to have emancipatory interests.

'A' public good is generally used in a much more closely defined sense. As several of our authors have suggested 'a public good' is at root a term used by economists to signify something to which the iron laws of classical economics do not readily apply in that if it is used or consumed by one person or group of people this does not prevent other people from enjoying it also. David Dill elegantly explains the issue in Chapter X:

> *Private goods are excludable; those who own the good can exercise property rights, preventing those who have not paid for the good from using it or consuming its benefits. Private goods are also rivalrous; consumption by one consumer prevents simultaneous consumption by other consumers. In contrast a 'public good' or service is neither rivalrous in consumption, nor excludable in ownership, and is available to all.*

This last phrase 'available to all', by implication also affordable by all, provides the starting point of much of the debate. If a good or service can be plausibly defined as public then it should be 'available for all' and nobody is prevented from enjoying it through lack of resources. But this is an issue of positive economics, not a value judgement. A product, once it exists, either is or is not available to all. Very few goods or services meet this criterion in its entirety. What do exist, and have been much discussed by economists for many decades, are products that have high fixed costs that must be met somehow but, once the product exists, the marginal cost of an extra unit is very low. Knowledge is one such item. The creation of new worthwhile knowledge is often very expensive. However, once the knowledge has been created my acquiring it does not prevent you benefitting from it also. Copyright and patent laws are one way of providing incentives for investment in invention and creativity but they result in what could be a (almost) free product available for all, becoming something that is expensive providing, often very substantial, rents for the holders of the copyrights or patents. This feature of knowledge points to a possible distinction between the university functions of knowledge dissemination and knowledge creation discussed later in the chapter.

There is also another difference between 'the public good' and 'a public good'. As Ron Barnett has pointed out in Chapter II:

> *the idea of a single public is also problematic for it could imply the formation of a monolithic society in which the diversity of opinion, publicly expressed, was far from encouraged...the idea of a public* [may imply] *the development of an educational system and the emergence of an educated class, capable of forming and articulating opinion, perhaps aided by the circulation of pamphlets, newspapers and journals. ...such a public could presage an unequal society with a narrow range of opinions coalescing around some taken-for-granted assumptions as to civil rights, respect for persons, obligations of persons as citizens to the common weal and so forth. In short this unitary public could be a harbinger of a lack and even a loss of intellectual and social freedoms.*

One cannot help wondering whether concerns about extreme forms of political correctness, as well as fears of totalitarianism, were not far beneath the surface of Barnett's thinking at this point.

According to Barnett the idea of an association between higher education and a common culture has appeared in evidence for around the past fifty years or so and he gives the Robbins Committee of the early 1960s the credit for highlighting it. However, the idea has been around for much longer than that. The public school ethos of Thomas Arnold, the Jesuits' educational policies, the battles over control of the universities during the Renaissance and Reformation and even the fate of poor old Peter Abelard were examples of the attempts to promote a dominant unifying culture in what was seen at the time to be the public interest. It is, in fact, impossible to separate particular ideas of a good society from the idea of education, including higher education, as a public good.

However it is also important to note Dill's stricture in Chapter X that

> literature suggests the policy reforms of the last several decades, which have introduced greater "privatisation" and market competition into higher education systems (i.e., so-called "neo-liberal reforms"), have also lessened the "public goods" provided by higher education institutions and are compromising academic activity within universities. This literature, written primarily by those who work within higher education institutions, makes valuable contributions, but has several limitations. First, it is largely rhetorical and qualitative, rather than empirical. When this literature is empirical, it is often focused on the views of academics themselves rather than on indicators of the outputs or outcomes of universities. Furthermore, in critiquing the impacts of current policies, many of these studies do not cite or assess the economic research on the increasing private and public returns produced by higher education noted earlier. While the impacts upon those actively involved in the production of higher education should certainly be included in any calculation of the public good and/or the social benefits derived from higher education, focusing primarily on the impacts upon producers may not provide a totally objective assessment of the public good.

My own starting point is Durkheim's proposition that educational systems reflect dominant societal ideologies because they are constructs built by society, which seek to reproduce in subsequent generations, their collectively held values, beliefs, norms and practices through the institutions they create for this purpose (Durkheim, 1956). Higher education can be seen as the final stage of this socialisation. Thus education cannot be theorised in isolation from theories of the wider society of which it is part, and higher education cannot be satisfactorily theorised except as a late stage of education generally. One of the knots in which many higher education commentators often tie themselves, encouraged by policy makers, is the belief that it can remedy most of the defects in society itself including those that emerge in the earlier stages of the educational system. Equality, technological progress, economic efficiency, cultural creation and transmission, an improved sense of citizenship responsibilities and a sustainable long-term global environment are all social aims which universities and colleges have had thrust upon them or have volunteered to pursue. Even Nixon, who makes wide claims in Chapter XI about what higher education should be doing, concedes that 'higher education cannot resolve all the ills of society'. But in the Durkheimian interpretation, if a society, for whatever reason, gives its main rewards for economic enterprise that results in more goods and services, but without much concern with how they are distributed, higher education institutions catering for large segments of the population will find it difficult to swim against the prevailing tide.

However, Durkheim's view presupposed a relatively stable or slowly changing society and economy, in which the wisdom of age could be passed down to new generations and each generation made incremental changes that slowly permeated the educational system. The public function of higher education was to ensure that change promoted by those who became the leaders of society was evolutionary rather than revolutionary. When social, economic and above all technological change is rapid, however, this model is less satisfactory. Commentators, such as Collini (2012) and Inglis (2013), along with many others in political and academic life, are not altogether happy about the change. There are calls to preserve or reinstate traditional curricula at the same time as incorporating new ideas and knowledge. These tensions become particularly acute when higher education participation encompasses a very wide cross section of society. The majority of those who graduate in a mass higher education system will not become leading members of government, business, the media or the arts. But they will, it is to be hoped, be citizens who contribute to the well-being of society through both their economic and social activities. Politicians and academics who wish the new enlarged systems to retain the substance and ethical virtues of the old systems clash with those who lay more stress on the acquisition of new knowledge and challenges to conventional wisdom.

The simplistic approach is to accept that the primary role of all education including higher is to enhance the life chances of all individuals by allowing them to develop their innate talents to the greatest possible extent. However, if higher education is about individual development in what sense can it be considered a public good? One possible answer is that those who have particular natural abilities should also acquire through their education a sense of responsibility towards others who do not have these advantages, just as professional athletes are expected to behave themselves in ways that set a good example to their admirers. It is not possible to ignore the clear evidence that different individuals have different interests and different intrinsic abilities but there are doubts whether in a healthy society the capacity to enjoy life should be closely related to the abilities as well as the material resources people inherit or are able to develop.

In a society in which all are respected and rewarded for their achievements whatever they are, and those who are lucky enough to have high ability in financially rewarding areas, accept the responsibility of sharing some of their benefits with those less fortunate, it clearly makes sense for every individual to be educated to the highest levels of which they are capable and society benefits from so doing regardless of whether everybody is able to receive these benefits. If I am successful and share the proceeds of my success with my neighbours there is no reason for my community not to educate me to levels that enable me to reach my full potential even if very few other people are able to reach that level of expertise. Cheng and Yang show that in traditional China the extended family and close neighbours played this role—as they still do in many countries. If one of its members shows high academic ability the family as a whole ensures that s/he is educated to the highest possible level and in return the graduate has a lifelong sense of responsibility to the family and village. In modern global societies there can be little resentment of the success of someone like Bill Gates if he uses a large part of his fortune helping those much less talented or lucky than himself. As Alfred Marshall remarked over a hundred years ago:

> *All that is spent during many years in opening the means of higher education to the masses would be well paid for if it called out one more Newton or Darwin, Shakespeare or Beethoven* (Marshall, 1961, Book IV, Ch VI, p. 26).

'From each according to his ability, to each according to his needs' is still a powerful slogan that could well underpin public higher education and the society of which it is part in the twenty-first century. The difficulty is that distributive equity usually conflicts with the pursuit of individual freedom which is a slogan at least as powerful, in most Western countries at least. Even the champion of free market economics Friedrich von Hayek conceded that 'we must face the fact that the preservation of individual freedom is incompatible with a full satisfaction of our views of distributive justice' (Hayek, 1948, p. 22). The debates about the public and the private in higher education exemplify a playing out of this dilemma amongst a particularly articulate segment of the population. In what sense can free universities serve the public, as opposed to the private good of many separate individuals?

Higher Education for the Public Good

The debate about whether the core function of universities is the intellectual and moral development of individuals or the service of a wider community through preparing these individuals for a place in society is very long standing. Newman's promotion of the idea of a liberal university education (Newman, 1852) mainly to civilise sons of gentlemen is much quoted in the literature. Matthew Arnold is another frequently cited nineteenth-century author who broadly supported Newman's ideas, especially in his *Culture and Anarchy* (1869). Less often noted in the literature on higher education are those with reservations about Newman's position by such as Herbert Spenser, Mark Pattison and, to some extent, John Stuart Mill (cited by Teixeira in Chapter VI) who saw education as having a clear utilitarian and social function. Many of the debates about higher education in the later nineteenth century were largely concerned with whether positivistic sciences belonged in universities, but much of it took a form that would be familiar today in that the traditional non-empirical arts appeared to be under threat from the philistine materialistic, positivistic scientific newcomers. Those debates took place under the shadows over the old religious certainties cast by the work of Charles Darwin and other evolutionary theorists. For people like Matthew Arnold the new world of science and technology, represented by the civic universities founded by industrialists to train people like engineers and chemists, was more a threat than a promise:

> *We are here as on a darkling plain*
> *Swept with confused alarms of struggle and flight,*
> *Where ignorant armies clash by night* (Matthew Arnold, 1867).

This digression into the nineteenth century is intended to show that, quite apart from the economists' debates outlined by Teixeira, the debates about the public or private nature of higher education are not new. In Britain it was clear that universities were private institutions that depended in large part on the income they earned, though in the case of Oxford and Cambridge this was buttressed by very substantial endowments acquired over centuries, to the disgust of Adam Smith who in the eighteenth century had compared them unfavourably with Scottish universities which depended to a much greater extent on fees paid by students. However, universities always had a legal status that required them to serve what was seen as the public interest of their day and, from time to time national governments intervened to tidy up practices which it believed were not in the public interest. The UK differed from most of continental Europe where the state played a much more active part in the establishment and the management of universities, though at least until the advent of Communism and Nazism, university professors in most countries enjoyed considerable freedom to pursue their scholarship and teaching as they thought proper.

However, the notion of the public role of universities changed dramatically during the twentieth century. In part this can be attributed to the rise of Socialism, both in its Marxist form and the more gradualist version of Social Democratic parties such as the British Labour Party, which was strongly influenced by such thinkers as R. H. Tawney, and in part to the previous expansion of primary and secondary education. Tawney's arguments for free secondary education for all made in the early 1920s at a time of severe financial crisis have a contemporary resonance even though the argument about the place of public funding has moved from secondary to higher education nearly a century later.

> *"(W)hat is prudence in the conduct of every private family can hardly be folly in that of a great kingdom." And, if a parent who neglects his children is liable to criminal proceedings, the burden of proving that the same action is highly meritorious when done by several million parents, in the name of economy, appears to rest on those who support that paradox* (Tawney, 1922, p. 132).

The battle for secondary education for all has been largely won, at least quantitatively, in most countries and it is accepted as a realisable aim across the globe: though there are a few countries where it still has to be fully accepted for girls. In the past half century the debate has moved to higher education. Many of the claims of those who make the case for higher education as a public good, including some of the authors in this volume, are essentially using this argument. It was one of the main arguments used by the UK Robbins Committee to justify expansion in the early 1960s.

There are, nevertheless, important differences between secondary and higher education. The word *parent* has little relevance when applied to students who are, in nearly all cases, legally adults and are in a position to make their own choices. Robbins used the argument at a time when much less than 10 percent of the population was able to undertake higher education and there was ample evidence that large numbers of school leavers both wanted higher education and would have been able to benefit from it. In an age when mass higher education has become nearly universal (to use Martin Trow's term) the case is not nearly so clear cut. It is reasonable to claim that the age of 18, which in nearly all countries is an age at which people are deemed to be responsible adults for nearly all legal and political purposes, is the point at which individuals' own choices should be dominant. Dill disagrees slightly (Chapter X). In his view the threshold is at the end of the first degree studies:

> *In contrast to the national markets for first degree-level education where the "myopic" choices of student consumers may limit the potential for user information to improve academic programme, the international market for research doctoral students appears to behave in accordance with classic economic assumptions.*

Inside Higher Education

Angela Brew (Chapter VII) mentions some of the conflicts of values and current practices within higher education institutions that act to confuse arguments about universities' contribution to the public good. She draws attention to the public–private tensions between meritocracy and equality, creativity constrained by positivistic ideology and the contradiction between collaboration and competition amongst students, staff and institutions. In Brew's opinion the most important question is not whether universities are contributing to the contemporary public good but whether they are helping to shape the society of the future and are likely to contribute to a good public in future generations. This draws attention to the intergenerational nature of higher education which I consider later.

Nevertheless higher education does make some useful immediate contributions to the public good. It provides interesting and often enjoyable experiences for most participants and offers a convenient alternative to idleness for those who are unable to find employment: universities are centres of expertise that can contribute to the welfare of local communities and the wider world. However, Brew is right to say that the main function of higher education institutions is to contribute to improvements in the societies of the future and the individuals who will be their members. It is the graduates and the outcomes of university research that will exert a powerful influence on the nature of their communities in the longer term. Brew regrets that

> *by being seduced by the loud voices of big business, economic rationalism, ideas about technology, and out-dated ideas about knowledge, and failing to listen to those with less power, universities are being reactive rather than proactive in shaping their future …There must be within society critical self-evaluation leading to change and this properly belongs to universities. To do this they must build on their inherent ideas of scholarly endeavour in more proactive ways* (Chapter VII).

From very ancient times speaking truth to power has been a task of academics and licensed fools. Universities have (nearly) always had the freedom to utter thoughts that others close to power feel inhibited about. Fools deflate pompous, socially superior characters. They are able to criticise kings. The use of the term 'academic' as a derogatory term signifying unrealistic, at least in England, comes close to this conception of the university. Professors promulgate interesting ideas but to ordinary people in the street trying to earn a living, or govern a nation, they remain interesting ideas until just occasionally they strike home. Lear's fool sees from the beginning how foolish the King was to give away so much of his property to his sycophantic daughters but was not heeded until it was too late. Universities are at their best when their members are licensed to speak the truth or at least the closest possible approximation to it, regardless of the consequences but they recognise the responsibility this brings. Many of the authors in this volume fear that this licenced fool function has been lost in a universal higher education system.

According to Brew, along with Macintyre and Blackburn, universities serve the public good by standing slightly apart from the societies to which they belong in order to develop new ideas and criticise the powerful. One problem with such contentions is that they are at variance with other claims, such as that of the Robbins Committee, that one of the important functions of universities is to help promote a common culture. Any healthy society needs to have some people whose criticisms and analyses cause the dominant majority to justify the contributions they are making to the public good. What is not so self-evident is whether this can be a primary function when universities cater to the majority of the population. While there may have been a case for the university as primarily a critic of the social order when it encompassed a small segment of the population it becomes less tenable when people with higher education comprise the majority of the population.

Brew's other claim that universities' primary responsibility is to future generations is also valid. However, it is not clear that it helps solve the problem of whether this is a public or private function. It merely moves the issue one step further back? If I put some money aside to contribute to the best higher education for my grandchildren, or if I remember my old Oxbridge college in my will, am I contributing to the public or private good? To what extent will the benefits be enjoyed by people as private individuals and to what extent will their benefits be as members of well-educated communities?

Civil Society

Peter Scott (Chapter IV) introduces the concept of the civil society in which he locates universities somewhere between the 'state', by which he means government in its broadest sense and the market. 'It is insulated from both political command-and-control and also from the immediate pressures of the market'. Certainly universities in most non-communist countries were in this comfortable position between 1945 and the 1980s though their legal position varied from substantial state regulation in France and almost complete legal freedom in the United Kingdom. What 'civil society' implies is a self-disciplined and tolerant state that allows considerable freedom to non-state organisations, but this goes along with an understanding, often tacit, that these organisations will not embarrass the state authorities too much. In the case of UK universities this was achieved through Royal Charters which treated universities as legal 'persons' able to do anything not explicitly forbidden by law. In this model universities serve the public good by being centres of expertise independent of government.

Scott also draws attention to one mechanism by which a degree of independence of universities in the UK has been assured, their charitable status. This gives them exemption from some taxes but in return requires them to be non-profit-seeking and to offer their services to those who need them or are

Reflections on the Debate

able to benefit from them regardless of their ability to pay. Similar provisions are in place in many countries.

This theme is taken up by Tapper (Chapter VIII) who analyses the policy issues involved in the English debate about whether higher education is a public good. According to Tapper,

> *perhaps the clearest understanding of why higher education was perceived as a public good is to be gained by examining the background as to why educational bodies should be accorded charitable status. Charitable status is awarded to those organisations that are deemed to provide a public benefit, and for pursuing that public good they are exempted from paying certain taxes. (p113 above)*

He points to analogies with the debate about the charitable status of private schools. Many of the great so-called 'public schools' in England were established by wealthy benefactors to provide free education for promising young boys from families who were unable to pay for private tutors. As time went on, particularly in the nineteenth century, many of these establishments became unable to be financially viable without charging fees to at least some of their students. They retained their charitable status by continuing to offer a certain number of free places to boys, and more recently girls, who obtained scholarships.

Tapper considers that universities are able to use the same argument. In principle anybody can go to any university provided they can show that they are likely to be able to benefit from the education provided. This rationale for universities as charitable institutions that provide a public service rests essentially on the principle of equality of opportunity, which ever since the publication of the Robbins Report in 1963 has been one of the main guiding principles of higher education policy in Britain. Since the 1940s equality of access to higher education has been a guiding principle of policy in most countries with encouragement from international organisations like UNESCO and OECD. The pursuit of equality was one of the main drivers of university expansion during much of the second half of the twentieth century. However, more recently the perceived role of higher education in helping to stimulate scientific and technological advance and hence economic growth has complemented and possibly superseded its function in helping to promote more equal societies (see e.g. Deem et al., 2008; Keeling, 2006). This may well have come to be an important public function but it is different from the rationale for treating universities as charities and hence as equitable purveyors of public services. The encouragement by many governments of legal profit seeking universities in many countries is one important recent extension of this principle.

Higher Education Institutions As Components of Wider Educational and Social Systems

Another weakness of many of the arguments about the public benefits from higher education is that they are often simply extensions of arguments that the education of children and adolescents should be a public responsibility. Teixera's useful historical account of economists' treatment of higher education for the past two and a half centuries (Chapter VI) often refers to education generally. Most of the arguments of Adam Smith and John Stuart Mill about education as a public service are concerned with schools rather than universities and so is much of what Marshall has to say. Teixeira asks why the mere provision of higher education should be seen as in the public interest. His tripartite answer based on cultural, social and political cohesion is essentially the same as Robbins' common culture argument. However, despite such eminent antecedents, these arguments amount to little more than the claim that education is good for a nation and that this applies to higher as much as to elementary education. There can be little doubt that societies in which the majority of the population are educated to a high level are, for the most part, more pleasant places to live than those in which there are smaller proportions of well-educated people or in which it is distributed more unevenly. However, the diverse and multifarious nature of mass higher education confuses the issue. Although there are many disagreements of detail and methods it is broadly clear what children and teenagers need to learn to enable them to become fully functioning adult members of their communities. Higher education is not nearly so clear cut. Those who undertake it are adults not children and they have a very wide range of interests and prior achievements. Clearly there are private benefits from possession of many of the skills that can be learned in universities. OECD figures, among many others, have consistently shown that the differential between graduate and non-graduate average earnings has remained substantial in nearly all countries despite the massive expansion since the middle of the twentieth century. In the early days of the economics of education it was often claimed that because of widespread ignorance about the benefits of education a less than optimum amount of resources would be devoted to it unless it was provided as a publicly subsidised service. In the twenty-first century the financial returns to individuals are so widely reported it is hard to make a convincing case that lack of knowledge about them will of itself lead to significant underinvestment.

Student recruitment in a diversified higher education adds another complication. Recruitment to any specific course is a two-way matching process. Universities seek to enrol students who are likely to complete a course successfully and enhance the university's reputation by their subsequent progress through life. Potential students match their own perceptions of their abilities and interests with the information on courses offered. Issues of equity are best tackled in lower levels of education, where students' interests and perceptions of their abilities and their general social and cultural attitudes are formed.

However, the issue of higher education as a public good is not only, and possibly not even primarily, a matter of equity in access to courses. There is a public interest in having sufficient numbers of graduates able to perform socially useful tasks at reasonable cost and also that they all have a sense of the public good in their professional and civic lives. It is not clear that an unregulated market can achieve this. Basic economic theory reasons that if there is a shortage of medical practitioners, they will earn high salaries and this will encourage more people to become physicians until some equilibrium is reached at which an appropriate number of people with the necessary inherent ability obtain the knowledge and skills needed. However, whether it is in the public interest that medical practitioners earn very high salaries so that only wealthy people or nations can afford their services is another matter. If the training of doctors is subsidised from public funds so that more people are willing to take up this profession at lower salaries there may be a public benefit not directly attributable to the private benefits of any modestly paid individual doctor. This is, of course, not an easy matter to determine and appropriate policies are almost certainly tinged with ideology as well as analysis.

It is comparatively straightforward to make a theoretical case along these lines for some subsidy of the training of medical personnel. It is not so easy for engineers or literature graduates. That there are benefits from having a population in which some people have essential high level knowledge and skills, and all people respect each other and do not break the law and vote for governments that make sensible laws is self-evident. It may also be the case that a country, or a city, or a globe in which most people obtain pleasure from the plays of Shakespeare or Corneille or Chekhov or the music of Beethoven, and can afford to enjoy them, is a pleasant place to live, but it is not self-evidently obvious that this is a general public benefit. In any society there is a great variety of tastes. It is easy to make the case that all higher education should have ethical underpinnings and that this is a public service. But which public should decide?

The extent to which higher education serves the public through its contribution to the common good, as opposed to the sum of all the private benefits it brings, depends to a large extent on its content. If higher education is merely training people to work more productively and graduates are, on the whole, rewarded for this through their higher lifetime incomes it is hard to make a case that there is a transcendent public good. There are well-attested wider benefits from higher education such as health and lifestyle (see e.g. Schuller et al., 2004), but many of these benefits, too, accrue to individuals' and their close acquaintances. Brew in Chapter VII claims that: 'universities should be exemplars of how to live and work in open democratic societies'. However, as well as being a value judgment, this includes acquiring the knowledge and skills needed to earn a decent living and thus leaves open the question of whether a higher education is or should be concerned mainly with enhancing individual economic and social capabilities or whether it makes sense for it to have wider social responsibilities as well.

It is difficult to escape the conclusion that the question of whether higher education is or ought to be a public good is primarily an economic and political issue. Several of the authors in the present volume have in practice conceded this. Philosophers, historians, sociologists, physicists and many others can show the world would be a better place if more people thought like they do and, therefore, public funds should be devoted to their field of study. Sometimes this is self-interest and sometimes it is based on a view of what they consider society should be like and the contribution higher education can, or ought to, make to help promote such a society. Often such arguments are valid but it is important to recognise that ultimately they are about resources. The claim is essentially that everybody, and not just those who receive it, obtains some benefits from higher education and therefore it is valid for at least some of it to be paid for collectively. The concluding section of this book is, therefore, concerned with an examination of the economic nature of higher education.

The Inter-Generational Economics

Traditionally students entered university soon after secondary or high school, before or very close to the beginnings of their working lives. They were dependent on financial support from others, both for the direct costs of their education and their living expenses while they were doing it. Subsequently they entered the labour force as (usually) well-paid graduates and had an obligation, moral and often legal through progressive taxation, to contribute to the costs of the next generation of students. Student financial support is in many ways the mirror image of old age pensions about which there is currently much policy discussion. Each generation must save and invest enough while it is productive to support the upcoming generation who will be producing the resources to maintain them in their later years of enforced idleness. So each generation goes through a cycle of: dependency—surplus generation—dependency. These inter-generational transfers can take place in several ways. In traditional societies it usually occurs within families: parents rear their children and do what they can to ensure they are educated well; then the children look after their parents in old age. Churches and other religious and community organisations, also, still perform these functions in many countries. Another source of resources for some universities in some countries is graduates who feel a sense of loyalty to their alma mater and want later generations to have similar opportunities as they have had. In a market system individuals borrow to gain knowledge and skills while they are young, save when they are working and run down their accumulated assets when they can no longer work.

In most of the twentieth century in most countries the state acting as a collective family took over many of these responsibilities 'from the cradle to the grave' as Winston Churchill put it when broadcasting to the British nation in 1943 announcing his government's acceptance of the 1942 Beveridge Report on Social Insurance and Allied Services (Beveridge, 1942).

Of course this model of higher education as a full-time activity early in people's lives that precludes students from earning while they are studying is not an entirely satisfactory picture of twenty-first century higher education. Many students earn while they learn and rapid technological change means that in many cases what students learn in their late teens and early twenties is soon out of date: a major function of modern universities is lifelong education. However, it remains the case that most policy debates about higher education are concerned with first-degree higher education and its students are attended mainly by young people before entry into their mainstream occupations. OECD figures show that in 2011 54 percent of women and 42 percent of men entered higher education before the age of 25 (OECD, 2013). This is about 80 percent of all entrants.

One useful way of looking at higher education from an economic point of view is, therefore, as a contributor to the redistribution of income and assets across the lifetime of individuals. Since everything that is consumed in any period is part of the current production of that period there is always some transfer of resources between productive and non-productive individuals. There are always debts being incurred and assets being accumulated and run down, whether financial, legal or moral. In an ideal society with equality between individuals over their lifetimes each person would incur debts, then create a surplus to share with other people, and then run down their assets, in real terms being subsidised by other people. Education is an intergenerational transfer of claims on resources. Obviously there are also inter-individual and intergroup transfers because some people are or become very wealthy and others are very poor. However, if the case for higher education as a public good is primarily an issue of equity, it is the life cycle of individuals that should be the starting point.

Higher Education and Equality

The question of whether higher education is a public good is the theoretical backdrop to the policy question of how it should be financed. Should the costs of higher education be paid for by taxpayers, by students and their families, by employers, by charitable organisations or by graduates? As already mentioned, most statements about its public nature are essentially claims that all or a significant part of its costs should be met from public funds, which means general taxation, and it is not surprising that they are often viewed as special pleading by ministries of finance and others responsible for the allocation of public funds, who receive similar claims from many other sectors of society.

In the final analysis the policy question boils down to one of the extent to which the benefits are confined to those who receive the education or whether they are shared indirectly with others who do not receive higher education themselves. There are various ways of looking at the indirect benefits. At one extreme, people who believe that everyone benefits from adopting certain beliefs, or living a certain lifestyle, religious and ideological groups for example, may legitimately claim that according to their principles society as a whole would benefit if everyone, and in particular society's leaders, were educated with these beliefs and ethical principles. This was one of the main rationales for church schools and universities and it has also been important in the use of education in state building in the nineteenth and twentieth centuries (see Green, 1990). Education certainly made an important contribution to the creation of the United States of America. Cheng and Yang in Chapter IX show the contribution it has made to the creation of a unified Chinese nation and culture. Most former colonies made the creation of at least one strong university a major nation building policy priority after achieving independence. This is essentially the basis of Durkheim's claim, referred to earlier, that educational systems are constructs built by society, which seek to reproduce in subsequent generations, their collectively held values, beliefs, norms and practices through the institutions they create for this purpose. The implication of this view is that all education is intrinsically public. However this interpretation of public also implies a considerable degree of collective control of the content of educational services and indeed in many countries of which France was the best-known western example, the state traditionally exercised influence over what was taught. In the Soviet Union the state ensured that universities made their contribution to the creation of a socialist society.

Currently equality is usually the underpinning ideological position of many of those who claim that higher education is inherently a public good and they regret the inequalities that appear to result from neo-liberal marketisation of higher education. In the present volume Nixon is explicit about this. His critique of recent trends in higher education policy concludes:

> *we consent, in the main silently, to a system that perpetuates these inequalities of access and inequalities of outcome: inequalities that have a hugely detrimental effect on the life chances of a significant proportion of young people in particular. Moreover, those inequalities are compounded by inequalities in the quality of provision—the inequalities of quality. Addressing the totality of inequalities is not, therefore, simply a matter of providing more public resources for higher education—important though that may be—but a matter of distributing those resources in such a way as to ensure equality of provision across the sector* (Chapter X).

Cheng and Yang come close to a similar position in commenting on recent trends in Chinese higher education:

> *Education used to be seen as a path for social mobility because it provided equal opportunities. The loss of its "public good" nature is now removing such a mechanism of social equilibrium, and education will soon become the culprit for social disparity* (Chapter IX).

The belief is that everyone would benefit from some form of higher education and they would emerge as more complete citizens and so there is a public responsibility to provide it to as many people as possible.

At the other extreme is the ideological position that has underpinned higher education policy during the past quarter century in several countries and is being promoted by the European Union and other international organisations in many others. This is that higher education is primarily an investment in future productivity and brings benefits to the individuals who receive it, primarily in the form of higher lifetime incomes but also in more fulfilling lifestyles as students and as graduates. Therefore it is appropriately treated as a private service with public intervention limited to those cases when clear external benefits can be shown over and above those received by individual students and graduates. Public intervention is permissible to help achieve more equitable lifetime distribution of incomes by enabling those who are unable to meet the costs directly to borrow the money needed on the collateral security of their probable higher lifetime incomes.

A problem with such an individual choice approach is that, as Standish points out in Chapter III, learning transforms people and they have different tastes and interests (as well as capabilities) after undertaking it. This was recognised by the utilitarian and libertarian John Stuart Mill in his widely quoted aphorism:

> It is better to be a human being dissatisfied than a pig satisfied; better to be Socrates dissatisfied than a fool satisfied. And if the fool, or the pig, is of a different opinion, it is because they only know their own side of the question. The other party to the comparison knows both sides (Mill, 1863, p. 13).

This is certainly rather elitist but it is ultimately the heart of the case why it is not appropriate to leave education, even higher education, entirely to the vagaries of the marketplace. Education increases knowledge and should widen horizons: choices made by those who are fully aware of the alternatives and their implications are more valid than those who are unaware of other possibilities. It is legitimate to claim that well-educated people have a special responsibility to help others achieve their own enlightened position because their education gives them greater awareness of the range of possibilities available.

A different argument pointing in the same direction is linked to the idea of endogenous economic growth. At the heart of these theories is the evidence that educated workers are more productive than those less educated, but this advantage is increased if they are able to cooperate with other educated people and use new technologies that result from the discoveries of highly qualified people. Several economic studies have shown this to be the case (e.g. McMahon, 1999). By analogy if I am well educated my enjoyment of life is enhanced if there are other educated people around me. The number of people who find long-term partners while at university is one homely example of this. Another familiar recent illustration is provided by social networking. When only a few people knew how to use email it was of some use for communicating with contemporaries who were in the know, but since most people were not it did not significantly reduce the need for paper-based communication. Now social media and electronic communication has transformed economic, social and cultural life. Not to be familiar with the techniques and conventions that have evolved over the past quarter century is to be cut off from many key aspects of modern life.

This brings us back to diversity and the content of higher education. The question arises of whether the public benefits, economic, social or cultural, are equivalent in all the activities that come under the heading 'higher education'. It may be that most of the benefits from the study of economics for example, which is consistently the highest paid social science discipline, accrue to the individuals who have acquired these skills. Literature, on the other hand, whose graduates are relatively poorly rewarded, may contribute more to cultural life over and above the earnings of individual graduates. The case can be made, as Dill comes close to making and as Mill did in 1863, that the best judges of this are those who are already educated to high levels. Only they can evaluate any particular educational activity in relation to the range of other possibilities.

Unfortunately, however, 'experts' also have their own particular vested interests to protect, whether it be Law, Medicine, History, Engineering or Literature. This, therefore, takes the debate out of the sphere of the market and into that of politics. Which groups can make the most convincing cases for their areas of interest? Whether political choices made by persuading representatives of the majority are more legitimate than market choices resulting from the sum of individual choices is ultimately a question of value. How the dominant values are arrived at in a democracy depend on the interplay of logic and rhetoric which were at the heart of the ancient Greek academies and are still the core of what many authors think higher education should be about.

Research

Much of this book has been concerned mainly with the acquisition of knowledge by students and the case for and against treating this as more than something with benefits, direct and indirect, that go beyond the individuals who receive it. However, higher education also has a knowledge creation function. Many higher education institutions also undertake research which has important public and private consequences. Here the relationship between the public and the private is particularly complex. Knowledge can be classified into two broad categories: that which once discovered can be codified and stored on paper (or in data banks); and that which is embedded in individuals who possess the knowledge or capability and cannot be separated from them. In the case of the former, once the knowledge has been codified it can be stored and made widely available at relatively low cost and often with comparatively little learning on the part of the user. It becomes non-rivalrous and, therefore, in the sense used by several of our authors, public. Embedded knowledge of the second type can be transferred from one individual to another but its acquisition requires as much education or training from each new generation as those who acquired it in the previous generation. Knowledge which needs to be embedded in individuals is intrinsically private; the London taxi driver, for example, acquires 'the knowledge' and is able to earn a living from it. A medical practitioner learns how to cure people or prevent them becoming ill and is able to profit from this knowledge. Both taxi driver and physician take several years to acquire the knowledge and there are few short cuts. On the other hand a new discovery which may take a large amount of resources to make can often be codified and made available to all at very low cost. The World Wide Web required great ingenuity to create, as did the plays of Shakespeare, or the music of Beethoven, but once created and written down or codified, they can all be made available to others at very low cost. Thus it can be argued that much research should be treated as an intrinsic public good.

Throughout most of the twentieth century, this was the model that was in the ascendancy. Research was largely paid for out of public funds and academic staff in universities published their results as soon as they could to advance their careers. The information was then available for all to use. There were a few patents claimed by universities: one of the most well known was the blood thinning drug Warfarin, which was patented by the alumni of the University of Wisconsin for their alma mater, but for the most part universities considered it desirable that the results of their research were made available as widely as possible.

In such a system university research depends on receiving funds from public sources. However, as part of the general ideological shift towards markets as the best mechanism for resource allocation the private benefit aspects of research as of most other aspects of higher education have become much more prominent. Furthermore, as Singh points out,

> *public good aspirations become even more complicated and diffuse in the context of the increasingly transnational settings within which many higher education institutions now operate. (p65 above)*

If the taxpayers of one country pay for research that is freely available globally this may be a global public service but, except for special circumstances such as medical aid to very poor nations, it is unlikely to be sustainable.

In research the growth of private interests has been manifested in the much more widespread use of copyright and patent laws that enable individuals and corporate bodies to profit for considerable periods from their discoveries and creations. Codified knowledge that is in principle non-excludable and non-rivalrous has been privatised along with much of the rest of higher education. Once again the issue comes down to policy choices, and these are for the most part global political choices. The argument for the privatisation of codified knowledge is that the possibility of high rewards encourages greater investment in research and creative activities: the arguments against are that dissemination of results of research is slower and more restricted than would be the case if they are freely available. Debates about the availability of recently discovered medicines in poorer countries are one widely debated example of this dilemma. More recently debates about the mandatory publication of research results and information gained during the course of publicly funded research are a manifestation of the public good—private rewards tensions.

Concluding Remarks

It is clear that higher education has the attributes of both public and private goods. That it usually brings considerable lifetime benefits to most people who undertake it is beyond question. That it should be organised in such a way as to allow all who can to benefit from it is a value judgment but one that is so widely held as to be almost beyond question. Some of the authors in this book come close to arguing that higher education is a basic human right and all should have access to it unconditionally. However, without going to such an extreme position there is good reason to accept that considerations of equity are one of the main public good aspects of higher education. The case is analogous in some ways with health services. There can be little doubt that most of the benefits of health care are enjoyed by individuals but there is a public health dimension in the prevention of epidemics, for example, that is accepted almost everywhere, and all but the harshest marketeers accept that those who are seriously injured or gravely ill have a right to high quality medical attention regardless of their ability to pay for it.

There is in addition the utilitarian rationale of John Stuart Mill. A society which is peopled by well-educated citizens is in general more aware of the range of life's possibilities and is therefore more likely to take wise collective decisions that one with less widespread awareness of human potential. This is of course an empirically testable hypothesis and the work of McMahon, cited earlier, has gone some way towards achieving this.

Beyond such general equity considerations it is impossible to escape the different conceptions of public as spelled out by some of our authors, and the enormous diversity of activities that are now accepted as higher education. This ceases to be merely a matter for intellectual debate when resources are involved since at any point in time resource allocation is a zero-sum game. More spent on one activity is less for others. Some activities of higher education institutions, research which leads to technological advance or improved social organisation, or those which result in more politically and socially aware citizens can make claims to advance the future public good in this way. Others are more likely to benefit mainly their direct recipients, at least as they are organised at present and can lay little claim to be public goods or services. By accepting that the main rationale for receiving public funding is that it advances economic growth higher education has laid a large part of its work open to this charge. It may well be that this shift towards belief in the private benefits obtained through higher education has brought it more resources from a grateful public of private individuals than would otherwise have been the case. But whether in so doing it has, like Dr Faustus sold its transformational soul to the devil in return for a few decades of prosperity remains an open question.

References

Arnold, M. (1867) On Dover Beach. In inter alia Jones, G. R. *The Nation's Favourite Poems*, BBC London, 2012, p. 13.
Arnold, M. (1869) *Culture and Anarchy*. New edition Oxford University Press, 2006.
Barnett R. (2013) *Imagining the University* (Routledge).
Beveridge W. (1942) *Social Insurance and Allied Services* (HMSO CMND 6404) London
Blackburn S., Review of Imagining the University (*Times Higher Education* 31.1.2013).
Deem, R., Ka Ho Mok and Lucas L. (2008) Transforming Higher Education in Whose Image? Exploring the Concept of the 'World-Class' University in Europe and Asia (*Higher Education Policy*, 21).
Durkheim D. E. (1956) *Education and Sociology*. Free Press, Glencoe, Illinois.
Collini, S. *What Are Universities For?*. Penguin, London. February 2012.
Green A. (1990) *Education and State Formation: The Rise of Education Systems in England, France and the USA*. Macmillan, London.
Hayek F. von (1948) *Individualism and the Economic Order* (University of Chicago Press)
Inglis F. (2013) Branded to death. *Times Higher Education July 18*.
Keeling R. (2006) The Bologna Process and the Lisbon Research Agenda: the European Commission's expanding role in higher education discourse (*European Journal of Education* Vol. 41, No. 2, 2006.
Marshall, A. (1961) *Principles of Economics* (9th Ed. Variorum, 2 vols.), with annotations by C. W. Guillebaud. Macmillan, London.
MacIntyre, A. (1990) *Three Rival Versions of Moral Enquiry*. London, Duckworth.
McMahon W. W. (1999) *Education and Development: Measuring the Social Benefits*. Oxford University Press, Oxford.
Mill, J. S. *Utilitarianism* (Originally 1863, page no. is from 2013 University of Adelaide e edition).
Newman J. H. (1852) *The Idea of a University*, reprinted Yale University Press 1996.
OECD (2013) *Education at a Glance*, OECD Paris.
Pattison, M. (1868) *Suggestions on Academical Organisation*. Cornell University Library, 2009.
Schuller T., Preston J., Hammond C., Brassett-Grundy A., and Bynner J. (2004) *The Benefits of Learning: The Impact of Education on Health, Family Life and social capital* (Routledge Falmer).
Tawney, R. H. (1922) *Secondary Education for All: A Policy for Labour*. George Allen and Unwin, reprinted Hambledon, London 1988.

Contributors

Ronald Barnett is Emeritus Professor of Higher Education at the Institute of Education, London, his work having focused on the conceptual and theoretical understanding of the university and higher education. His books include *The Idea of Higher Education*, *Higher Education: A Critical Business*, *Realizing the University in an age of supercomplexity*, *A Will to Learn* and, and most recently the first two volumes of a trilogy, *'Being a University'* (Routledge, 2011) and *'Imagining the University'* (Routledge, 2013). He is a Fellow of the Society for Research into Higher Education, has been awarded a higher doctorate of the University of London and has been a guest speaker in over 35 countries. **Email:** r.barnett@ioe.ac.uk

Angela Brew is a Professorial Fellow in the Learning and Teaching Centre at Macquarie University, Australia. Her research is focused on the nature of research and its relation to teaching, learning and scholarship, models of research-led teaching and undergraduate research. She has published over 200 articles and seven books including: *The Nature of Research: Inquiry in Academic Contexts (RoutledgeFalmer 2001); Research and Teaching: beyond the divide (PalgraveMacmillan 2006);* and *Academic Research and Researchers* (McGraw Hill 2009, with Lucas). Email angela.brew@mq.edu.au

Kai-ming Cheng is Chair Professor of Education at the University of Hong Kong. He was Dean of Education, Pro-Vice-Chancellor and Senior Advisor to the Vice-Chancellor. He did his doctoral study at the London Institute of Education, after teaching in schools for 15 years. He taught at the Harvard Graduate School of Education as Visiting Professor, 1996–2007. He works on policies and reforms of education in various jurisdictions, and has paid special attention to changes in society and their impact on education. Email kmcheng@hku.hk

David D. Dill is Professor Emeritus of Public Policy, The University of North Carolina, Chapel Hill. He research has explored the regulation of academic quality, markets for higher education, policy instruments for higher education, and research policy. He has published comparative analyses of national policies, been an assessor of academic quality assurance in numerous countries, and advised policymakers in Asia, northern Europe, and the US. Email david_dill@unc.edu

Ourania Filippakou is a Senior Lecturer in Education at the University of Hull. She is a Co-Director of the Postgraduate Taught Programmes in the Faculty of Education and also leads the specialist route on 'Higher Education' in the Professional Doctorate EdD. After her first degree at the Aegean University she obtained a scholarship from the Athens Academy to do postgraduate studies at the Institute of Education. Her PhD thesis, The *Legitimation of Quality in Higher Education*, looked at the quality assurance regimes in England and Greece within the wider context of the European Union and the Bologna Process. Her main areas of interest are in higher education policy analysis and social theory. Email o.filippakou@hull.ac.uk

Jon Nixon has held chairs at four UK universities and is currently affiliated to the Hong Kong Institute of Education as a senior research fellow. His most recent book is *Hannah Arendt and the Politics of Friendship* (2015). Previous books include *Interpretive Pedagogies for Higher Education* (2012), *Higher education and the Public Good* (2011) and *Towards the Virtuous University* (2008). He is a founding co-editor of the Bloomsbury *Perspectives on Leadership in Higher Education* series. He is currently working on a book entitled *Rosa Luxemburg and the Unfinished Revolution*, a study of Luxemburg's continuing legacy within the field of political thought and analysis. Email nixonjon@live.co.uk

Peter Scott is Professor of Higher Education Studies and co-director of the Centre for Higher Education Studies at the Institute of Education University of London. He was formerly Vice-Chancellor of Kingston University, Pro-Vice-Chancellor and Professor of Education at the University of Leeds and Editor of 'The Times Higher Education Supplement'. He is a Fellow of the Academy of Social Sciences and Member. Email p.scott@ioe.ac.uk

Mala Singh is Professor Extraordinaire in the Centre for Higher Education Research, Teaching and Learning, Rhodes University, South Africa. She was previously Professor of International Higher Education Policy in the Centre for Higher Education Research and Information at the Open University in the United Kingdom. She has published in the fields of higher education studies and philosophy. She is a former Fulbright Scholar, a member of the Academy of Science in South Africa and serves on the Council of the United Nations University in Tokyo. Email singhmala9@gmail.com

Paul Standish is Professor and Head of the Centre for Philosophy at the Institute of Education, London. His work spans the range of philosophy of education. He is interested particularly in tensions between analytical and continental philosophical traditions and the creative possibilities that arise from them. His most recent books are *Stanley Cavell and the Education of Grownups* (2012, Fordham University Press) and *Education and the Kyoto School of Philosophy: Pedagogy for Human Transformation* (2012, Springer), both co-edited with Naoko Saito, *The Philosophy of Nurse Education* (2007, Palgrave Macmillan), co-edited with John Drummond, and *The Therapy of Education: Philosophy, Happiness, and Personal Growth* (2006, Palgrave Macmillan), co-authored with Paul Smeyers and Richard Smith. He is Associate Editor and was Editor (2001–2011) of the *Journal of Philosophy of Education*. Email: p.standish@ioe.ac.uk

Ted Tapper spent nearly all his academic life at the University of Sussex, retiring in 2005 as Professor of Politics, and Chair of the Department of International Relations and Politics. Much of his career, both research and teaching, was built around two interests. Firstly, the politics of secondary schooling with particular reference to the protracted campaign to undermine the private, fee-paying sector. Secondly, the governance of British higher education with the focus on the decline in academic autonomy in the face of an increasing policy input from the state, incorporating in recent years the broad political push to make the higher education system more responsive to market pressure. Email kmtapper@aol.com

PedroTeixeira is Professor of Economics and Vice-Rector for Academic Affairs at the University of Porto. He is also Director of CIPES—Center for Research in Higher Education Policies. His main research interests are on the Economics of Education and the History of Economics. He has published several journal articles in higher education and economics journals and has edited several collective volumes. Email pedrotx@fep.up.pt

Gareth Williams is Emeritus Professor at London University Institute of Education. He founded and directed its Centre for Higher Education Studies from 1985 to 2001. An economist by training he has worked mainly on HE policy and finance since publication of *Changing Patterns of Finance in Higher Education*, 1992. He is a past chairman of the Society for Research in Higher Education and was director of its Leverhulme project on the future of higher education in the early 1980s, which anticipated the direction of many of the changes of the 1980s and 1990s. Recent publications include 'Some Wicked Questions from the Dismal Science' in *Universities in the Knowledge Economy* (Ed Paul Temple, Routledge 2012; 'A bridge too far: An economic critique of marketization of higher education' in *Browne and Beyond: Modernizing English Higher Education,* Eds Claire Callender and Peter Scott (IoE press 2013) Email g.williams@ioe.ac.uk

Rui Yang is Professor at the Faculty of Education in the University of Hong Kong. With his BA and MEd respectively in 1985 and 1988 from China and his PhD from Australia in 2001, he has worked in China, Australia and Hong Kong. His research focuses on education policy sociology, comparative and cross-cultural studies in education, international higher education, educational development in Chinese societies, and international politics in educational research. Email yangrui@hku.hk

Index

A

Accountability 6, 29, 53, 59, 62, 67, 150
Australia 8, 100, 103
Autonomy 43, 53, 67, 86, 117, 121, 123, 146

B

Bourdieu 6, 19, 32, 39

C

China 9, 53, 95, 127–139, 172, 184
Civil Society 16, 18, 42, 44, 55, 166, 192
Courses 101,102, 107, 122, 150, 168, 194
Culture, cultural 19, 22, 23, 29, 42, 46, 52, 55, 64, 66, 67, 68, 96, 115, 116, 127, 129, 132, 133, 135, 138, 149, 150, 159, 166, 171, 185, 188, 192, 194, 200
Curricula 24, 25,38, 65,70, 103, 107, 108, 129, 132, 133, 149, 174, 187

D

Democracy, democratic 6, 8, 10, 41, 44, 53, 60, 64, 66, 68, 96, 97, 100, 103, 104, 106, 130, 163, 166, 173, 184
Derrida 34–38, 183

E

Economy, (see also knowledge economy) 22, 37, 43, 50, 59, 76, 96, 128, 131, 133/4, 138, 146,155, 166, 186
Economic growth vii, 46, 49, 52, 96, 99, 101, 121, 142, 152, 193, 200, 204
Economics 75–90, 184, 188, 194, 196, 200
Egalitarian 133, 237, 172
Elite, Elitism, Elitist 22, 43, 45, 48, 79, 82 ,85, 104, 108, 118, 168, 172, 184, 200
Employment 120, 122, 134, 142, 148, 166, 191
England, English 8, 16, 47, 51, 52, 114–126, 167, 182, 192, 193
Equality (inequality) 8, 10, 64, 96, 105, 164–177
Equity, 88, 96, 146, 166, 182, 184, 188, 193, 195, 198, 199, 203

F

Fees (tuition) 9, 49, 51, 56, 81, 114–117, 120–22, 124, 130–32, 134–7, 145–7, 157/8, 168, 170, 172, 189, 193
Finance, Financial 22, 43, 51, 83, 95, 115, 119–121, 124, 129, 132, 134, 136, 145/6, 151–3, 193, 196, 198
Funds, Funding (see also public funding) 6, 8/9, 49, 63/4, 75, 79, 81, 83–5,

88, 106/7, 124, 145, 147, 149, 151–155, 157, 164, 168
France 164, 192, 199
Friedman, Milton 83–86, 88

G

Germany 52, 163
Global, globalisation 5, 15, 18, 20, 22–7, 42/3, 50/1, 54, 60, 65, 98, 104, 110, 146, 155, 158, 164, 170, 172, 174, 187/3, 202
Government, national (see also state) 3, 4, 8, 10, 29, 42, 45, 54, 66, 70, 76, 77, 78, 80, 81, 83, 84–8, 97, 98, 100, 103, 107, 108, 110, 114, 118–21, 123, 129, 130, 134, 137/8, 143, 145/6, 151/2, 155, 157/8, 165–7, 171/2, 189, 192, 193, 197
Governance (of HE institutions) 43, 53, 56, 66, 119, 157

H

Habermas 17/8

I

Inclusive, Inclusion 8, 37, 64, 97, 99, 109, 163
Intellectual Property Rights (IPR) 47, 152/3

K

Knowledge economy, society 7, 11, 19, 43, 46, 50, 54/5, 59/60, 69, 101, 115, 123
Knowledge, technology transfer 151, 152–155, 201/2

L

Lyotard 29–33, 37, 40

M

Manpower planning 131, 134
Market, marketization 6–11, 15–17, 21, 33, 41–44, 47/8, 50–54, 56, 69, 76, 81, 83–8, 103, 119, 121–125, 133–137, 142–8, 151, 152/3, 156–8, 167, 170–2, 174, 188, 192, 195, 199, 200/1
Mass higher education viii, 12, 45, 46, 50, 54, 103, 104, 173, 187, 190, 194
Mill, John Stuart 78–81, 87, 89, 188, 194, 200/1, 203

N

Neo-liberal 21, 23, 41/2, 44, 46, 55, 60, 62, 66, 67, 69, 101/2, 142, 144, 148, 199
Netherlands 154, 155, 157, 158, 159
New public management 7, 42, 53, 67/8, 119
Nineteenth century 6, 8, 43, 45, 52, 53, 78, 84, 114, 116, 129, 182, 188, 193, 198

O

OECD 142, 144/5, 151, 153, 155, 157, 193, 194, 197

P

Performance indicators 7, 29, 36, 67, 146, 153/4, 155
Performativity 6, 29/30, 32, 38, 67
Private benefit viii, 49, 50, 56, 64, 87, 96, 99, 113, 128, 136, 141, 142, 146, 148, 156, 157, 194/5, 202, 204
Private funds, funding Viii, 124, 170
Private good(s) 3, 4, 8, 48, 66, 67, 75, 88, 100, 113, 117, 119–123, 127, 135, 136, 137, 138, 141, 183, 188, 203
Private HE institutions 45, 47, 49, 54, 63, 77, 79, 81, 130, 172, 189, 192
Private interest(s) 10, 60, 66, 67, 68, 80, 96, 142, 150, 157, 165–167, 173, 202
Private provision (of education) 81, 83, 85, 87, 88, 123, 125
Private rate of return 50, 141, 184
Private sector 42, 43, 55, 77, 81, 85, 88, 89, 133, 134, 141
Professor, role of 6, 38/39, 101, 143, 181, 189, 191

Index

Public (definition), Publics, multiple 5, 6, 9, 10, 15–20, 23, 43,4, 46, 55, 57, 62–65, 69, 164–7, 181–3, 184, 203
Public funds, funding viii, 3–5, 8, 9, 42,/3, 46, 51, 56, 66,-68, 79, 81, 89, 117, 118, 119, 120/1, 123, 145, 153, 158, 170, 195, 196, 198, 202
Public goods 6, 10, 15, 18/19, 47–51, 56, 86, 88, 141, 163/4, 183, 184, 200
Public (HE) institutions 42, 49, 77, 78, 81, 130, 142, 146, 147, 172, 173
Public sector 41/2, 46, 70
Public service 9, 10, 41, 75, 154, 155/6
Public sphere 15, 17/18, 21, 23–27, 69, 88, 181, 184

Q

Quality, quality assurance 11, 39, 64, 67, 71, 79, 87, 95, 97, 123, 145, 147–151, 152, 153/4, 157, 170–2

R

Regulate (universities) regulation 9, 10, 42, 46, 50, 51, 52, 55, 57, 61, 62–70, 76, 81, 86, 87, 88,95, 114, 119, 121, 123, 143,/4, 145–150, 153, 156, 158, 192, 195
Research (function of universities) 10, 12, 25, 39, 46, 50, 52, 54, 57, 61, 70, 71, 97–99, 102, 103,104–6, 107, 108, 118/9, 125, 143, 144, 145/6, 148–152, 155/6, 168, 171, 182, 201–3
Research (into higher education) 9, 19, 29, 62, 100, 106, 109, 129, 142, 143, 144, 145, 155, 171
Research assessment, evaluation 59, 142, 144, 151, 153–5, 157/8, 171, 172,
Rivalrous, non-rivalrous 18, 47, 86, 141, 164, 184, 201/2

S

Social benefits 7, 48/9, 56/7, 60, 75, 77, 86–8, 142, 144, 146, 148, 156, 200
Social capital 19, 168
Social justice 52, 54/5, 115
Social mobility 37, 52, 114, 118, 128, 130, 138, 171/2, 199
Social policy 24, 33, 43, 46, 123
Socialism, Socialist 15, 25, 131–3, 138, 189, 199
Social welfare 42, 48, 123
Student Loans 51, 56, 115, 120, 124, 135/6, 171
  Theory, Theoretical approaches 3, 5–8, 17, 19, 23, 31, 47, 61, 65, 76, 87, 89, 101, 103, 129, 148, 153, 156, 186, 195, 198, 200
State, (see also government and welfare state) 1,3, 4, 6, 9, 11, 16, 22, 41, 42–55, 62, 63, 66,/7, 69, 76–89, 95, 117–9, 121, 123/4, 127–138. 146, 157, 165, 170, 189, 192, 197, 199
STEM subjects 54, 102, 150
Students(s) 4, 6, 8, 10, 15, 20/1, 23–26, 37,44, 45, 50, 51, 54–7, 64, 67, 85, 95, 97, 99, 101–110, 114/5, 118, 132, 134/5, 137, 141, 144, 158, 163, 168/9, 170–2, 174, 199
Student achievement 169, 174
Student choice, Student demand 9, 44, 122, 125, 147/8, 152, 190, 193,
(per) Student costs, funding 144, 145, 147
Student fees vii, 170, 120, 189, 198,
Student numbers, student population 54, 106, 114, 121, 123, 163/4, 164
Student recruitment 194/5, 196/7

T

Technology, Technological 10, 11, 18, 22, 25, 46, 52, 54, 98, 100, 102, 103, 129, 130, 150, 156, 182, 186/7, 189, 193, 197, 200, 203
Technology transfer (see knowledge transfer)

U

United States (USA) 44, 46, 52, 84, 150, 151, 152, 153, 172, 198
United Kingdom (UK, see also England) 9, 15, 21, 22, 37, 42, 46, 54, 55, 84, 100, 104, 108, 113, 142–8, 151, 153, 154, 157/8, 163, 165, 166, 170–2, 174, 189, 190, 192

V

Value(s) 8, 10, 12, 17, 19, 31, 33, 39, 60, 64, 68, 70, 84, 97, 98, 115–7, 127, 129, 136, 138, 141, 157, 164, 183, 186, 196, 198, 201, 203

W

Welfare state 4, 41, 42, 43, 46, 50, 84, 156

GLOBAL STUDIES IN EDUCATION

A.C. (Tina) Besley, Michael A. Peters,
Cameron McCarthy, Fazal Rizvi
General Editors

Global Studies in Education is a book series that addresses the implications of the powerful dynamics associated with globalization for re-conceptualizing educational theory, policy and practice. The general orientation of the series is interdisciplinary. It welcomes conceptual, empirical and critical studies that explore the dynamics of the rapidly changing global processes, connectivities and imagination, and how these are reshaping issues of knowledge creation and management and economic and political institutions, leading to new social identities and cultural formations associated with education.

We are particularly interested in manuscripts that offer: a) new theoretical, and methodological, approaches to the study of globalization and its impact on education; b) ethnographic case studies or textual/discourse based analyses that examine the cultural identity experiences of youth and educators inside and outside of educational institutions; c) studies of education policy processes that address the impact and operation of global agencies and networks; d) analyses of the nature and scope of transnational flows of capital, people and ideas and how these are affecting educational processes; e) studies of shifts in knowledge and media formations, and how these point to new conceptions of educational processes; f) exploration of global economic, social and educational inequalities and social movements promoting ethical renewal.

For additional information about this series or for the submission of manuscripts, please contact one of the series editors:

A.C. (Tina) Besley: t.besley@waikato.ac.nz
Cameron McCarthy: cmccart1@illinois.edu
Michael A. Peters: mpeters@waikato.ac.nz
Fazal Rizvi: frizvi@unimelb.edu.au

To order other books in this series, please contact our Customer Service Department:
   (800) 770-LANG (within the U.S.)
   (212) 647-7706 (outside the U.S.)
   (212) 647-7707 FAX

Or browse online by series:
   www.peterlang.com